SOW
THE SEEDS
OF HEMP

By Gary Jennings

Sow the Seeds of Hemp
The Terrible Teague Bunch
The Rope in the Jungle

nonfiction:

The Treasure of the Superstition Mountains
The Shrinking Outdoors
The Killer Storms

SOW
THE SEEDS
OF HEMP

Gary Jennings

W · W · NORTON & COMPANY, INC ·

New York

Copyright © 1976 by Gary Jennings
First Edition

All Rights Reserved

Library of Congress Cataloging in Publication Data

Jennings, Gary.
  Sow the seeds of hemp.

  I. Title.
PZ4.J532So [PS3560.E518] 813'.5'4   75-42202
ISBN 0-393-08733-6

Published simultaneously in Canada
by George J. McLeod Limited, Toronto

This book was designed by Jacques Chazaud.
Typefaces used are Plymouth and Baskerville,
set by Fuller Typesetting of Lancaster.
Printing and binding were done by
American Book–Stratford Press, Inc.

Printed in the United States of America

1 2 3 4 5 6 7 8 9

this book is
for Glenda
who brought it to life

Contents

Foreword

Time was when the names of John Murrell and Virgil Stewart were famous in America—or infamous, depending on the point of view. It is a considerable loss to American folklore that their story, their adventures, their names should have been buried these many years in the bone yard of a few obscure histories, biographies and academic theses. This attempt to redress the slight is a work of fiction, compounded of about equal parts of fact, legend and imagination. But Murrell and Stewart—and practically every other character in this novel—really lived and did the things they do here.

The book and I are indebted to a number of people for aid, support, encouragement, criticism and other contributions during its long gestation. Among them: my brother Hiram Jennings, Edie Keaton Williams, the late Charles Brown, Elizabeth Lucas, R.N., Victor Avers, Marilyn Marlow and Francesca Todaro.

G.J.

Here I sow hemp seed, hemp seed I sow.
He who would catch me, come after and mow.

—*children's game, early 1800s*

Hemp for rope to bind a nation,
Rope to toll its fun'ral knell.
There ain't room in all Creation
For decent folk and John Murrell.

—*from "The Ballad of John Murrell"*

Book One

THE SEEDS

Stewart's old mare whickered and did a tired dance step to express her anxiety about something. Stewart, half asleep in the saddle, spoke a consoling word, patted the horse's neck and kneed her on southward through the summer twilight.

The mare was blind in her off eye and hadn't seen whatever it was she had scented. The pack mule trailing behind did. He balked, turned and jerked viciously on the lead rope. Stewart, awakened suddenly from his doze at the other end of the rope, had to choose among three alternatives. He could let the mule yank him out of his saddle, or hold tight and maybe have his shoulder dislocated. Or he could let go of the rope and chase the mule while it distributed the contents of his packs through a mile or two of canebrake. He took the easiest course and toppled philosophically over his horse's rump, to land on his back in the mud of the trail. The mule took the opportunity to haul him around for a while. Stewart finally regained his feet, moored the muttering beast to a willow tree and went off, muttering himself, to see what had spooked his animals.

The trail here ran close along the east bank of the Yazoo, and the land differed from the river only in being slightly less wet and slightly more overgrown with cattails, scrubby willows and reeds. Stewart sloshed back along the furrow he had plowed with his tailbone, expecting to find something about as mon-

strous as a dead possum or polecat. But, at the place where the
mule had dumped him, he stopped and looked out toward the
river in some puzzlement.

Here there was a long open swale uninterrupted by trees,
where the reeds marched down to, into and under the water.
Stewart could discern a ragged path through the reeds, as if
some huge and ungainly animal had churned up from the
river. The alley through the reeds did not reach quite as far as
the trail where he stood, but at this nearer end of it the reeds
were agitated—and a flock of parakeets, flame-bright even in the
twilight, circled and squawked peevishly—indicating that the
beast was slowly progressing, or perhaps wallowing there.

Stewart hesitated, then squelched away to where his horse
was unconcernedly grazing. He untied the saddle thongs to get
his long rifle, primed it with a cap and returned to the riverside swale. He didn't plunge directly into the reeds, but
made a cautiously circuitous way around the still-agitated patch,
to come up on it from the rear.

This was no neighborhood to go openly into the face of the
unknown. Aside from the ordinary wildwood perils, it wasn't
unlikely that there were still some unconverted Choctaws in
this corner of the Purchase who were disgruntled at the sale of
their tribal lands and had refused resettlement in the Indian
Territory way out West. But if this was one of the holdouts, and
he was looking to take out his grievance on the first white who
came along, he was certainly setting a clumsy and un-Indian-
like ambush. The alley he had made for himself through the
reeds was trampled and matted and wide enough for a buffalo.
One broken reed flaunted a telltale tatter of brown cloth. Stewart fingered it and found blood on his hand. He pushed on
along the pathway until he came to its landward end, where
the reeds were still waving.

A big black man lay there, his outstretched hands weakly
fumbling to part the reeds and drag himself farther toward the
trail. Stewart knelt, laid his rifle aside and put a hand on the
man's coat shoulder. It was wet with blood and river water.
The Negro slowly turned his head to look up at Stewart and
his lips moved. All the blood seemed to have been drained from
his veins long before. His lips were pale lavender and the near-
black of his skin seemed no longer the color of life, but an over-

lay, like blacking on the dead metal of a gun barrel. The man groped for Stewart's hand and made unintelligible noises. It was doubtful that the glazed eyes could see anything, but they held a last light of urgency.

"Hold on," said Stewart. "Let me see if there's anything I can do."

He was talking to a dead man. The eyes lost their light as suddenly as a blown-out candle, and the huge black hand dropped away from his. Stewart frowned and stood up to consider his find. There was no boat or raft floating about on the river, no sign of how the Negro came to be here. The Yazoo was too shallow and sluggish at this season for him to have fallen in somewhere upstream and been swept here helpless.

Stewart stooped again, got his hands under the man's chest, turned the upper body half over, and found what he was looking for. The Negro wore a rough-woven brown jacket, but no shirt under it, and the bullet hole in his chest stood out blacker than the skin around it. Stewart grunted and let the body sag back onto its face. He looked around, decided that it would be full dark in half an hour and impractical to continue traveling. He might as well take time to give the dead man a decent burial of sorts, and then seek higher, drier ground to camp for the night. He made his way through the reeds and down the trail, to get his short-handled shovel from one of the mule's packs.

It was clear enough what had happened. The Negro was a runaway slave who had been tracked down, shot, and lived long enough to make it to the river and float out of reach of his pursuers. Odd, though. It did seem that, if one of his trackers had got close enough to face the Negro and put that hole neatly in his middle, he could have captured him just as easily. The slave looked too valuable to be shot just out of pique for his running away.

But Stewart got a nasty shock—and had to dismiss his reconstruction of the event—when he returned to bury the body. He had decided to dig a hole right where it lay, in the soft muck where digging would be easy. But when he rolled the corpse out of the way and it flopped over onto its back, he dropped the shovel, involuntarily stepped back and stared in disbelief. The Negro's clothes had fallen away, slit and torn down the front of the body. The body itself was likewise slit, from just below the breastbone to the groin. And out of that gaping crevice spilled a stuffing of gravelly dirt.

.

Novelty and excitement were rare enough in any back-country Mississippi town that the mere passing through of a stranger was sufficient to convene the population for a look at him. Stewart's arrival in the hamlet of Tuscahoma on an August afternoon, with a corpse slung across his pack mule, created something of a sensation. He rode in with a tight rein on his horse and a close hold on the mule's lead rope. Both of the animals objected to the dead man's smell and the mule was particularly aggrieved at the extra load.

Stewart was already leading a considerable parade by the time he entered the village's central street. A dozen or more children of varying age, sex and towheadedness, but unvarying volubility, trailed in his wake, having been collected from outlying farms. Back up the road, their mothers and fathers were severally tying on poke bonnets and abandoning their grub hoes to follow.

Stewart had struck the road, such as it was, about three miles back. The town of Tuscahoma amounted to not much more than a widening of it. Along either side of this main thoroughfare ran a meager row of stores and shops. Their street fronts were mostly whitewashed clapboard, and some had mullioned windows of real glass. But the backs of the buildings were of hewn logs or rough-cut timber, unfinished; and the rearward windows, where there were any, showed only oilpaper panes or flaps of hide scraped thin to translucency. The merchants had laid board sidewalks over the mud that lapped at their doorsills, and had erected board or canvas awnings that made an unbroken, street-long arcade. Out from the shade of this canopy came shoppers, loafers and shopkeepers, to peer at and then join Stewart's cortege.

He spied the place he was looking for, midway down the street. The sign said GENERAL STORE and the building front boasted a large, unmullioned sheet of show window that had to have cost a pretty penny to haul into these backwoods.

That would be the local showplace, post office, gossip center, polling place, town hall, and Stewart's logical destination.

He was right. When he turned his team and made for the hitching rack in front, the crowd gathered around at a respectful distance and the excited jabber died to an expectant murmur. Latecomers were still scampering from around corners, clattering down the outside stairs of the few two-story buildings, and hurrying out of privies with their galluses dragging. But the General Store's proprietor—no doubt the town's chief citizen—was evidently waiting a dignified while to emerge.

Stewart dismounted and flung his reins and the mule's rope over the pole rack. The proprietor finally appeared and stood wiping his hands on the hem of his apron. He was a short, bald, butter-fat man, an imposing and self-important belly with some eyes and things at the top.

"How do," he said.

"Howdy," said Stewart.

The storekeeper peered over his temple spectacles and said, "Stranger in town, ain't you?" as if he were having trouble placing Stewart among the hundred or so inhabitants.

"That's right," said Stewart. And, in polite recognition of the communal curiosity, he added, "Down from Tennessee, bound for the Trace and Natchez."

"Well, you're welcome to Tuscahoma, Mississippi, young feller," said the fat man expansively. "Reckon to stay long?"

"Hadn't reckoned to be here at all," said Stewart. It occurred to him that this sounded churlish and might hurt the community feelings, so he tacked on, "I didn't know there *was* such a place," and made it worse.

"Humph," said the storekeeper with some hauteur. "Growing town. Biggest in Yalo Busha County."

"Is that a fact?" said Stewart admiringly. "Well, you're got the climate for a coming piece of country. Soil looks good, too," he added, with a glance at the trampled mire into which he was perceptibly sinking. "Reason I stopped, mainly, was to ask for a little information."

"Glad to be of service if we can, young man. Ask away."

"Well . . ." said Stewart, and motioned toward the body draped over his mule's packs. As one man, the collected population shifted their gaze from Stewart to the dead Negro, and the fat man widened his eyes as if the cadaver had just that instant come on the scene.

"Well!" he said. "You're toting an unusual freight, stranger."

"Found him last evening, up on the Yazoo. I brought him to see could I learn where he belonged. Do any of you-all happen to recognize him?"

The fat man let himself down heavily into the street. He waved away the gathering flies, took hold of the Negro's hair, looked at his face, let it drop and shook his head. After him, the other men stepped in and, one by one, did the same. "Big buck," Stewart pointed out. "Must have been worth good money to somebody." But they all shook their heads and left it to the fat man to deliver the consensus.

"Appears you brought him to the wrong place," he said to Stewart. "Meaning no offense, but do you always concern yourself so with dead darkies?"

"He'd been shot," Stewart explained. "It struck me as a peculiar way to treat valuable property."

The storekeeper snorted. "Runaway, most likely."

"That's what I thought at first," said Stewart. "But there's something else." He began to loose the rope that held the body on the mule, then paused, looked around at the crowd and cautioned, "I'll have to undo some of his clothes." The men in the crowd made shooing noises at the women and children. The women moved off with ill-concealed disappointment to a discreet distance; the children stayed staunchly where they were. Stewart finished untying the rope and let the corpse flop onto the ground on its back. He bent over, parted the tatters of clothing and revealed the ruined body.

"Godamighty," someone breathed. "He's empty!"

"He wasn't when I found him," said Stewart. "He was stuffed like a sawdust doll—full of about a bushel of dirt. You can still see some of it in there if you want to look."

One of the men verified it. "Well, if that don't damn all!"

"Somebody shot him," said Stewart, "then gutted him, filled him up with countryside to make sure he'd sink, and dropped him in the river."

"Nobody'd treat a runaway like that," said the storekeeper.

"String him up in a tree, maybe, for a warning to the other niggers. But not that."

"The damndest thing is," Stewart went on, "he was still alive when I found him. How he managed it I don't know—with a bullet in him and not much else—but he got out of the river and about six rods through the reeds before he gave up the ghost."

"If he had that much vim in that condition," someone said, "he must of been a prime worker. A top hand, prob'ly worth more'n a thousand on the hoof. Damn shame."

"Well, laying there in the hot sun ain't likely to improve him," said the fat man. "Here—one of you kids run and get them two niggers from the livery stable to come and plant him."

"There's one more thing," said Stewart. "He managed to croak out something at me before he died. Sounded like 'Muriel, Muriel.' His owner maybe?"

This remark brought a sudden silence. Stewart looked at the crowd, then at the fat man, the only one who met his eyes. The rest of the men glanced sidelong at one another and shuffled uncomfortably.

"Muriel," Stewart repeated. "You know any lady named Muriel he might have belonged to?"

"It wouldn't of been 'Muriel,'" one of the men told him finally, almost reluctantly. "What he must of said was . . . 'Murrell.'"

•

"It ain't that it's bad manners to tack Murrell's name onto a killing," said the fat man. "This one sure looks like his work, all right."

"I got the impression I'd introduced an unpopular subject," said Stewart.

They were inside the General Store, leaning at each other across a clear space of counter, and the proprietor had poured two mugs of buttermilk, cold from the spring box. Outside, the livery-stable hands were gingerly and unhappily rolling the dead Negro into a winding sheet of coarse canvas, while the rest of the community stood around and watched.

"It's no secret what John Murrell is and what he does," the storekeeper went on. The buttermilk had given him a white mustache that waggled distractingly as he talked. "But even a man like that has friends and connections. You never know who, or where. So people don't like to talk out against him, or be put in a position where they might be expected to take sides."

"Just so I'll know which way to lean, myself," said Stewart, "who or what *is* John Murrell?"

"Believe you said you hail from Tennessee," said the fat man. "Whereabouts up there?"

The hint was not too subtle for Stewart; he rode along with the change of subject. "Madison County was my last address," he said. "I had a little farm near Jackson. Sold out a few months ago, put my money in goods, and I've been trading along the Mississippi since."

"Well, a brother tradesman!" the storekeeper exclaimed in a jovial boom. He stretched across the counter and stuck out a plump hand. "Around here we make it a point not to ask a man his monicker, but we don't mind volunteering our own. Mine's Ed Clanton."

"Virgil Stewart." He shook the proffered hand. It was like squeezing a fistful of link sausage.

Now that Clanton had identified the stranger as a colleague, he gave some attention to sizing him up. What he saw was a tall young man—not yet out of his twenties—lean-built, straw-haired, snub-nosed and blue-eyed. Any notion that Stewart might ever attain the shrewdness and sharpness to be any great shakes as a trader would be given the lie by those mild eyes and manner. Right now his appearance was more that of an itinerant fruit picker than a traveling peddler. He was appropriately rough-dressed for hard journeying: a linsey-woolsey shirt, buckskin trousers tucked into heavy country boots, a flat-crowned hat with a brim that flopped down to keep the sun off his face and neck.

"Tell me, Mister Stewart, what kind of merchandise do you deal in?"

"Just about anything that meets my two specifications. I've got to be able to carry it. And I've got to be able to sell it. I don't reckon I'd stack up as competition against an emporium like you've got here."

Clanton swelled even fatter with proprietary pride. "Well, I try to anticipate the needs of this growing community, and keep up with them. And supply a few of the luxuries of life as well. I send all the way to New Or*leens* for coffee and salt, for instance. I stock just about everything a body hereabouts could want."

"Sure and you do," said Stewart, looking around. "Me, I'm just carrying some bolts of calico, bullet molds, assortment of tinware, needles and pins. But I've got a real fine line of cutlery. Easy to pack along in quantity, and it practically sells itself."

He abruptly left the counter and crossed the cluttered room to where a rack of knives and scissors hung on the wall. He came back turning a wooden-handled butcher knife in his fingers and speculatively testing its edge against his thumb.

"My best grade," said Clanton. "Three dollars in that size and guaranteed for——"

The counter was made of puncheons—half rounds of logs set side by side, the split sides up and adzed to an approximation of smoothness. Stewart stuck the point of the knife in the chink between two logs and gave it a twist. With a discordant twang, the blade broke in two.

"It wasn't made for prizing up stumps!" the storekeeper blurted in exasperation.

"Bad temper," murmured Stewart.

"Well, now I didn't mean to sound——"

"I meant the knife. Here, let me give you one of mine for it." And he went outside to rummage in one of the mule's packs.

The impromptu funeral had moved to the top of a hill on the other side of town, where the two stableboys were testing who could dig slowest, and everybody else was still watching.

"Take a look at that," said Stewart, returning to plunk the point of a new knife into a counter log.

"My, that *is* a pretty thing!" exclaimed the storekeeper.

Stewart slapped its haft. The knife vibrated in a blurred arc and hummed a musical note. "There's temper for you. That's what a good household knife should be—not a flaked-down pickax. And look at that edge, Mister Clanton; sharp enough to shave with and wouldn't nick a baby's backside. The handle, now, that's ironwood. Comes all the way around the Horn from California, and it'll last as long as the blade."

"Say, you did get a good buy, young fellow. You maybe could teach me a thing or two."

"I've got a full line—for everything from dehorning a bull to paring a lady's toenails. A few razors and scissors, too."

"You know," mused Clanton, "this might just turn out to be an advantageous stopover for you. How about if I bought out your whole stock of this here cutlery? I mean, of course, if you can see your way to making a trade discount. At that, you'll profit by not having to retail it piecemeal from door to door."

"Ye-es," said Stewart uncertainly. "Reckon I would. But hell" —he grinned—"there would go my whole reason for making this trip. With nothing else but calico and odds and ends to sell, I might just as well head back and load up on cutlery again."

"Back?"

"That ain't *all* of my worldly goods," said Stewart, indicating the pack mule at the rack. "Most of my inventory is stored up at Memphis. I work out of there, carrying just enough at a time so I can go where I please—overland or on the river, as the mood takes me."

"Hard to tell whether you travel to sell or sell to travel," said Clanton good-humoredly. "Well, you don't have to make up your mind this minute. Lookahere, it's getting on for sundown——"

"I was just thinking I'd better look for a campsite."

"And I was just going to say there's no call for you to eat something cremated over a deadwood fire when you can have a good home-cooked supper along with me. I take my meals at the Vesses', and I reckon Hester Vess can always squeeze another spoon onto the board."

"Well . . ."

"I won't hear no. The Vess house is the nearest thing we've got to a hotel in Tuscahoma. You can put up for the night for four bits. The meal is on me. Or you can sack down in the loft at the livery stable. Vess runs it." He bustled toward the door. "I'll whistle up a boy right now and have him take your animals down to the stable."

•

"Hester, I'd like to make you acquainted with Mister Virgil Stewart. This here's Miz Hester Vess."

Hester Vess was something new and improved in the line of boardinghouse landladies, as Stewart knew them. She was not plump and white-haired and smelling of fresh-baked bread, like some, nor grim and battle-ax gaunt and smelling of asafetida, like others. She was about his own age, red-haired and vivaciously pretty, and she smelled of flowers.

"I'm happy to meet you, Mister Stewart," she said, as if she meant it. "I watched you ride in."

This was unremarkable; only the stable mice hadn't. But Stewart was pleased that she made it sound like a personal and private interest on her part.

"Come in here in the parlor and sit, Mister Clanton, Mister Stewart." She opened one of the doors leading off the hall. "Supper'll be ready in two shakes."

She flitted about the room, lighting candles. Stewart sidled in and stood stiffly in the middle of the parlor, not daring to settle his travel-stained breeches on her prim furniture. Clanton joined him and the redheaded woman disappeared toward the back of the house.

"Now what do you know about that?" said the storekeeper, with a conspiratorial wink. "She's gone and tooken a shine to you already. Ain't everybody she'd invite into the parlor room on their first visit."

"Wish I'd changed clothes," Stewart said uncomfortably. He picked up a book from a chairside table, winced at its muletrain title— EXTRACTS IN PROSE AND VERSE *by a Lady of Maryland, Together with a Collection of Original Pieces of Prose and Verse Consisting Principally of Pieces of Moral Instruction, Descriptions of Fine Scenery, Delineations of Distinguished Characters, &c.*—and hastily put it down again. Then he started, as a long, hoarse, sheeplike bleat sounded from outside.

"Supper horn," said Clanton casually. "She blows it to call Vess. The stable's at the other end of town."

The other end of town being something like a long spit distant, her husband's arrival was almost simultaneous. There was a crashing on the front porch which heralded the entrance of a grizzled, iron-jawed, bullish man. Clanton introduced him as William Vess and, after Vess had mangled Stewart's hand, he invited them to partake of his house's hospitality. "Might's well eat" was how he put it.

The kitchen was a big-beamed lean-to on the rear of the building, like an afterthought. But it was roomy, cheerily candlelit and well appointed. It had a sink with a pump, right there inside the house, and a good-sized wood stove.

Hester Vess was again untypical in that she set a bountiful table, and there was no hesitancy or finicking in the way the men pitched into the burgoo of squirrel and deer meat and mixed vegetables. For Stewart it was the first food he'd eaten in more than a week that hadn't been iron rations. And to judge from their build, their grunts and their two-handed technique, both Clanton and Vess were men who gave Hester's meals the undivided attention they deserved.

The woman spent most of the time trotting between the table and the stove, occasionally pausing to drop a remark into the arena of activity: "Do pass the red gravy, William. Can't you see Mister Clanton has sopped up the last on his plate?" And now and then Clanton would halt his millstone grinding to toss in a testimonial for his store: "You'll note this here is real South American coffee, my boy"—hoisting his half-quart mug—"none of that dried peapod stuff you'd have to put up with elsewhere. I see to it Hester here has a well-stocked cupboard."

When the last heel of cornbread had squeegeed the last plate of its last smear of burgoo, the men leaned back with sighs of repletion. Vess picked with a horny thumbnail at the edge of the table until he pried off a splinter, and began to prospect among his teeth for anything overlooked. Clanton gathered his flesh in preparation for getting up.

"Young Stewart, I'm gonna go back and open up the store. You set awhile. The boys'll want to gather 'round after supper and talk you over, and they can't do it if you're there. But hear me; I want to discuss business with you afore you leave town. I sleep in back of the store. You stop by there, whatever time in the morning you're fixing to leave. Now, will you do that?"

"I will, Mister Clanton. I sure wouldn't sneak off without saying good-by."

Hester paused in her clearing of the table to ask, "Mister

Stewart, would you like me to make up a room for the night?"

"I reckon not, ma'am. I ain't—er—washed in some days. And anyhow I ought to stay by my animals and gear."

"There's an empty stall next to the one your mule's in," said Vess. "I'll throw some straw in it when I go down."

After Clanton had left, Vess produced two clay pipes and offered one to Stewart. They lit up and smoked for a while in silence, studying each other out of the corners of their eyes. Then the heavy gray man put his elbows on the table, leaned across it and grinned chummily.

"Don't reckon you're aiming to make a habit of picking up after Murrell, hey." Stewart couldn't tell whether the man had framed a question or a prophecy.

"Not unless he makes a habit of leaving his used-up bodies in my path, I'm not." Vess grunted and went back to sucking on his pipe. "Murrell seems to be kind of a household word in these parts," Stewart ventured. "Maybe I'm pure green, but I never heard of him before."

"If you're aiming to travel the Natchez Trace," Vess said, leaning forward almost eagerly, "you'll find out about John Murrell, all right. You might even find out firsthand, like that nigger did. Ever hear of Mason? Or the Hares? Or Big and Little Harpe?"

"Yes. What they called land pirates. But they were all cleaned out some years back. I heard that Harpe's head is still nailed up in a tree somewhere, from when they caught him."

"Well," said Vess, "if they stuck his head there to discourage imitators, they might as well of used it for a doorstop. Because Murrell took up where them others left off, and it looks like he'll lay over the whole bunch of 'em for pure rattlesnake meanness."

Stewart murmured that, for just one man, this Murrell seemed to have got a pretty tight stranglehold on this neighborhood.

"Not just here. The whole Trace is his hunting ground— from Natchez to Nashville and God knows where else besides. And he's not just one man, neither. They say he's got a whole army behind him. Killing, robbing, stealing livestock and slaves, passing bad money. Just about any lowdown crime that happens, they say it was done by him or for him."

The storekeeper had mentioned that people didn't like to take sides when Murrell was discussed. But it seemed to Stewart, from this man's almost lip-smacking account of the bandit, that it wasn't hard to tell which side Vess would like to be on.

"And there's no law to stop him?"

"Hell, he owns the law, too. Murrell is a rich man now, and a powerful one. More than a few peace officers and judges are spending his money—and looking the other way when there's a Murrell henchman to be hunted or tried."

"It does seem to me," said Stewart, after some cogitation, "that a man like that is a nuisance that ought to be stomped on." No sooner had he said it than he stiffened at a sudden command from behind him.

"Put up your hands, Mister Stewart."

Without turning, he numbly raised his hands chest high. But it was only Hester who came around in front of him, smiling, and looped a hank of yarn over his hands. "Would you be a gentleman and help me wind this skein?" she asked prettily. "William never will sit still for it."

Vess got up from the table, with a disdainful look at the suddenly domesticated Stewart. "Don't go stomping after Murrell with your hands tied like that," he advised. "I'm going down to fix the stable for the night."

When he had clomped out of the house, Hester stopped winding and said, "Why're we sitting here in the kitchen? Let's go in the parlor and have a real visit."

Stewart followed at the end of her woolen leash-string and sat down—protesting his unworthiness of these hygienic surroundings—on a spindly little bench she placed for him. Hester also sat, her knees almost touching his, in a Windsor chair that had a peg lamp stuck in a socket in its arm. The soft blend of candle and lamp light on her auburn hair, creamy skin and butternut dress made a warm picture that pleasantly disturbed Stewart's senses.

"Tell me about Tennessee, where you come from," she invited softly, and taking her time with the winding.

"Why, it's——" His voice came unstuck rather more loudly than he had intended, and his sudden demonstrative gesture spilled some of the wool in a tangle. "——pretty much the same as here," he finished lamely, rearranging the skein across his hands.

"Well, that's interesting," she said, as if it was. "You ought to feel right at home here, then. Yes, if you're ever aiming to settle, you could do worse than Tuscahoma."

"I'm—more the fiddlefoot type. Been meandering ever since I left my folks' place back in Georgia, when I was sixteen."

"High time you put down some roots, then. I'm sure William and—and *I*—would welcome having you for a neighbor."

"Well, uh, thank you, Miz Vess."

"My first name's Hester, if that's easier to remember." She wrinkled her pert nose. *"Missus* Vess is my mother-in-law."

"Hester. That's a mighty fetching name. We had a colored washerwoman back home named Hester." Something was wrong with that. "I mean, I always thought the name was too nice for a ——"

"Virgil is a nice-sounding name, too. You're named after a—a Greek warrior, I think he was."

There ensued a silence, time enough for a Roman poet to twirl in his grave. Stewart said the only thing he could think of: "Is that a fact, ma'am?"

"Yes. I believe he fought with Ulystus." Another pause. "Virgil Stewart, are you always so bashful around female folk? Here we are, friends I hope, and nearabouts the same age I *know*. And you keep calling me missus and ma'am like I was about to thimble your ears."

"I—it's just that I don't often meet up with——"

"Now you can't tell me there ain't some little girl pining for you back in Tennessee. And a traveling man like you, why, I bet you've got a sweetheart in every settlement betwixt here and Memphis."

"Well, there's a girl in Madison County that I reckon you could call . . ."

"I knew it! So you *can* charm a lady when you want to. I'm sure she must be a real belle."

Stewart was saying yes, she was, when there came the thunder of William Vess at the entrance. Stewart seized this opportunity to make his escape, and fled down the empty, moonlit street to the sanctuary of the livery stable. His mule, in the next stall, loudly broke wind by way of complaint at being disturbed. There were things to be said against mules as bedfellows, but at least they didn't *flirt*, by God, like Hester Vess. Or, like everybody else in this town, go on and on about that fellow Murrell.

•

"I just don't see any reason you could say no to this kind of a proposition," said Clanton. It was the next morning, and Stewart was being treated to another show of flirtation, this time by the storekeeper. As promised, he had come by at dawn to say good-by, and the fat man had bounded out of bed and into a sales talk.

"But I'm all saddled and packed, ready to go," said Stewart.

"Fine. You can lead your mule right up here and unload." Clanton, wearing an apron over his long underwear, was bustling about the store, pinning back the window curtains and unbarring the street door. "You realize what I'm offering you, young man? A partnership!"

That did truly sound fine, Stewart conceded, but he just hadn't figured to settle.

"*Now* you talk like I'm binding you into indenture," said Clanton. "Any time you feel like it you can pack up and move on. But this way you'll have something to jingle in your jeans when you do."

It wasn't, Stewart admitted to himself, that he felt so strongly about moving on southward. Nor that he felt strongly against staying here. For that matter, he had to admit that he had never, so far, felt strongly for or against anything much. For five years or so, he had been drifting from one occupation to another, from one opportunity and one place to another, as capriciously as a milkweed puff, feeling no particular regret for yesterday nor any unrealistic optimism about tomorrow. The little farm in Tennessee had cajoled him for a while with a vision of the Good Life Found. Then that had bored him and he'd given it up—despite the wishes and advice of a girl who did have a certain stake in his future. Now the wanderlust had brought him this far. And Clanton's argument was making footlooseness sound like a phase he ought to put behind him.

"A partnership," Stewart said thoughtfully.

"You might knock it and say it's only a *junior* partnership,"

Clanton put in hastily. "But how many other young fellows you reckon would like to say they own a piece of this thriving merchandise mart?" He waved an arm to take in the whole store. "Why, not to mention the stock in trade, just regard that show winder. Bet there ain't another that size this side of Natchez."

Stewart had to agree that it was a mighty fine window. Clanton seized on the intimation of surrender.

"We'll work it the way I said, then. You contribute your merchandise to the stock. We'll settle on a fair valuation of it, and figger from that what percentage of the business you're entitled to call yours. At the end of each week, we'll split the profits according to that percentage. And since you'll be clerking here, you can count every picayune that comes in and see that I don't take any advantage. Once you've tried it for a while, if you like it, you can sashay back up to Memphis and bring down the rest of your goods. And we'll figger a new and bigger percentage. Now what could be fairer?"

"Nothing, Mister Clanton. But I'd reckoned on seeing something of the country. Natchez and New——"

"Don't waste your time," Clanton said flatly. "Nothing in Natchez but gamblers. And foreigners in New Or*leens.*"

"I've never seen a foreigner," Stewart said, rather wistfully.

" 'Course you have. What do you call niggers? And Injuns? Anyhow, here it is almost September. Be winter afore you know it. No time to travel for pleasure." Stewart started to point out that September was still three weeks off, and that in these latitudes winter might be expected to occupy all of Christmas Day, but Clanton plowed on unheeding. "You'd go slogging through the canebrakes, just hoping to stumble on a cabin where some drudge might or might not buy a scrap of cambric to make a nose hankercheef, and probably pay you in gourd seed. That is, if you don't run into Murrell or one of his gang along the way, and end up like that darky out yonder. While all the time you could stay here and have your cake and eat on it, too. Meaning you get full value for your whole pack, you get a sharehold in a going business, and you join right in as a leading citizen in a substantial community. How's that sound, partner?"

Stewart fidgeted uncertainly. The sun was high now, and the

street outside beginning to show activity. It seemed that, by lingering and foregoing his early start, he had already tacitly agreed to stay.

"A minor point," said Clanton, "but there *is* that dead nigger of yours. If you stick around till the judge comes to town, you can tell your story about that. Otherwise—never can tell—he might have to fetch you back from wherever you'd be, to testify."

Both of them knew it was preposterous to suppose that any lawman, however duty-bound, would go to that much trouble over an unknown and unclaimed Negro, but Stewart obligingly said yes, that was something to consider.

"Well, I've done said my piece," Clanton summed up. "I think I've discoursed on every consideration, so I ain't going to push you none. Now, is it *partners* or ain't it?"

With a brief, not really plaintive sigh, Stewart dismissed for the time being his ambitions of distant horizons. He grinned, shrugged, and took Clanton's outstretched hand.

"I reckon so. Partners it is."

The fat man beamed, and shook the clench long enough to affirm it to his satisfaction. "Now then, junior partner." He wasn't going to let the qualifying adjective get lost in this. "Now then, this calls for a drink."

"Before breakfast?" Stewart said to his senior partner's back as it vanished through the rear door.

"Buttermilk," said Clanton, coming back with two mugs. "Best thing in the world in the morning. Peels the moss off your teeth." Stewart subdued a grimace, clinked mugs and drank to the new affiliation. "Now just let me get some britches on, Virgil—I can call you Virgil?—and we'll mosey down to the Vesses' for breakfast. Settle the arrangements for you boarding there, too."

"Do I have to?" asked Stewart.

Clanton looked at him in mild perplexity, and asked if he aimed to go on living in the livery stable. "Not to throw off on your taste in company and accommodations, but the customers here might not take to having a hostler ladle out their molasses. The back room yonder wouldn't hold two even if I was as rawboned as you, and the Lord knows I'm getting heftier if I'm getting anything."

"Ain't there no place else?"

"Oh, you could put up on one of the farms round about, I expect. But you'd likely have to share a shuck pallet with four–five kids and a sprinkling of even itchier livestock. And one thing's sure. Nobody else sets a table like Hester Vess. What's the matter?" His eyes narrowed slightly. "Her old man spook you someway?"

"Not him. Her."

Clanton chuckled and leered. "That sorrel hair got you, huh? Afeared you won't be able to keep hands off?" Stewart's face flushed, and for a moment his eyes lost their good-humored mildness. The fat man said quickly, "No offense meant, partner."

"No offense taken," Stewart said, after a brief silence. "All I meant was that she likes to talk, and I ain't much on palaver."

"Shucks, is that all? You'll get used to her. Bill Vess did. Now let me go and get dressed."

Stewart went outside and stepped off the boardwalk for a good look at his new store. He backed all the way across the street for a perspective view, murmuring meanwhile, "Clanton and Stewart . . . Clanton and Stewart," and occasionally, "Stewart and Clanton." As he walked up and down to regard the building from various angles, he was peeked at shyly from around the rim of numerous coal-scuttle bonnets, and stared at more frankly by the loafers who were already taking up their tilts against walls and doorways. Stewart didn't quail under this battery of scrutiny; he knew it would abate when word got around that he was now just another townie.

He went back across the street to give a close inspection to the contents of Clanton's vaunted show window. The display had obviously been there, unchanged and undisturbed, for a good long time. It was thriftily composed of items that had been slow sellers to begin with, or had become totally unsellable through the action of time, direct sunlight and flies. Stewart saw little advantage in using this extravagant glass window to advertise the dubious attractions of faded yarns, curdled patent medicines, mildewed leather goods, warped tallow candles, dusty and discolored crockery, and several million flyspecks. He would put in a card or two of his cutlery. The sun wouldn't harm the knives and they would shine out commandingly enough to attract attention—and customers. It wouldn't hurt, either, to paint a sign on the window. "Clanton & Stewart, General Wares" would look good.

•

Hester expressed surprise and delight when the two men showed up for breakfast. "And here I thought you'd gone off for good without even stopping to say good-by!" she exclaimed. "I'm so proud you decided to stay, *Mister* Stewart."

Clanton cocked an eyebrow at this, but said only, "He'll be wanting a room. I reckon you got one?"

"I have two, both real nice." She took him upstairs to let him choose between the two available rooms. They were identical, but Stewart—perhaps harboring some unconscious desire for an open avenue of flight—chose the one that looked out on the kitchen lean-to's roof.

That night, to celebrate the new addition to the household, Hester really spread herself at mealtime. There was pea soup cooked with a ham knuckle, fried rabbit, fried deer liver, baked yams, poke greens cooked with a slab of fatback, white-flour bannocks, snap beans, pickled watermelon rind, chokeberry jam, peach cobbler for dessert, bottomless mugs of coffee and, at the end, thimble glasses of Vess's homemade raisin cordial.

"By the eternal!" Clanton spoke for the table at large, when even he could eat no more. "If Virgil's coming is like to inspire this kind of meals, I'm sure glad he settled." Stewart said so was he. Vess belched and said so was he, but he might have to hike the rent to afford his wife's bountifulness.

After supper, Vess and Clanton went off to tidy up their separate establishments for the night, while Stewart sat on at the table and painstakingly wrote a letter; the weekly post rider was due tomorrow. Hester, busy with the wash-up, sang lightly while she worked around the room. When Stewart folded the paper, sealed it with a dab of candle wax and addressed the outside of it, she came to peek over his shoulder, said "Naomi Henning, is that her name? We had a colored washerwoman back home named Naomi," and laughed delightedly at his discomfiture.

•

At the first week's accounting, the lesser half of Clanton & Stewart was a trifle disappointed to discover what a minuscule share of the receipts his percentage entitled him to. But it did pay for his room and board and left him a mite over. And, he reminded himself, his share would increase when he invested the rest of his goods. Meantime, he could best improve his dividends by simply working harder and making the whole enterprise more profitable.

He was good for business. His slow, earnest way of talking up an article was more believable than Clanton's overblown puffery. He was a sight more patient with the ladies, when they handled the goods and poked and pinched, than Clanton had ever been. Stewart was unfailingly courteous, even when they didn't buy, so that they eventually came back and did. He could swap a bawdy joke with the men and he knew it wasn't profligate to pass around an occasional free chewing plug to the loafers out front.

It wasn't long before Virgil Stewart was as much a community fixture as his senior partner, considerably more warmly thought of, and deferred to almost as often during cracker-barrel discussions. The ladies thought him handsome, and began to bring along their nubile daughters when they came into town to shop. Stewart even learned to take Hester's joshing and teasing as just that. But still it made him uncomfortable to have the pretty redhead fuss over him, and, especially when Bill Vess was away from home, he would flee to his room or to the store whenever her laughing advances seemed more than playful.

He didn't have to wait long for a reply to his letter to Tennessee. Naomi must have written immediately on receiving it, because the post rider brought a letter from her on his second next trip around, just two weeks later.

August 20th, 1833

My dear Virgil,

It is a great pleasure to me to learn that you have settled in Tuscahoma, Mississippi, and already have found such a gladsome place for yourself there.

Your sponsor, Mr. Edw. Clanton, sounds like a fine person, as do your hosts, the Vesses.

Papa and Mama are both pleased that you intimate that

this will mean a fulfillment of our plans, and so am I. I look forward to hearing that you *have* found the situation you wanted, and promise that I shall like the Southwest as much as you do. Please, I should like to hear all about it from your own lips. Cannot you come up for the Christmas holidays, even if that will be too early for me to go back with you?

May the angels attend your continued success and bring you hence for an early reunion, is the sincere supplication of your affectionate friend,

Naomi (Henning)

Scrawled across the bottom, in a heavier hand, was:

My Boy, we have Missed you. We are all Praying that you have found the Grail you sought, and found it, praise Heaven, not too far distant from us. God bless and Keep you. Your devoted friend (and Father-in-law?),

(Rev.) M. Jno. Henning

•

The day after that was high carnival for Tuscahoma—County Court Day, when circuit-riding Judge Awdward came to town and held court in Clanton's General Store. Not long after dawn, the wagons began rolling into town from lesser settlements and farms all over Yalo Busha.

It wasn't for courtroom drama that Court Day was so popular. The calendar seldom boasted anything more titillating than the usual run of pissant boundary disputes, damages by unsupervised livestock running loose, small-claims collections, assault and battery, and an occasional child-support suit. No, the entertainment value of Court Day was mostly in the excitement of having a lot of people gathered together: strangers you'd never met from far corners of the county, as well as acquaintances you seldom saw except on this one day a month.

For the women it was a great chance to trade recipes and sewing patterns; to tot up the latest score of betrothals, marriages, jiltings, childbirths, miscarriages and misalliances; to learn whose heifer and whose daughter had just freshened; to swap details of their various gynecological complaints; and to disapprove of the goings on among the gathered men.

The men occupied themselves mainly in sampling one another's jugs of home-distilled concoctions, in getting up gambling games, organizing impromptu horse- and foot-races, pitching horseshoes, waiting in line for a "real" haircut at Doc Mooney's, and occasionally fighting. Sometimes, when a professional gambler happened to be in town on County Court Day, one or two of the visiting farmers would be left with no farm to go home to.

And there were all the little ordinary, everyday hazards and excitements of urban society. At least one drunk would fall into a horse trough. A dog tormented by children would bite one of them. Some underage and overeager maiden would become a woman in the underbrush of the burying ground. A mule would kick somebody. A bunch of young hellions would drop a lucifer match into some dozing oldster's whiskers. At noontime, as usual, friends and families would gather together in a shady copse, swap around the contents of their baskets and picnic there; and several of them would break out the next day in poison-ivy rash. Some self-anointed expert on sin would, as usual, lead a prayer meeting in a handy barn, attended solely by pious women and irreverent chickens.

This day the court business was somewhat enlivened by young Stewart's performance, when he was called to give testimony in the case of the dead Negro. The store was packed, and the overflow crowd pressed close against the building. Stewart knew and was known by just about everyone there, but the massed eyeballs stared at him, sitting on the witness barrel, as if he'd been an imported professional tragedian. This gave Stewart stage fright at first, and a case of the mumbles. But he was so obviously being admired and envied, and he had told the story so many times already, that toward the end he was rattling it off like a born raconteur.

Judge Awdward, who knew at least as much about pleasing an audience as he did about upholding the law, milked Stewart's story for all it was worth, having him repeat some of the more sensational portions and questioning him on various inconsequential but gory details. When the performance came to an end, the judge handed down the verdict that everyone had expected: "Murder of a colored person unknown by a person or persons unknown," and closed the book on the case. All present agreed that good old Judge Awdward had been impressively sagacious and judicious. No one brought up the name of Murrell.

•

At sundown, the out-of-towners said warm good-bys, split up into family groups and, after beating the bushes for strayed young ones, piled back into their wagons and headed sleepily homeward, agreeing that a good time had been had. As was customary, Judge Awdward honored Hester's supper table with his presence, and spent the night in one of her rooms. The next day, he packed his logs, ledgers and lawbooks in his saddlebags and pointed his horse for his next sitting, over in Tallahatchie County. Stewart, who had an errand at one Abe Ableworthy's farm, rode with the judge as far as the river, driving the bright yellow wagon with the big signs on the sides: "Clanton's Store."

He found Ableworthy before he got to the farmhouse. The dried-up little man was sitting on the ground beside the road, his back against a burned-out stump, gazing out over his acres with something less than pride. Stewart pulled up his horse, waved farewell to the judge, and leaned down to say, "Howdy, Mister Ableworthy. I fetched out that wardrobe trunk your wife ordered from the catalogue."

" 'Bout time," said Ableworthy.

"It just came in last evening."

Ableworthy sighed, got up and dusted the seat of his pants. "Take it up to the house. I'll ride along." He didn't climb to the seat beside Stewart, but hitched himself up onto the tail of the wagon, his legs dangling. Stewart clucked the horse onward.

"Figure on storing some stuff away?" he called back, just to make conversation.

"Yeah," snorted Ableworthy. "Far away."

"How's that?" Stewart said loudly, over the creak and rattle of the wagon.

"We're packin' to move," Ableworthy shouted. "Gettin' out o' this Christ-bitten country."

"Oh," said Stewart, and let the conversation drop.

He reined in his horse again at the farmhouse. It was actually a one-room shanty of logs, with the mud chinking falling out. Obviously all of Ableworthy's talents, energies and ready money had been plowed into the soil; the cabin was a sort of by-the-way, scrimped so as not to take too much ground that could be planted to cotton. If any thought had ever been given to repairs or comforts in the cabin, it didn't show. Ableworthy evidently wasn't particular about the surroundings where he ate and slept, and his old lady was still spry enough to skitter around the leaky spots when it rained. The woman came to the door just then, gumming a corncob pipe, and Stewart told her of the trunk.

"Just hold it a minute," she said, flustered. "Lemme sweep off a place in hyar where you can set it."

She attacked the dirt floor with a scraggly willow besom, and Stewart joined her husband, who was now leaning dejectedly against the side of the wagon.

"How come you're leaving, Mister Ableworthy? Looks like a right tolerable piece of property to me."

"Jee-zuz," said the farmer, with a scornful look. "I never tilled a swawmp afore. The land's all right, but that goddamn river yonder's got it in for me. Three years I been here, and every blessed spring that river floods and rots my seeds and seedlings right in the ground!"

"That much rise to it?" murmured Stewart.

"Christ, it comes right up to the road. I suspicion that our house here must of drifted a rod or more from where I built it. Wake up any morning in springtime and your pallet is floating round 'mongst loose piggins and pipkins. And I got the only chickens in the Choctaw Purchase what know how to swim!"

"Seems to me," said Stewart meditatively, "if you built up a levee and dug a couple drainage ditches . . ."

Ableworthy hawked and spat. "I tried throwing up a beaver dam six miles or so up where the river narrers atween two bluffs. That held the water back just long enough to collect a goddamn ocean. Then *it* all broke loose and drownded two of my cows that was pasturing on the flats."

"I wonder——"

"I'd plow the whole damn place under, if there was anything

to plow it under but *it!"* Ableworthy was getting shrill and a little hard to follow. Stewart occupied himself with wrestling the wardrobe trunk off the wagon.

"Far as I'm concerned, Pres'dent Jackson can give the whole misbegotten Yazoo Speculation back to the Choctaws!"

"You want to sell?" Stewart dropped in quietly.

Ableworthy gave a little jump. "What do you think?" he said. "I been looking for a buyer all summer. Figgered I'd move along anyway, and let the Land Agent handle it for me."

"Well, I might be minded to consider it, Mister Ableworthy," said Stewart, settling the trunk on his back.

"Call me Abe. Here, son, lemme give you a hand with that. Where you want this thing, Aurlene?"

They dumped the trunk on the pounded-earth floor and left the old lady to start her packing. Ableworthy nudged Stewart in the ribs and said out of the corner of his mouth, "Ride me back down to my stump, son. We'll talk there."

His reason for this became apparent when he hauled out a clay jug from the hollow of the stump and pressed it on Stewart.

"You gotta admit I been honest about talking the *dis*advantages of this here place," he said. "Now lemme tell you some of its good p'ints."

So they sat on opposite sides of the charred stump, handing the jug back and forth, while Abe expatiated on the virtues of Ableworthy Acres. ("Used to have a signboard up over the way with that name writ on it, but it washed—but I tooken it down.") He pointed out the merits of its size and location: "One hunderd fourteen and a half acres of good, black bottom land, and—uh—well watered." Its fertile arability: "Rich with loam and silt laid down here by the river waters." Its furnishings and appointments: "One stout hewed-log house, notch-and-saddle construction; split-shake roof; one glass winder and one door, one clay-top chimbley. One stable-barn that, uh, needs some work."

Eventually they got around to talking price. Stewart had *some* money put by, he said, including a wee bit already saved from his stint at the store. They settled on a price and agreed that Stewart would lay down half the amount right away, and pay the balance to the Purchase Land Agent when he took oc- cupancy, "in the spring, when I bring my wife down from Tennessee." They had a drink to seal the bargain, then a drink to Stewart's Naomi, then a drink to Abe's Aurlene—who was going to be "mighty s'prised and pleased" at the news, if Ableworthy could still walk back to the cabin to tell her—and then three or two more drinks apiece just to finish off the jug.

Stewart slept soddenly on the wagon seat most of the way back to Tuscahoma, and found that somehow the news had got there before him. Probably some passerby on the road had seen him and Abe Ableworthy with their heads together, and had mentioned the fact in the storekeeper's hearing. For Clanton and the Vesses were at supper when Stewart unstead- ily entered, and Clanton's first words were, "Reckon you'll be wanting to get your money sack out of the strongbox, eh, Squire Stewart?"

"Reckon I will," Stewart said with a grin, and sort of fell into his chair at the table. Hester discreetly slid a mug of black coffee before him.

"You might of asked around afore you sprung something like this," said Clanton, good-naturedly pointing out Stewart's social blunder. A matter of selling or buying land was custom- arily thrashed out, hedged around, pawed over, argued about and advised on in innumerable discussions with innumerable unconcerned parties before being consummated. "The boys'll be hurt that you didn't feel you needed any advising. Howsom- ever, I think you made a good deal." The fat man's eyes glittered mischievously behind his spectacles. "Mainly on ac- count of I was waiting for Ableworthy to leave town so *I* could snap up that holding."

Stewart looked up from his mug. "I think I got a prime buy. Mister Ableworthy didn't half appreciate what he had."

Vess nodded dourly. "Never was a man misnamed as bad as that work-brickel bushnipple. So lazy he had to lean up ag'in a tree to cuss. Abe Pisspoorly, he should of been called."

"Mister Vess!" objected Hester.

Clanton agreed with him. "If Abe couldn't stick a seed in the ground and have it sprout right up, harvest itself, sell itself, and poke the money in his pocket itself, he wasn't farming."

"Claimed it was the river ruined him," said Stewart, now feeling a little more awake. "Why, anybody could see that all his land is so flat that just a foot of rise would flood it. All it'll take is a little low levee—I can build it and keep it up single-handed—to hold that river back."

"And that good black muck would grow bananies at the North Pole," Clanton added. "I wish I'd of grabbed it earlier, but I can't say I begrudge you getting it. Except"—he looked momentarily worried—"you ain't figgering on retiring from trade?"

"No, no," Stewart assured him. "I just aim to putter around out there whenever I can spare time. Get the levee up, dig some ditches. Then when I bring Naomi down I'll put in a little garden for truck and yarbs. But I won't really farm it till I can afford to buy a couple hands to work it for me."

"Well, I'm glad to know I ain't going to lose me a partner!" boomed Clanton. "And, by damn, the whole town's going to feel good that you're buying into the community. Settling down for real."

"Unless I'm going to lose such a nice tenant," Hester pouted. "You moving to the Ableworthy cabin?"

Stewart shook his head emphatically. "That might do for hogs when I get some. If they ain't too choosy."

"Say now!" Clanton crowed. "Know what I'm gonna do? I'm gonna get the townies together for a *house* raising, Virgil! Make a big party of it. All the men together, we can whomp up a reg'lar plantation mansion for you and your bride. How about *that?*"

It sounded good, and the fact that it never quite came to pass did not lessen Stewart's gratefulness to Clanton for having thought of it.

•

A week later, the Ableworthys and their belongings, namely the wardrobe trunk, a solitary cow and a straggle of chickens, were poled off on a flatboat, bound for the Mississippi and points otherwards.

During the weeks thereafter, Stewart could usually be found at the farm when he wasn't at the store. It was too long a ride away for him to accomplish anything there in the dawn and dusk hours during the week, but he went out every Sunday and whenever he could spare a Saturday afternoon. The house-raising party turned out to be a sometimes thing, limited to a handful of town loafers who rode out with him occasionally. They helped him dig and line the foundations for a three-room house and a privy. Clanton contributed some good lumber and nails, and they got as far as erecting the house framing and part of the roof before the loafers' enthusiasm dissipated and they went back to their more accustomed dissipations.

The river was accommodatingly low at this season. Stewart spent most of his time chopping down saplings and driving them deep in the mud at spaced intervals along the water line. Between these he bedded other sapling poles and all the deadfall branches he picked up. Croker sacks, brought from the store, he shoveled full of dirt and wedged among the poles and branches. Eventually his levee snaked a respectable distance along the river boundary of his land. It was high enough and sturdy enough to hold back anything but a flash flood. The water would gradually nibble away at it, of course, and he'd have to shore up portions of it from time to time. But someday he'd have his own Negroes to replace the whole thing with solid, cemented rock. In odd moments, he cleared the cabin of the Ableworthys' left-behind trash and repaired the holes in the roof, so he had a shelter for nights when the weather turned bad or he was just too tired to make the trip back to town.

One bright Sunday in November he quit work on the levee in midafternoon; he had dulled the edge of his ax and forgotten to bring a whetstone. When he trudged across the fields to his cabin he discovered that Stewart Acres was entertaining its first visitor. One of Vess's stable nags was tethered alongside his own mare, and a trickle of smoke rose from the chimney. He shouted a halloo and the visitor came to the cabin door. It was Hester, in woolen shirt, soft kid breeches and beaded moccasins. As well as he could remember, this was the first time Stewart had seen her in sunlight. Her red hair, unbound, was like a sudden fire against the gray vista of fallow land and winter-bare trees. A man ought to go galloping up to welcome a guest like that; Stewart plodded up with some misgivings.

"Well, howdy," he said.

"Well, howdy." She smiled at him. "You didn't come home last night, and when it started getting late today I thought maybe you'd starved to death out here."

Stewart said she shouldn't have worried; he had raided her kitchen before leaving and had some jerky and cornbread in his saddlebag. Hester said tartly that a white man couldn't work on Injun rations.

"I'm fixing you a hot meal. Anyhow, I thought it was about time I took a look at your new plantation."

"Well, you're sure welcome, Miz—uh—Hester. Just let me wash off a little, down at the run."

When he returned he found a meal set out for him, on a plate she had brought herself, on the flat of a stump outside the door. There was fried beefsteak and fried beans, a sweet potato and a johnnycake both baked in the fireplace ashes, and a steaming pot of coffee.

"You'll have to drink out of the coffee pot," she said. "I forgot to bring a mug." He thanked her and set to with a will. She sat on the ground, hugging her knees, and watched him with warm brown eyes. "When you're finished, you can show me around." Stewart mumbled, through his mouthful, that when you'd seen one hunk of flat land, you'd seen them all.

"You know, Virgil, you've sort of set an example of ambition. Now William is all fired up. He's fixing to build another lean-to on the house and open up a tavern."

"Good idea. More and more people traveling through town every day. And travelers get thirsty."

"We'll have a full-fledged hotel before you know it."

"Growing town," said Stewart. "Get in on the ground floor and grow with it."

The conversation so far might have been between two strangers meeting in that tavern of Vess's. Stewart somehow felt that the conversation had better be kept on that arm's-length basis.

"You going up home for Christmas?" Hester asked.

Stewart shook his head. "Talked it over with Mister Clanton and we figured I better stay for the Christmas business at the store. I'll go up right after, for a week or two."

"You bringing your Naomi back with you?"

"No, not yet. I'll have too much else to take care of. Got to go over to Memphis and get the rest of my trade goods for the store. And there's the house here to finish. I'll ride back up in the spring again, for the marrying."

"Bet you can't hardly wait." Hester seemed suddenly in a merry mood, but her eyes weren't. "Bet you'll get your fill of spooning and sparking while you're up yonder."

Stewart bent to his dish with exaggerated attention. Hester laughed, stood up in one graceful movement, and wandered back into the cabin. When Stewart had finished eating and wiped his mouth on his sleeve, he followed and stood in the doorway. She was standing over one of the quilted pallets, guardedly poking at it with a slim moccasined foot.

"Is that a *bed?*"

"Shuck pallet. Miz Ableworthy's."

"Feels more like cobs than shucks. And they didn't even have the gumption to shore it up off the ground. I'd be scared to see what must be living underneath." She roamed restlessly around, inspecting the rest of the shanty. There wasn't much to inspect.

"You got a picture of Naomi, Virgil?"

"No," said Stewart. "Not here. I got a crayon picture she had done in Nashville, but it's in a big frame and I couldn't carry it on the trail."

"She must be pretty."

"Right handsome."

Abruptly, in that teasing mood again: "You're breaking the hearts of half the young women in Yalo Busha, I hope you know." Stewart could think of nothing to reply—to this one of those young women. "Any girl hereabouts would be pleasured to give you her hand. You're a good-looking man." Stewart coughed a self-deprecating cough. "A hard worker. You've made a passel of friends. You've got a good situation, land of your own. Building a fine new house."

"I don't think that counts too much with Naomi, things like that. She promised herself when I had a lot less."

"She's got good sense," Hester said, and her face was wistful for a moment. She began to gather up the utensils from the meal. "Sometimes, you know," she went on, "a woman will settle for a lot less than a real man, just to get all the rest of it. The things she *can* count instead of the things that *do* count."

After she had scoured the dishes with wet sand, Stewart led her on a walk-around of the farm. She admired the levee, and indicated a spot where she suspected a good fishing hole. She praised the wooded site he had picked for the house, still just a skeleton of framing, and pointed out the places she thought best for planting shrubs and flowers and the kitchen herb patch. And all the time she seemed to have her mind on something else. Back at the cabin, when they were tightening their saddle cinches preparatory to riding to town together, Hester suddenly turned to him.

"Virgil," she said, almost urgently. "You've got a whole, good, sunshiny future waiting for you to take it and enjoy it. You and—and Naomi." She put her hands on his shoulders, and her eyes searched his as if she could read there about something that hadn't happened yet. "Whatever you do, don't let anybody spoil it for you. Don't let anything change what you *are*."

With that, she stretched up, roguishly pecked a kiss on his cheek, released him, and bounded into her saddle as lithely as a boy.

"Come on!" she laughed down at him, as she wheeled her horse. "Race you to the fork!"

•

They gathered at the livery stable that crisp January morning when Stewart took rein for Tennessee: Hester and William Vess, Ed Clanton and a few otherwise-unoccupied loafers. One of the stable Negroes made a great show of conscientiousness, adjusting and restrapping the pack on the back of the saddle. Stewart wasn't taking his mule along; he could make better time without it, and he would be bringing his goods back by flatboat.

He shook hands solemnly all around. Clanton said, "Don't forget now; the boatman's name in Memphis is Sawney Hawkins. He's freighted down to me before." Vess gave him some ribald suggestions as to the hottest spots to visit in Memphis's

Pinchgut. Hester said only, and almost under her breath, "Hurry back."

Stewart climbed into the saddle, raised one hand in a farewell salute and kneed his mare to a walk. He had reached the end of the street when Hester called something after him, but he couldn't make it out. He turned in his saddle without stopping, and cupped a hand behind one ear. Clanton repeated it for her, bellowing. Stewart acknowledged it with another wave and stolidly rode on. That last piece of advice was: "Ride clear of Murrell!"

•

He could see her from the road. Cold as the day was, Naomi stood in the unsheltered dogtrot between the main house and the kitchen building. He wondered how long she had been waiting there—her not knowing exactly when he would arrive. Standing there so tiny but so straight, in her blue bombazine dress, she looked as pert and spunky as a wood violet that had sprung up betimes out of the frozen January ground. She saw him, too. When he turned his horse in from the road and dismounted to unhook the gate, she bounded off the dogtrot and came flying down the hill, her skirts billowing and her black hair tossing.

"Virgil!" She flung herself on him with an abandon that almost toppled them both. Laughing, they swayed, regained their balance and locked for a time in a long kiss.

"I was hoping you'd be here yesterday," she said breathlessly. "I've been popping in and out of the house every few minutes." She touched a hand to his face. "You're blue with cold. Come in and get warm."

"You're warmth enough for me," said Stewart, hugging her closer. "I would've been here yesterday," he explained, "but I stopped off in Jackson to buy something, and it got late, so I stayed the night there." He handed her a small paper-wrapped box. "Here."

"Oh, Virgil. How sweet." She gazed up at him, her eyes the color of the wood violet.

"It's a belated Christmas present, or a betrothal present, call it what you want."

"It's beautiful!" she said, taking out of the box a heart-shaped locket on a cobwebby golden link chain. She snapped it open.

"I couldn't think what to get to put inside," Stewart apologized.

"I know just the thing," she said. "There's a man in Jackson who cuts your silhouette out of black paper. I'm going to have him make one of you and one of me, and put one in each side of the locket. So that when I close it"—she slowly swung the two hearts together—"we'll kiss."

They were at the house verandah now. Naomi called and a black boy came to take the horse to the stables. Mrs. Henning burst out of the house, almost as impetuously as her daughter had, and enveloped Stewart in a bosomy and motherly embrace. The two women hustled him into the front hall, calling out excitedly for "Papa!" to come and see who was here. Parson Henning seemed absent-minded in his greeting, lacking the exuberance of his womenfolk. His handclasp was warm enough and his expressions of welcome as sincere, but Stewart sensed distraction in his manner.

John Henning was a bantie of a man, not much taller than Naomi, and easily lost in the shadow of his buxom wife. Someone had once remarked on his facial resemblance to Andrew Jackson, and he had taken to wearing his white hair brushed up in a cockscomb, to heighten the resemblance and his stature as well. Now the hair was disheveled, so that he looked more like an elderly thistle than like Old Hickory.

Naomi led Stewart upstairs to his room. There she whispered to him, "Don't mind Papa, Virgil. He's—had a little problem on his mind recently. He'll be himself again before long. Now you hurry, so we can talk before supper."

Downstairs again, spick and spruce, Stewart met a snow-storm of questions. The Hennings wanted to hear all about his adventures during the seven months he'd been away, about Tuscahoma and the people there, about his store and his farm. It being before mealtime, Stewart considerately omitted any mention of the prime precipitator in his new situation—the horribly mutilated Negro he had stumbled on. As for the rest, he discoursed far beyond his usual reticence, and held the family enthralled until supper, throughout the meal, and afterward. He described Tuscahoma in terms that would have gratified (and, in fact, echoed) Ed Clanton. He gave his impressions of everybody he had met along the way. "That Miz Vess, now, she's a mighty pretty redheaded woman, and awful nice to me" —which brought the sought-for tinge of green to Naomi's wood-violet eyes. Oddly, though, Stewart felt a tweak of guilt at using Hester to tease Naomi. To cover his momentary confusion, he picked up a chunk of charcoal and drew little maps of his new farm on the hearthstone, and showed them how he intended to make it a Yalo Busha showplace.

Through all this the two women my-myed and cooed appreciatively. Parson Henning tossed in an occasional query, but would then withdraw into himself. Stewart could probably have orated all night, but there were other things he'd rather have been doing. Mrs. Henning, good soul, obviously noticed how he was more and more talking only to Naomi. The woman rose, gathered herself and her not-quite-sociable husband, and announced that it was time old folks were abed.

When they had gone upstairs, Naomi slipped about the room snuffing all the candles, and then she and Stewart sat close together on a settee, bathed in the romantic light from the fireplace embers. But when he leaned to kiss her, she stopped him with a coy gesture.

"You may think I missed it, *Mister* Stewart," she said primly. "But I caught that light in your eye when you were talking about your landlady."

"Miz Vess?" he said offhandedly. "What about her?"

"Pretty. Redheaded. Nice to you. Those are all *your* words, *Mister* Stewart. Just what kind of carryings-on have you been up to?"

"Oh, thunderation, Naomi! I'm not——" Then he caught the mischievous grin she was trying to hide, and said, "Well, I'd have been right lonesome down there, hadn't been for Hester."

Naomi's grin wavered. "Hester, is it? And her a married woman!"

"Heck, her husband's old enough to be her daddy," said Stewart complacently.

Naomi's grin was all gone now, and her eyes were wide. *"Virgil!* Here I just meant to josh you about her! I didn't know I'd hit on the absolute truth!"

Laughing, Stewart pulled her onto his lap.

"Let me go, you—home wrecker! Philanderer!" She fought, twisted, kicked and bit. But not so hard as to hurt. And when the top two buttons popped off her shirtwaist, it might almost have been a natural result of the struggle. "Now look what you've done!"

Stewart looked. He looked pleased. Naomi hastily re-covered the glimpse of satin skin.

"What kind of a lunatic have you turned into?" she said angrily. He kissed the tip of her nose; she wrenched away. They glared at each other for a moment, then began simultaneously to hiccup with suppressed laughter. In a moment more, they were back in each other's arms, and Naomi forgot about her gaping blouse. Stewart didn't.

After a considerable time, the girl murmured, "Is she as nice as me?"

"Naw," Stewart assured her, and added, holding a straight face, "Never put up half as good a fight."

"Ooooh—you *wretch!"* But this time her struggles were weaker and briefer.

•

Stewart slept late the next day, more tired from his trip than he had supposed. He missed breakfast and might even have missed the noonday meal, had not his assigned boy been sent to wake him. When he came to the table, Naomi and Mrs. Henning smiled at him, while Mr. Henning wore the same woebegone look of yesterday. After some desultory conversation about how he'd slept, and what a beautiful day this was, and how if winter came spring sure couldn't be far behind, Stewart announced, "Thought I might saddle up this afternoon and ride over to take a look at my old place."

To his surprise this caused a sudden silence. Then Parson Henning said, "It's been sold again. I don't know if you heard."

"Is that a fact, sir? Well, I don't reckon the owner'll mind me looking at it."

A quick communion flickered between Mr. and Mrs. Henning before the parson said, with a hint of reluctance, "Why, no, I don't imagine so. He's got a big place there. Your farm is just the latest addition."

"Is there——?" Stewart cleared his throat. "Excuse me, but is there—something amiss between you and him?"

The parson reddened and stirred things around on his plate. "Why, no, Virgil. No feuding, if that's what you mean."

"Papa," Naomi spoke up. "Stop being mysterious. Tell Virgil what's made you so dauncy."

Parson Henning gazed gloomily at his guest. "Well, I hadn't wanted to sour your visit, Virgil, with a tale of my woes." Without much gusto he forked a piece of ham into his mouth, chewed and swallowed. "It's just that a couple of my hands have disappeared. Stolen, I'm afraid."

"The hell you say!" Stewart blurted—and hastily excused himself to the ladies.

"My field foreman and my blacksmith," Henning went on. "Caesar and Rustum, the most valuable hands I owned. Easily worth more than a thousand dollars apiece. Just vanished. On Christmas Eve."

"Why, I never heard of anything like that in Madison County!"

"There are a lot of unwelcome things in Madison County these days," Mrs. Henning said ominously.

"I sent out search parties," said Henning. "I advertised, posted bills. Not a sign or a word of them. I'm not a poor man, thank the Lord, but those two Nigras are going to be ruination to replace."

"You sure they didn't just run off?"

"On Christmas Eve, Virgil?" exclaimed Naomi. "When the entire quarters were looking forward to their presents and the party and all?"

"Those two were happy here," Mrs. Henning put in. "They had the most responsible jobs on the place. They were held in higher esteem than a good many white men in this world."

"I had a real nice present fixed up for Rustum," Henning said mournfully. "It was supposed to be a surprise, but I don't doubt he knew about it, or suspected it at least. I'd made arrangements to buy his wife and little boy from Wavely Dooley, over Columbia way."

No, a slave would hardly run away if he had a treat like that to look forward to, Stewart had to admit.

"Oh, no question they were stolen," Henning said.

"Not only that," said Mrs. Henning, with a sharp glance at her husband. "We know who stole them." Stewart raised his eyebrows. Naomi sighed. Henning pushed back his chair and gave his wife a look of patient despair. "It's true, John, and you know it. I vum, you'd take up for the Old Harry himself!"

"The fellow's our neighbor, Blanche. And a man of the cloth besides. We can't go scattering unfounded accusations."

"Man of the cloth," Mrs. Henning sniffed. "A wolf in sheepskin, that's what he is."

The parson threw Stewart a contrite glance. "I'm afraid, Virgil, we're talking about the man who bought up your old holding. A fairly newcomer hereabouts and therefore, it appears, susceptible to suspicion."

"Susceptible, my grandmother!" Mrs. Henning persisted. "Am I the only one suspects him? All that land, that grazing herd, those fancy horses. Where'd he get them, without ever doing a lick of work?"

"By all the saints, Blanche, that's nobody's business but his own! He's doubtless a gentleman of private means."

"Private *meanness!*" she snorted. "Gentleman, indeed!"

Stewart, embarrassed at being spectator to a family quarrel, was hurrying to clean his plate and take his departure.

"Blanche, I promise you," said Henning, in a sort of wail, "I'll have it out with Mister Murrell as soon as he comes back from his trip."

Stewart had his fork halfway to his mouth. Whatever was on it fell off. He really didn't take in any more of the conversation until he was roused out of his meditations by the scraping of chairs away from the table. He was the last to stand up, and when he did he found Naomi looking at him curiously. She followed him out of the dining room, across the front hall and into the parlor. She closed the folding doors behind them to shut out the sound of her mother and father, still bickering somewhere in the back of the house.

"You know something about him, don't you?" she said quietly. "About that man Murrell?"

"I've heard the name before," he admitted. "Not much else. Nothing that'd be of concern to you-all. Likely there's other people named Murrell, and I heard about somebody else."

"There's enough talk about this one that another word or two won't matter. Do you know——?" She lowered her voice. "The woman that's his wife, she's a real coarse, unrefined sort. Nobody else will have anything to do with her, or pass a word with her. They say that Mister Murrell was disappointed by his true love and so he just went and *picked* this woman out of a—out of a house of ill repute, and married her just like *that,* and made her mistress of his whole estate. All out of pure spite."

"Now, Naomi, they said some pretty low-down things about President Jackson's wife, too, right up to the day she died."

"Well!" Naomi compressed her lips. "A man that'd do a thing like that—and him claiming to be a preacher, too."

There came a cautionary cough from the hallway, and then the doors parted to admit Parson Henning.

"Forgive the intrusion, young people," he murmured. "Naomi, my dear, I wonder if you'd excuse us for a few minutes. I'd like to talk to Virgil."

"Certainly, Papa." She curtsied formally and left the room. Stewart stood stiffly at attention before the mantel. The parson took a chair and waved him to another.

"Take your ease, my boy. I know you've actually just had your breakfast, but perhaps you won't balk at sharing a little libation with me?" In answer to some subliminal summons, a black houseman appeared in the doorway. "Lance, bring us a couple of toddies, please." The Negro bowed and backed out of the room.

"I reckon you want to talk about me and Naomi," said Stewart tentatively.

The parson halted him with a nervous gesture. "You and Naomi, yes. We'll come to that. What I really wanted—I felt you deserved an apology for that distressful scene at the table." Stewart made forget-about-it noises and started to stand. "No, no, sit back. It's unfortunate that we had to air our family linen before an honored guest. But now I might as well give you the whole story."

Stewart obligingly put on a doleful expression to match the parson's.

"It's true that this new neighbor of ours, this John Murrell, is something of a mystery. He's not a fraternizer; keeps to himself and keeps his own counsel. He moved in about the time you left, Virgil, and began buying land—paying spot cash for it—until now he's got the biggest piece of property in the county. Then he brought in a herd of blood horses. He raises Thoroughbreds—races them himself, I've heard. And fine cattle, Durham shorthorns, every head with a lineage better documented than my own. He's built a house that must be the equal of Jackson's Hermitage."

Lance slipped silently in and set down a pewter mug for each of them. Into each he poured from a cut-glass decanter a generous dollop of Bourbon County whiskey, sugared it, filled the mugs with boiling water from a jug, and stirred the potions with a stick of cinnamon bark. "Leave the tray, Lance," said the parson; the Negro bowed and departed.

"About Murrell. As Matthew makes mention: he sows not, neither does he reap, nor gather into barns. Oh, I suppose he sells some of his breed stock occasionally, and derives some income from stud services. But he doesn't farm his land or market his beeves. And that's what has got the whole country-side gossiping—where does he get his money? He's often away on long, unexplained trips, and when he comes back they say his saddlebags are full and jingling. I've preached, God knows, against the iniquities of idle chatter, but it would take Gabriel's own horn to silence some of the tongues hereabouts."

Stewart sipped at his hot drink and kept his silence.

"Murrell's wife is another thorn in the community flesh," Henning continued. "They say she's a, well, a fallen woman from the Memphis Pinchgut, and that he married her—if he did—just to have a housekeeper. Whether that's true or not, she's hardly the consort for a preacher." Henning steepled his fingers. "Yes, John Murrell lets on to have a Call. I guess you'd describe him as a nondenominational lay preacher. I understand he's taken the pulpit at a few camp meetings here and there, though I've never gone to hear him."

"What—what is he like personally?" Stewart interrupted.

The parson replenished his mug before answering. "Younger

than I expected. Certainly young for a gentleman farmer. In his late thirties, early forties, I'd estimate. From our one or two conversations, I'd hazard that he's had an education. I remember we had quite an interesting discussion on the significance of the sixes and sevens in Revelations. And that's been about the sum of our social intercourse."

Stewart helped himself to another dash from the decanter. There was silence for a while, Stewart stirring his cinnamon stick, Henning gazing apathetically into the fire.

"I'm afraid," the parson finally said, "Mrs. Henning is all too prone to accept the popular tattle about Mister Murrell. He is aloof; he walks alone; ergo, he is an object of suspicion. I feel as bad as she does about the loss of Rustum and Caesar. But, good Lord above, if the man *is* independently wealthy, or secretly wealthy, or even criminally wealthy—would he *steal*? And would he be so foolish as to steal from his next-door neighbor?"

"Might be that's the way he'd like you to think," said Stewart.

"What?"

"I think he stole your two hands, Mister Henning."

"*What!?*"

"I think he stole 'em. I think it makes no difference to him whether you know it or not."

"Virgil! This is outrageous!" Henning's face was brick red. "You're worse than my wife. How can you idly malign a man you'd never even *heard* of before today?"

"Oh, I reckon I could be wrong," said Stewart placatively. He reached again for the bourbon and made them each a fresh toddy. "But if this is the same man, and I believe it is, I've heard of him before. Let me tell you what they told me down South about John Murrell."

•

"Fantastic!" gasped Henning, some half hour later. "Can this possibly be the same man?"

"Could it be anybody else?"

With an unsteady hand, Henning sloshed more whiskey into his mug. "Here, a prosperous squire," he murmured. "And there, a—thieving murderer? Fantastic. Fantastic."

"You might put the law on him, and let them find out."

"What charges do I bring? What proof do I have, beyond my wife's—intuition—and some wild stories you've brought out of the Choctaw lands?"

"Well," said Stewart, being practical, "if all the neighbors are already inclined against him, I reckon everybody could club together and boot him out of here."

The parson began to stride mechanically up and down the buffalo hearthrug, his mug in hand, his head bowed in deep thought. When he did speak, it was apparent that the unaccustomed plenitude of toddies had begun to affect him adversely. His eyes were unfocused, his voice slurred.

"Want to know something, m' boy? Believe it or not, this is a situation—an opportunity—I've been waiting for all my life."

Stewart sat silent and let him take his time.

"People first told me I looked like Andrew Jackson," Henning said suddenly, " a long time before Jackson became a hero. Back when he was just a pettifogging lawyer here in Tennessee. I've always liked that. Looking like Old Hickory and looking up to him. *I* felt good whenever he made another step up. Tennesee's first congressman, our senator, our general. I did everything I could to look more like him, be more like him. But there wasn't any way I could stretch my runty body, and there didn't seem to be any way I could emulate his exploits. I couldn't fight the British or the Indians."

He stopped pacing and leaned heavily against the fireplace bricks, his head barely topping the mantel.

"Oh, I've had my little set-tos, my little battles and feeble triumphs. I've spoken from the pulpit on unpopular subjects, championed the underdog occasionally, raised my voice when it would've been easier not to. But that's nothing. I talked about sin, but I never tackled it in open combat. I fought the devil, but the devil never fought back. I was always just a little man, who could snort and rampage because the pulpit made me taller . . ."

Stewart was acutely uncomfortable. He made an attempt to restore some of the man's dignity. "You've made a good life for yourself and your family, Parson. This fine plantation——"

"My wife's father built it," Henning interjected, "and my slaves run it. No, I can't point to any single accomplishment

I've ever done on my own. And my vicarious enjoyment of Jackson's heroics has never been any substitute."

He teetered on his feet and smiled wryly into his mug. It was empty again. He refilled it and drank it off, all in one motion. Stewart got ready to catch him.

"That's why I say that thish—this Murrell situation is one I've waited for all my life. Not for me the defense of New Orleans or the pacifying of Florida. But here at last is the enemy, the devil incarnate. *Here* is sin alive, triumphant, unopposed. And it not only exists. In Murrell it has reached out and touched me, invaded my home, challenged me personally. *Me.*"

For a moment, Henning seemed to increase in height and breadth, but then he deflated as suddenly—into a little, elderly, gentle, rather unhappily intoxicated man with a ridiculous topknot of white hair.

"And where is my sword and buckler?" he muttered drunkenly. "Where is my sling and my stone?" He tottered again. Stewart hastily rose and helped him into the hallway, where he found the black man Lance. They each took an arm of the old man, led him upstairs without being observed, and stretched him out on his bed.

"I take keer o' him, Mas Stewart," said Lance. "You best keep de ladies ennertained."

Stewart left the room, hoping the parson wouldn't remember, when he awoke, how he had so indiscreetly turned his innermost self out for inspection. He found Naomi in the dining room, busily embroidering away at a sampler frame. She turned it for him to see. On a ground of naïve arabesques, colorful flowers and equally colorful lambs was the simple inscription, MATT 6:21.

"Mighty pretty. What's it mean?"

"Godless man," she chided him, and quoted, " 'Where your treasure is, there will your heart be also.' Isn't that a nice motto for our new home?" Stewart said yes, it was. "Well, now," Naomi said briskly, putting the sampler aside. "How did the talk with Papa go? Is everything settled? Is he going to marry us or give the bride away?"

"Whoa. Whoa," said Stewart. "We—uh—didn't get around to the marrying arrangements yet. We talked about—well, just man talk."

"Meaning I'm not supposed to pry. I bet it was about that man Murrell."

Stewart neither confirmed nor denied. He appeared to be occupied in counting the stitches of the sampler.

"Very well, then," she said stiffly. "I won't pry. But you know I do have some interest in what plans are made—if they ever are. Just so I'll know whether to go on sewing on my new nightgown, Mister Stewart, tell me please, do you still want to marry me in the spring?"

"No."

"*No?*" Her prim sarcasm evaporated.

"I mean I'd like to marry you right today if I could."

She sat back limply in her chair, with a sigh that registered somewhere between relief and exasperation.

"Putting it off till spring just seems like a waste of several months that we ought to have together."

This reason was plausible enough, but something must have warned Naomi that it wasn't the real one. She studied the profile of Stewart's averted face before she spoke. "Virgil, you've always been so easygoing about things. A few months won't make that much difference, when we've got the rest of our lives."

"I just have this funny feeling, Naomi, like something's clouding up to storm. I don't know why. But—some way—I'd like to get you safe under my own roof before the storm breaks."

"I'd go with you this very minute if you asked. If it means that much to you. I do wish you weren't going back alone. From what you've said about that Hester Vess, if she so much as wiggled a finger, I bet you'd forget all about me."

"Lordy, Lordy," said Stewart. He went back to pondering the sampler, trying to remember what she had said it meant.

"Virgil Stewart, you know you've always been as changeable as a weathercock. Look how you flitted from one thing to another before you lit in Tuscahoma. How long is that going to hold you? How long am *I* going to hold you?"

"God willing, Tuscahoma'll be our home for a long time. And you'll always be the only woman for me."

His bluff sincerity softened her. "Darling, I do worry sometimes. Maybe I have the same feeling you do. Like there's something telling me, too, to hurry and not waste any precious time. But it's silly."

"I reckon."

"We've got to be practical," Naomi said, in her best grown-up voice. "There's the house to finish. You've got to freight your goods down from Memphis. Oh, there are so many arrangements to be made. Trousseau. Furniture. Why, the time will go like nothing!"

"I reckon."

"So let's us have no more of this foolishness about storm clouds. Really, what could happen between now and May?"

•

"Mister Henning isn't feeling well," his wife explained at supper. "He begs you to excuse him, Virgil, Naomi. He's taking a tray in his room."

When she had to make the parson's excuses again at next morning's breakfast, Mrs. Henning spoke directly to Stewart, in a tone implying that whatever he had done to her hapless husband he had done with a vengeance. More to escape her unspoken accusations than for any other reason, Stewart suggested to Naomi that the day was an unseasonably warm one and just right for a ride. So they had the stableboy saddle up for them and rode into Jackson, Stewart slouched on his crow-bait mare and Naomi towering above him on the sidesaddle of a rawboned seventeen-hands hunter. Suddenly and inexplicably, Stewart found himself remembering Hester, not in demure skirts, but in sleek kid breeches and riding astride, like one of those old-time goddesses.

That vision had vanished by the time they got to town, where Stewart let himself be led, suffering, through the billowy snow-drifts of a bridal costumery, where the proprietress simpered at him and Naomi pointed out the merits and demerits of every single gown. Then they went to the portraitist's cubbyhole studio and took turns sitting rigid while he snipped away at black paper with tiny scissors and a delicate etching knife. The artist fixed the two miniature profile silhouettes in place on the blue velvet inside the hearts of the locket. As Naomi closed them together, very slowly, she gave Stewart a secret smile.

The houseman Lance was waiting for them in the parlor when they got back, with a steaming cup of sassafras tea for Naomi and a hot rum punch for Stewart. "De Mas Henning say soon's you got de chill off, suh, he be pleasured to speak wid you in he room."

"Now, please, for my sake, Virgil," said Naomi. "Pin Papa down on the plans for the wedding. Don't let him get you onto anything else."

Stewart promised and went upstairs.

"My boy," said Henning weakly from his nest of pillows. "I seem to see you only to apologize for one thing after another." Stewart again made forget-about-it noises. "Inexcusable," the parson insisted. "My behavior."

"Well, you were worrying about Caesar and Rustum, sir. I can underst——"

"I'm glad you brought up the subject. That's what I wanted to talk about. Our Mister Murrell." Stewart felt an internal stir of apprehension. "I said some wild things yesterday—about vengeance and beating the devil." He turned half on his side, away from Stewart. "In the light of reason, of course, I can recognize what a fool I must have sounded. If ever I did invite a challenge from life, the time for it is long past; the challenge has come too late. I'm too old and rickety to play the role of Jackson-at-the-barricades."

There was a long, uneasy silence in the room. Stewart wished he was anywhere else.

"When Rustum and Caesar disappeared," the parson resumed, "I wrote to Mister Murrell. Blanche would have had me accuse him outright, but I merely asked whether he could shed any light on the mystery. Circumspect, you understand. Well . . ." Henning rummaged under one of his pillows, produced and unfolded a sheet of paper. "This is Murrell's reply. Brief and bland. He is occupied with preparations for a journey. He departs on the twenty-fifth instant, to visit Randolph on business. He begs my indulgence for the delay, but will call upon me immediately he returns, and—humph—do what he can to assist me in the retrieval of my property." Henning looked up at Stewart. "The twenty-fifth is a week away. You had planned to visit with us until about then, hadn't you?"

"Well, yes, I reckon so."

"And then you're going to Memphis. Randolph is just a few miles north of there. Suppose you contrived to encounter Murrell en route, and rode part way with him?"

"I reckon it's possible. I don't say I druther. Anyhow, what good is this supposed to do?"

"Just get to talking to the man. He doesn't know you from Adam, doesn't know you're acquainted with me. He might let something slip. Incriminate himself in some way about Caesar and Rustum."

"Mister Henning," Stewart protested. "It's about all I can do to hold up my end of most conversations. I'm not your man for prizing secrets loose from somebody. Even if he did tell me anything, do you think he'll wave good-by when our road forks, and let me ride off knowing it?"

"Heavens, Virgil, I don't expect him to give you an affidavit of confession. I only hope he'll let *something* drop, some little thing. You make a note of it, of anything he says that might have *any* bearing on this business, and post it back to me when you get to Memphis. It could be something for me to use if I charge him and bring suit. Something more than mere suspicion and hearsay."

Stewart sighed profoundly. "I reckon."

"Then you'll do it?"

"I reckon," Stewart said glumly. "There's just one condition I'd like to make, sir."

"And that is?"

"Well, Naomi's been pumping me to find out how come I'm so interested in Murrell. I've stayed stubborn and haven't repeated anything I've told you. By now she probably thinks I'm in cahoots with the man. I wish you'd tell her about this scheme of yours. Don't make it sound dangerous or anything —but just so she'll know whose side I'm on."

"Surely, Virgil. Blanche would worm it out of me eventually anyway. I'm feeling much improved now. I'll come down for supper and explain then."

When Stewart returned to the parlor he was confronted by the distaff Hennings in congress assembled.

"Well," demanded Naomi. *"Now* is everything settled?"

"Er . . . not quite."

Naomi began to swell. Her mother chipped in, "Did you settle where and when the wedding's to be *held*, Virgil? And is Mister Henning going to perform the ceremony?"

"I don't know," Stewart admitted humbly. "That is, we didn't talk about it."

"Oh, *damn!*" Naomi said, very precisely. Both Mrs. Henning and Stewart regarded her with shocked alarm. "What *did* you talk about?" she almost shouted.

"He—he'll tell you himself," mumbled Stewart. "At supper."

Naomi spent the rest of the day sulking in her room. Her mother seemed inclined to suspect Stewart of an inscrutable attempt at breach of promise. Though she spoke not, he found her lurking in whatever room he wandered to that afternoon. The parson's chirrupy arrival at the supper table did little to melt the prevailing frost. As soon as the soup was laid on and Lance had absented himself, Mrs. Henning demanded to know what her husband and the apparently reluctant bridegroom were "up to."

Henning proudly disclosed, with suitable elisions, his plan to skewer the slippery Mr. Murrell. "So you see, my dear," he concluded triumphantly, "I *am* doing something about the situation."

His wife said grudgingly, "It seems to me like going a long way around the bush to pick one little berry. But if it works . . ."

Naomi had sat quiet throughout her father's recital of his plan, but her violet eyes were fixed coolly on Stewart. The parson asked, "And what do you think of it, my child?"

"I think that only a couple of scapegrace little boys could have hatched such a hookem-snivey," she said unfilially. "Virgil, why don't you dye your face with walnut stain and go as an Indian?"

Henning turned pink and harrumphed. Stewart likewise flushed under Naomi's disparaging stare. In modesty and good sense he couldn't trade on her emotions by telling her that, from what he knew, had heard and surmised, this venture might turn out livelier—or deadlier—than any little-boy game.

The parson mollified Naomi slightly, by switching the conversation to the long-neglected subject of the upcoming nuptials. From the way the women had been fussing about this, Stewart expected the planning session to take all night. As things turned out, under Henning's expert chairmanship, every possible detail had been proposed, discussed and affirmed or rejected even before they finished the meal. Stewart's only role in all this was that of goggling spectator; they might have been discussing some other couple's wedding for all the attention paid to him.

The wedding was to take place at four o'clock on Saturday, May the somethingth. It would be held in Henning's church, but he would subordinate himself to giving the bride away. The ceremony would be conducted by the famous Reverend Somebody-or-other, who had long been promising to come out from Knoxville and inflict his renowned pulpit personality on Henning's congregation. Naomi would wear such-and-such. Miss Yes-she-simply-must would be maid of honor. The bridesmaids would wear such and such. At some point, Stewart didn't gather exactly where, he was to be briefly injected into the ritual. The reception would be an at-home, and would consist of thus and so. The wedding night would be spent in the bridal suite of the Whatsis Hotel in Jackson. Next day the couple would take the stage to Memphis and a suite on the You-know, that brand-new steamboat, to Vicksburg, thence by keelboat up the Yazoo and Yalo Busha rivers to Tuscahoma.

Mrs. Henning was so vivified at having effectually settled the arrangements at last that she pattered directly off to her sitting-room desk to Make Lists. The parson gave Stewart a cigar and his condolences and went off to compose his invitation to the upstate minister. Stewart was left alone with Naomi and the remains of dessert. She sat looking at him for so long that he began to fidget, and finally excused himself to escape to the parlor and smoke his cigar. He felt her stare follow him. Shortly, so did she, but still silent, still staring.

"If you're waiting to find out my opinion of the plans," he offered, "I think everything sounds fine, just fine."

Stare, stare.

"Way it sounds, this wedding ought to set Madison County on its ear."

Stare, stare.

Stewart puffed valiantly at his cigar, possibly hoping to lose himself in a smoke screen. Finally Naomi spoke.

"Just like a weathercock. That's what I called you and that's what you are."

"Why, hey, now," Stewart blustered. "I agree to everything. Fine. Dandy. Wouldn't change a smidgen of it."

"Any old wind that blows, you swing right around with it!"

"Naomi," he pleaded. "What have I done now?"

"That idiot scheme of Papa's!" she flared. "*How* did you ever let yourself get talked into that? You know Papa's just playing general, and you're his troops."

"Well, let him have his game. I don't mind."

"*I do!* What kind of goody has he promised you if you'll play? What sugarplum is he going to give you for it?"

"You."

"I!" Naomi was momentarily taken aback.

"I'm taking his only child away from him. I owe the man something in return. If he wants to act General Jackson, it's a small thing for me to play along."

"It is not!" Naomi regrouped and attacked again. "Not when you're involving a third party, by sniffing after Murrell like a bloodhound. He could make you—me—all of us—the laughingstock of Madison County." She abruptly switched weapons; a bright tear welled in each eye and she melted down onto the settee beside him. "Virgil, this plan of his is not only ridiculous. It could be dangerous."

"No, it couldn't," he mumbled, wondering how much he lied.

"If John Murrell is a thief, he could be worse things as well."

"What the heck, I'm not exactly helpless."

"You are, you are!" She flung her arms around him. "Virgil, you're brave and you're good and you're honest. So honest that you won't suspect less of any other person. You won't believe that Murrell or anybody could do you any harm. You won't see that Papa's just using you—for the big man he wishes he was."

Stewart had the sudden, disturbing notion that Naomi was more perceptive than either he or her father had ever imagined.

"You just bumble along," she went on, "and let him or any-body else twist you around their fingers."

"Like you do?" he asked humorously.

"I declare, Virgil," she said, "you're so foolish that if *I* had any sense I wouldn't hitch myself in double harness with you. Except out of the goodness of my heart—because I think you need a keeper."

"You'll have the keeping of me for a long time," he reminded her. "Once I've done this little errand for your daddy, I'll be beyond his beck. Don't take on about it, Naomi. I promise not to take any chances or embarrass any of us while I'm about it. When it's over, *you'll* have the say-so about whatever I'm to do or not to do. Forever after."

Put this way, it partially conciliated her. She covered her retreat with a nominal show of fuss, but finally relented with a shrug of her shapely shoulders. "All right," she sighed. "I don't know how I could stop you."

•

The rest of Stewart's week was smooth and pleasant. Now that the wedding plans were firm, Mrs. Henning had all sorts of urgent and important trivialities to keep her busy and happy. The parson mooned about in smiling serenity, his gloomy aspect gone, now that Stewart had promised to attend to the Murrell matter. Naomi seemed determined to be sweet and charming and beautiful and desirable.

In the afternoon of his last day there, Stewart let himself be led up to the parson's room again, where Henning produced a map, much thumbed and scrawled upon.

"I've spent some time and thought," he said, "planning the interception of our quarry." He tapped the chart. "There are different roads he could take out of town, and a choice of routes on the other side of the Hatchie River. But he's got to cross the river at the Estanaula toll bridge. You wait for him there, on this side or the other, it doesn't matter. Now don't forget—he doesn't know you from Adam and he mustn't suspect that you know me. If it becomes necessary to name yourself, make up something. He might remember that a Virgil Stewart once owned that piece of his property. And don't ask too many questions." He laid a fatherly hand on Stewart's shoulder. "I don't want him to get riled at you. Let him do the talking, but remember and make a note of anything he says that might be held against him. Here. Here's a little memorandum book of mine that you can fit in your pocket. And write me immediately you get to Memphis. Is everything clear, now?"

Stewart nodded numbly.

"Fine. Fine. Now kneel down here beside me, dear boy, and let us ask our Lord's blessing on this momentous venture."

•

Once more, Stewart and Naomi found themselves alone together with the parlor fire. Naomi responded to Stewart's farewell kisses with a startlingly fierce, urgent, last-time passion that made him get up from her side and retreat as far as the fireplace. He turned slightly away from her, as if studying auguries in the embers, and hoped that his perturbation didn't show through his clothes.

"Plague it," he muttered angrily, "it *is* going to be hard to wait."

He saw Naomi smile, a trifle wickedly, then she called him. Stewart faced her, and got a pleasant surprise. Considering that a woman was naturally and well-nigh impregnably cocooned in baleen stays, corset cover, petticoats, chemise, pantalettes and Lord knows what else under her dress, it was surprising how vulnerably naked Naomi could make herself appear, just by wishing it so—and undoing a few buttons.

When Virgil came, wondering, to her, she lay back and drew his head to her breast. "I don't know if it will make the waiting easier," she whispered, clasping him tightly, "but there are some things we don't have to wait for . . ."

•

When the pale sun cleared the hills next morning, Stewart was seated half frozen on a stump on the far side of the Hatchie River, watching his old mare crop lethargically at the withered January grass. He had had to rouse the disgruntled tollkeeper of the Estanaula bridge out of a sound sleep, which indicated that no previous traveler had crossed it that morning. Now he sat waiting, far enough along the way that he was out of sight of the bridge, but could survey a segment of the road a ways back, where it emerged from a thicket.

He sat and sat. His horse finally despaired of gleaning any nourishment from the local weeds and stood rocking gently, fast asleep on her feet. By midday Stewart had about given way to despair himself and was beginning to fear that his quarry had found a private way across the Hatchie at some other place. But then all his senses were jolted alert, and his involuntary jerk on the reins rudely woke his mare. He had spotted a movement in the thicket across the river.

The movement resolved itself into a horse and rider, moving down the far slope toward the bridge. Toward him. Toward Virgil Stewart's finally meeting John Murrell.

Book Two

THE SOWING

Stewart hastily mounted and put his horse to a trot. He wasn't overly eager to face Murrell, true, but that wasn't why he hurried ahead; just that it might not look good to be found lurking right by the only river crossing. He put half a mile between himself and the bridge before he slowed and searched for a likely place to lie in wait. He found it where the road bent sharply around a high rock outcrop, and dismounted on the far side. When he heard the clip-clop of the follower, he knelt and took one of his mare's forehooves onto his knee.

The other rider rounded the bend and reined in so abruptly that his stallion reared in protest. Stewart looked up, grinned amiably, and went on prying under his mare's shoe with his clasp knife. The other man quieted his horse, then sat like a statue, silently watching. Stewart ostentatiously produced, examined and tossed away a pebble. He stood up, closed his knife and stuck it back in his pocket. "I think she picks 'em up a-purpose. Anything for an excuse to laze."

The dark man continued to stare down at him without any show of interest or curiosity, but Stewart could feel the probe of his eyes. He swung himself into his own saddle, and his horse obliged by sighing tragically.

"You sure she's lazy?" asked the man at last. "And not just in rigor mortis?"

"Can't blame you for poking fun, mister," said Stewart, with a silent apology to his loyal old mare. "But it ain't my fault I'm nigger mounted like this." Without a word the other man started his stallion walking again. So did Stewart, right beside him. "My other horse was stolen. A good one. I've been out two days now, looking for him. But I don't reckon there's much chance of me catching up to a horse thief on this old lady."

"Unless it was just some tramp who rode off with your horse," Murrell said indifferently, "it's probably on a barge right now, halfway down the Tennessee. If it was a professional gang, they wouldn't risk hanging just for your one nag. They'd make off with a sizable herd and rendezvous with a boat. Water leaves no trail."

"Drat," said Stewart. "Reckon I've been wasting my time. I didn't suspicion there'd be a whole gang. Though there has been a considerable rash of thieving here lately."

"That right?" murmured Murrell. Everything about him implied boredom, except his eyes, which were fixed sideways on Stewart.

"Damn right that's right. And you hear all kinds of stories. Road agents, land pirates, travelers waylaid. My wife tried to talk me out of making this search by myself. Tell the truth, I was kind of glad to see you ride up. Road agents won't hardly bother two together. You mind if I kind of ride at your stirrup till our trail forks?"

"I've no objection," said the dark man, indifferently, "if it'll make you feel safer."

"Oh, I'm not *too* worried," said Stewart. "Me, I figure most of the fellows outside the law got there because they were tired of grubbing at life, like I am. I respect their gumption. And I reckon, should I meet one, he'd be as easy on a poor man as I'd be in his place."

"Bless me," said Murrell, "a wilderness philosopher."

"No, I'm no deep-thinking man. It's just that—well, I don't mind admitting that there's been times in my own career when I had to shy a little downwind of the law myself." He laughed ruefully and added, "Not that I made that pay any better than honest drudgery. Not enough to make tongue and buckle meet."

"Excuse me, sir," said Murrell, seeming to warm up somewhat, "but I didn't catch your name."

Stewart reminded himself of Henning's assurance ("He doesn't know you from Adam") and said, "Er . . . Adam."

"Adams?"

"Adam. Adam Hughes."

"Brother Hughes." The dark man gave him a look of having spotted this for an alias but respecting it. He extended a gloved hand. "I'm John Murrell, traveling preacher."

"A pleasure, Reverend."

Murrell made a pious demurrer. "I don't rate the honorific. My labors in the vineyard are my own undertaking, not yet ordained by any established presbytery. I merely endeavor to emulate my namesake, that disciple whom Jesus loved best. So please, no 'Reverend.' Brother I call you—and brother to all men *I* am."

They rode on a way in silence. Though Hughes-Stewart was intensely curious about this man of whom he had heard so much, he forced himself not to stare or show any overt inquisitiveness. But in quick, infrequent side glances he managed to take in all the details of the man's appearance. He was tall, Stewart could see, taller than himself. Afoot he would be uncommonly lithe, wiry and smooth moving. In the saddle he made a commanding figure. He was darkly tanned, with a clean-shaven face that women probably liked to look on. His black hair was worn short and impeccably brushed; his eyebrows were crisp black accents, one of them bisected and quizzically quirked by a tiny white scar. His eyes were gray, so oddly pale in his dark face that when he turned them on you it was like the focusing of two beams of light.

Murrell favored black in his dress. Black jacket with flap pockets and buttoned-back wide cuffs. Black leather gloves. Slim-fitting black trousers that had little loops at the bottom to hold them down over burnished black boots. A black string tie flowing over a shirt front of blinding whiteness. A black hat of a style not often seen in these parts, with a blocked-in crease in the crown and a soft roll to its brim.

The aspect of a more than ordinarily well-to-do preacher was a little faulted by the fact that his jacket was hiked back on either side over the butt of a pistol holstered on each thigh. But they were as ornamental as everything else he wore; the grips were white ivory, mounted and chased with silver. His tooled and inlaid saddle and accouterments were as fine as his blood horse. And that high-stepping chestnut stallion was one to make even prize Thoroughbreds look puny; it made Stewart's poor old mare look like ambulating dog meat.

"I wouldn't be surprised," said Murrell suddenly, "but that I know who stole your horse." This was so reminiscent of recent other remarks that Stewart almost expected him to accuse Parson Henning in his next breath. "I'm not unacquainted with goings on hereabouts," the man continued. "A traveling preacher hears things."

"How about letting me hear?"

"Oh, no good my naming the man," said Murrell coolly. "You'd never get your animal back from him. You might end up going downriver yourself. If it's the man I think, he could do it."

Stewart said he'd appreciate the opportunity to give the bastard cause to try. He reined to a halt and pretended bluster. "Where do I find him?"

Murrell laughed and beckoned him on. "Come along, Brother Adam. You'd look ridiculous charging off after anybody on that spavined old skate."

Stewart fell in beside him again, glowering. "Maybe you feel it ain't right for a man of the cloth to promote violence, is that it?" To his surprise, Stewart felt himself assuming quite easily the character of a hard-used man. He was even more surprised, and startled, when Murrell lifted his voice and addressed the countryside in a sonorous chant: "Thou shalt give life for life, eye for eye, tooth for tooth, burning for burning, wound for wound!"

"Well, that's just about what I was getting at, Brother Murrell. You tell me who the thief is and I'll apply the Golden Rule—treat him just like he's treated me."

The dark face split in a flashing white smile. "Let me tell you about—about this man. You've said you have a certain tolerance for outlaws. When you've heard this one's story, you ought to have a positive admiration for him."

Murrell nonchalantly tossed one leg across the pommel of his saddle, to half face Stewart as he talked; his horse strolled gracefully on, unbothered by the shift in balance.

"This fellow—we'll call him, oh, Jones—was born here in Tennessee. Father unknown, or unprovable. His mother ran a wayside inn over near Columbia, and she gave that boy a most extraordinary upbringing. Trained him to rifle the bags and traps of everybody who stopped at the doggery—and, when they stayed over, to go through their pockets as they slept. The old hen hussy warmed their beds first, to make sure they slept the sounder."

He paused as they crossed a broad but shallow creek, so cold that the horses whinnied, and even Stewart's hurried.

"But that was the only trade she could teach him. So the boy Jones ran off when he was sixteen, and tried to enlarge on his skill. He learned gambling, horse theft, robbing, counterfeiting." Murrell shook his head despairingly. "Even blasphemy. He posed as a preaching child prodigy so as to pass the queer at revival meetings."

"Pass the queer?"

"A rogue's term for foisting off bad money. Jones killed his first man before he was twenty—in a quarrel concerning the prevalence of face cards in a faro deck. He was never prosecuted on that score, the deceased having been even more of a blight on the public weal than he was. But then Jones made a foolish mistake and got himself hauled up in Nashville on a charge of horse stealing. The mistake he made was in borrowing an animal about as vivacious as that one you're straddling. It couldn't outrun the pursuit. Well, I suppose he was lucky to get off with his neck intact. But at twenty-one a year's jail sentence can look like an eternity."

Murrell's voice began to take on an edge, as cold as that creek they'd just forded; until, toward the end of his narrative, his words were coming out separate and hard as the ring of his stallion's iron shoes on the frozen ground.

"Before they even had the kindness to retire him to prison, they mortified Jones by dealing him thirty lashes of the cat at the Market Street whipping post. Then they branded the letters H T into his left thumb with a white-hot iron. Most of the genteel ladies among the onlookers swooned at the sizzle and the stench. But Jones just earnestly damned the eyes of every torturing wretch that had anything to do with it. I think that hot brand burned into his soul deeper than his flesh. I think he'd rather have swung than been put to that inhuman humiliation."

Murrell rode on in a black, beetling silence, seeming oblivious of Stewart's presence. The silence lasted for a quarter of a mile or so, while they zigzagged through a winter-bare beech grove, the silver-gray branches like an untidily piled bone yard. Then Stewart and his horse flinched simultaneously, when Murrell shook his fist defiantly to the eastward and his voice rose again to a trumpet blare: "And the Philistines laid hold on him, and bound him with fetters of brass; and he did grind in the prison house!" Stewart was beginning to get accustomed to Murrell's delivering remarks—whether emotional or casual—in this theatrical play-to-the-balcony fashion.

He went on, less dramatically, "That year in prison was the best thing that ever happened to Jones. He didn't see it so at the time, but it was. Somewhere along the way he had learned to read, and the prison had what passed for a library. A few Bibles and a slew of come-to-Christ tracts contributed by well-meaning old ladies. And an assortment of lawbooks with which the prisoners amused themselves by trying to find loopholes in their convictions. Well, Jones read them all. And he got his kid brother to fetch him others from the outside. More lawbooks and more scriptural works. Literature, too. By the time they set him loose, he could quote a chapter of Ephesians or a commentary of Blackstone or a canto of the Inferno with prodigious ease."

Murrell broke off to interpolate, with a reminiscent half smile, "Hadn't been for that brother, Jones would still be no better than a pistareen lout of a crook. That brother was mighty good to him." His face fell and his voice grated. "I'd hate to tell you how that brother ended up. What the law-abiding and esteemed and respectable folk of a certain village did to him. But I *can* tell you that you won't find that village on any map any more."

Afraid that he was in for another Biblical bellow, Stewart commented, "With all that book learning, couldn't Jones have gone into trade or something when he got out?"

"He could have. But the most important thing Jones brought

out of Nashville Penitentiary was a revelation. He had come to realize that an outlaw alone—or the motley rabble of a criminal gang—was absurdly easy prey. Why, all over the West, when pickings were poor for a gang, they'd make up for it by picking on another. And fighting amongst themselves just made it easier for the law to nobble them. No, what Jones determined to provide was organization, along the lines of a legitimate business venture. As soon as he was turned loose, he hunted up every scalawag he'd ever worked with, and made them all the same proposition."

There was a pause, as their horses took different sides around a buttonwood tree that was at least forty-five feet in circumference.

"Well, they all came in with him. And *they* talked him up to others. Pretty soon he was the kingpin of a far-flung team of outlaws, some of them working solo, some in gangs, but all of them working for him. Now, instead of individual thieves having to peddle their booty where and when they can, for a fraction of its worth, they turn everything over to him. He's able to pay them a fair price and still retain a handsome bit for himself." Murrell laughed. "People prate about the 'headquarters of crime' being in Memphis's Pinchgut, or Natchez-under-the-Hill, or the New Orleans Swamp district. By damn, the headquarters is under Jones's hat!"

"But ain't it likely," Stewart suggested daringly, "with his doings so all spread out, like you say, Jones is apt to run up against an *honest* man some day? One that'll give him away?"

"One . . . honest . . . man . . ." Murrell murmured, as if the concept was new to him. "One white hen in a flock is a pretty thing, but the black ones are safest when the hawk flies over the yard." He shrugged. "Anyhow, what is there against Jones? You lose a horse, a bank in Mississippi discovers that half its paper is worthless, a post rider is held up on the Natchez Trace. What is there to connect with the man Jones? To all outward appearance, on his home grounds, he's a respected and respectable citizen."

"You mean he never takes part in these doings any more?"

Murrell chuckled. "Oh, he's still enough of a rascal to enjoy the game for the game's sake. Like freeing slaves. Notice, I don't say stealing. That's against the law, and Jones is too well versed in the law to break it idly. When he comes across a likely looking Nigra, he merely persuades him to run off. Promises him freedom up North, or an overseer's job in some nice climate, or just knocks him on the head if all other inducements fail. Then Jones tucks him away for a while in one of his hideouts, and waits till it's safe to sell him elsewhere. He may liberate that same slave half a dozen times."

"Don't the poor darky get a little shopworn and tired of this?"

"Hardly. Each time the fellow is sold *he* gets to pocket a small share of the sale price. And he's grateful. You understand, Jones is kindly helping the Nigra build a stake for setting himself up when he finally gets up North."

"Even so," said Stewart. "After a while, the whole nation would be plastered with bills advertising for the same runaway."

"True, Brother Hughes. Comes the day when it's dangerous for Jones to be seen leading this Nigra around, he does give him his freedom."

"Sends him North?"

"A trifle farther." Murrell raised his eyes to heaven. "And even in that, Jones adds a unique and most practical touch. So they say, though no living man has ever seen it."

Stewart was rather uncomfortably reflecting that one other living man had looked on Jones's unique and most practical method of disposal; but what good did that fact do anybody? And, he reflected further, Parson Henning's scheme was working out far beyond any reasonable expectation; but what good did *that* do anybody either? Also, did this personable if sinister gentleman unburden himself to just any handy listener, purely to enjoy his own braggedyness, and then erase his indiscretion with a unique and most practical touch? No, somehow Stewart thought not. Even on such short acquaintance, and knowing full well what Murrell was, he found himself enjoying the villain's company, and suspected that the feeling was reciprocated. Somehow they two had struck an immediate communion—but how and why he couldn't yet imagine.

"So you see, Brother Adam," Murrell concluded languidly, "while I have no doubt that Jones is the man responsible for your missing horse, I do doubt that he has any more idea where it is than you do. He'll merely enjoy a profit on the transaction and probably never lay eyes on the horse."

"Well, maybe there's nothing *I* can do," said Stewart, with grudging resignation. "But there's more and more law coming into this border country all the time. Mister Jones can't rule the roost forever, if it takes President Jackson himself to wring his neck."

"If President Jackson knows what's good for him," said Murrell in a steely voice, "he's probably satisfied to have Jones go on just as he's doing."

Stewart was genuinely staggered. "Why—how can you possibly say a thing like that?"

"Because," said Murrell, "Jones is big enough now that, if he wanted, he could be bigger." His eyes narrowed, and he spoke to himself instead of Stewart. "He could be one hell of a lot bigger. He could be bigger than Jackson."

•

Murrell had pretty well talked the afternoon away. The road dwindled out straight ahead of them to a vanishing point on the distant horizon, and on that point the red ball of sun was magically balanced. They were in a rolling countryside of chocolate-brown pasture land, now dotted with piles of hay, and Murrell cast a professionally calculating eye—whether that of a serious cattle breeder or that of a prospective purloiner, Stewart couldn't tell—on every field full of beeves they passed. The cleared land was dotted with copses, groves and occasionally sizable woods of bare-branched trees, each bunch consisting almost entirely of a single species—catalpa, buttonwood, locust, black ash, infrequently still-green pine—as if the trees had decided, in the manner of men, to congregate by kind and isolate themselves from alien types.

"Well," said Stewart wearily, "that old sun's going to be quenching itself in the Missassip before long. One more blame day I've wasted on this fool's errand. Reckon I'll sack down in the pineys yonder, and head back for home in the morning."

"A January night is not the most felicitous time for camping out," said Murrell. "If I'm not mistaken, there's an inn about four miles on. We can make it by nightfall."

"Thankee for the information," said Stewart, who would

have welcomed a bed, but was committed to playing the poor man. "Even had I the money I wouldn't squander it just to have a roof over me. I've slept out before. Barring an invasion of bobcats, or your Mister Jones, there's no harm in it."

"He maketh me to lie down in green pastures," said Murrell. He rubbed his chin in meditation, then grinned boyishly. "Blessed if I don't think I'll join you, Brother Hughes. Where I'm headed I'll have to camp out often enough; I might as well get used to it. That is, if you'll put up with a continuance of my company . . ."

Stewart had heard far more than enough to relay to Parson Henning, and so spur him to action, if the parson was so minded. Stewart had completed his mission, and he'd rather have been shed of this man. But he'd also rather not get shot for saying so.

Not far from the road, they came to a small glade among the trees, comfortably carpeted with a fall of soft, dry pine needles. They made up springy, sweet-smelling beds of fresh-cut pine boughs, with their saddle blankets slung over them, and their saddles for pillows. They fed their horses grain from their traveling provisions. Murrell had no saddlebag provender for himself; Stewart kindly volunteered to share his rations.

When they hunkered down by the fire to eat, Stewart asked, "Ought you to be sitting on the ground in them fancy duds?"

"The clothes'll have to get used to the ground, same as I do."

"Sure is a natty outfit. Was I you, I'd save it for dance parties."

Murrell said, with his mouth full, that he'd found that a preacher did well to set himself apart from his flock—and a little above them—in costume as in manners and spirituality. When a congregation looked up to its pastor, his preachments seemed to come from that much higher up. "I deem it a good investment to order my clothes custom-made for me. My shirts come from New York, my suits from New Orleans, my hats and boots from Philadelphia." He stretched his legs out straight before him and proudly contemplated the high-polished, pointed black leather boots. Stewart said it seemed kind of an extravagance, to have one's footwear tailored left and right like that.

"Why?" asked Murrell, puzzled. "That's the way everybody

wears them back East. One made for the left foot, one for the right."

"But then, when they begin to wear over on the heels, you can't swap 'em around to even out the wear."

Murrell laughed tolerantly. "When they wear down I give them to some deserving Nigra and order myself a new pair."

"That's what I mean," Stewart murmured. "Extravagance." He stretched out his own legs and regarded, with the complacency of a thrifty man, the identical heavy, blunt, round toes.

"Well," said Murrell. "We might as well get bedded down while there's still firelight." He began scouring his tin dish with a handful of pine needles.

Stewart agreed, and cleaned his own utensils. When he packed them away again in his saddlebag, he loosed his old rifle from its thongs and laid it handy alongside his pallet. Murrell raised his eyebrows inquiringly.

"My squirrel rifle. In case any beastie comes nosing around the food scraps during the night."

"Squirrel rifle? A half-inch bore is kind of massive for squirrels, wouldn't you say? Like swatting flies with a two-by-four."

"You never heard of what they call barking a squirrel?" said Stewart lazily. Consciously or not, he was trying to impress this man who had already considerably impressed him. "I bounce the ball off the tree trunk next to the critter's ear. The concussion stuns him and he drops right into my hands. No mess, no clotting, no lead to bust your teeth on when you eat him."

Murrell's eyebrows went up even higher. "A veritable Nimrod Wildfire."

"Speaking of armament, that's a nifty brace of hardware you're sporting."

"Ah!" breathed Murrell, pleased. "My Jonathan," he said, slapping his left holster, "and my David," slapping the other. "They're of English manufacture, Brother Hughes. Made by H. Egg of London. Fifty-four caliber, but as cunning and exquisite as dueling pistols. Converted from flintlocks they are."

"A bigger ball than my rifle," said Stewart. "Ain't that a bit hefty for fine shooting?"

"See that leaning pine yonder? The one with the scar?"

Simultaneous with the last word, Murrell's two hands dropped to the pistol butts. The word was barely past his lips when the pistols were alive in his hands, and the single blast was his punctuation mark. The deafening thunder of the guns racketed back and forth through the woods. A cloud of acrid blue smoke filled the glade. Stewart's mare danced uneasily. Murrell stood up, beckoned to Stewart and led him to the tree, some dozen paces distant. It wasn't much more than a sapling, still quivering; it bore a single, splintery hole, breast high to a man.

"It appears that either David or Jonathan has a mite of drift," Stewart said tactfully. He was sufficiently impressed that Murrell had been able to pick out the slender tree across the glade, let alone snap-shoot through the flickering firelight, the smoke and heat-wave refraction, and hit it with even one of his bullets. But Murrell had produced a clasp knife with a corkscrew attachment and was winding it into the hole in the tree. After a minute's silent work he extracted and dropped into Stewart's palm two separate, distorted gobbets of lead.

"I win a few bets that way," he said modestly.

Stewart stared at the impossible evidence, then at him, in frank astonishment. Murrell beamed and went back to the fire. Stewart followed and plunked down on his saddle, still tossing the balls in his hand.

"Dog my showing off," Murrell growled to himself. "Now I suppose I ought to clean these things before I reload them. And I wanted to go to bed."

"Don't trouble," said Stewart, in a quiet voice. "I prefer 'em empty."

Murrell looked up, and the eyebrow with the little scar notched up on his forehead. Stewart's rifle was across his knee, and the big black eye of it stared solemnly at the middle of Murrell's chest. In the sudden silence, the click of the hammer cocking back sounded almost as loud as the shooting earlier.

"What is this?" said Murrell. He barked a short laugh. "Don't tell me you're Mister Jones!"

Stewart shook his head without relaxing his gaze. He leaned forward and held out his clenched left hand, thumb extended, into the firelight. "Let's see you do that, Brother Murrell," he commanded.

Murrell's quizzical frown melted into a wolfish grin. There was a very long pause. Murrell considered Stewart's set face and the unwavering rifle barrel, then with another laugh dissolved the tension. He too leaned forward and held his left thumb in the light. The letters H and T on its ball were dead white against his dark skin.

•

"It was a jape, Brother Hughes, just fun and games. You'd have to be a natural-born idiot to have swallowed all that about Jones without suspecting I was talking about myself. And you're no idiot. You're no simple bushnipple either. A farmer you may be, but you've been other things as well. You admitted that yourself. And, my boy, I could see hell dance in your eyes the minute I started talking."

Stewart said nothing. He was asking himself why the dickens he had so impulsively blown the game wide open like this. A twitch of his finger on the trigger was the most practical next move, but how would he ever explain shooting the good Reverend John Murrell, Esquire, in cold blood? And yet, now that he *had* drawn a bead on him, what alternative did he have?

"All the time I was spinning that little rags-to-riches story, I could see you cogitating—and I'll bet Jonathan and David against your four-dollar blunderbuss I know what you were thinking. Now tell me true. Weren't you wishing you could trade your worthless farm and your grubby prospects for that kind of romantic and prosperous career?"

Stewart remained silent, mentally flipping a coin. But if Murrell suspected that his continued existence was under consideration, he gave no sign.

"I'm happy to say that you show the proper mettle for such a career, Brother Adam. Should you outlive the hangman, you can tell your grandchildren that you were the only man ever to get the drop on John Murrell. But I tagged you for my kind of man some ways back. This little trick of yours just confirms my opinion. Now if you'll put up that rifle, I've got an offer to make you that I don't make to just anybody."

He dug in a coat pocket. Stewart's trigger finger curled tighter, but relaxed when Murrell's hand emerged with nothing more lethal than a black Dosamygos cigar.

"I'm not funning you now, Brother Hughes. I've got a proposition that could be the making of you." He stopped and lit his cigar with a brand from the fire. "Being it's late and cold, I was going to save this confabulation for tomorrow. But your sour demeanor prompts me to broach it now. Put up the iron, friend. My sting is yonder in the tree, and my oratory isn't likely to prove fatal."

Stewart communed with himself and came to the conclusion that a stretch of listening would at least postpone his having to decide how to settle this tetchy situation. After a moment he thumbed the rifle's hammer gently down onto the nipple and laid the gun aside. Murrell smiled, produced another cigar from his pocket and flipped it across the campfire to Stewart.

"The name Jones was a feeble fiction, of course, but everything else I told you was true. This country hereabouts is riddled like an anthill, with a great spread of organized deviltry working away underground—and I am, I modestly submit, the head devil. There are places where you can't speak the name of John Murrell without making people shiver as if the winter had come sudden and unexpected. But even the people who know and fear the name don't know just how much they have to fear. I told you, back there on the road, that Jones was big enough now to grow a lot bigger if he chose. Well, John Murrell chooses. The whole Southwest is already mine in fact; I aim to make it so in name."

Stewart was already beginning to regret not having pulled the trigger.

"Perhaps I made our organization sound like a scurvy bunch of scamps and tramps conniving to keep each other out of jail. It's more. It's as solid and well run and powerful as anything this side of Washington City—and a damn sight more so than any of the state and territorial governments out here on the frontier."

Either because of his own whipped-up excitement or because of the night's rapidly encroaching cold, Murrell stood up and began to stride up and down before the fire. Stewart felt the chill, anyway; he stripped the blanket off his pallet and draped it around his shoulders.

"Ignorant country jakes call us the Murrell gang. *We* prefer to call ourselves the Mystic Confederacy, or sometimes just the Clan. See, Adam, it's set up along the lines of a secret brotherhood. We have our passwords and handshakes for recognition, because there are so many clansmen by now that they can't possibly all know each other without something like that. And besides, all this rigmarole impresses the Nigras."

"The Nigras?" Stewart echoed, uncomprehending.

"Ah, despise them not, Brother Hughes. They comprise an important part of the Mystic Confederacy." He took a long drag on his cigar. "Now, here's how the Clan works. I am the chief of an inner circle: the high priests, the presidential cabinet, call it what you will. There are only a dozen, all cofounders—the men who clave to me way back when I first came out of the Nashville pen. They in turn oversee the activities of eighty subordinate officers—who each command a troop of their own. Should need be, I can mobilize the entire Clan on a few days' notice. An army, Adam, an *army!* Under my command, at this very instant, I have—in addition to the chiefs and subchiefs I mentioned—more than three hundred white men and a thousand blacks!"

"How do the blacks fit into all this?"

Murrell came around the fire and squatted down in front of him. "Think, Brother Hughes," he said breathlessly, "what would be the most terrible disaster that could hit this western country right now?"

Stewart thought. "Another war with the British?"

The dark man shook his head. "They'll never try again."

"The Choctaws and Chickasaws fighting for their land back?"

Murrell snorted contemptuously. "Think, man! The settlers out here in this country are here on sufferance. But whose?"

Stewart looked at him blankly. "Yours?"

"*The blacks'!* This country is chopped up into plantations and farms and piddling townships, each peopled with a handful of whites and a hell of a lot of slaves. The Nigras outnumber the whites three or four to one! Were the blacks to rise up, all at once, in all their numbers, they could squirt the white man out of the Southwest like an orange pip from between your fingers!"

The pervading cold in the glade now was not solely that of January. Stewart tugged his blanket closer. Murrell bounced up again and resumed his pacing, gesticulating dramatically, his pale eyes reflecting red from the campfire.

"Think of it, Adam! All the blacks that are working on the river, in the towns, in the fields—all of them churning up together at the signal. Slashing out with their scythes and boat hooks and pickaxes! Burrowing into haymows for the guns I've given them! Halting a hog butchering to butcher the master! Firing the cotton fields and the cane fields and the bales on the wharves! Hacking, chopping, slaughtering without let or ruth, like the savages they are! Their black hands turning red!"

Stewart glanced at his rifle.

"All the white men, unprepared, unbelieving, unresisting, wiped out in one flash flood of blood. All but me, Brother Adam, all but me and mine! For us—a whole land, an empire, a dynasty. The busy river towns, the rich city of New Orleans, the wide countryside all cleared and cultivated and waiting *our* seed. Everything, man—from the Mississippi delta to the Ohio!"

Stewart cleared his throat and said, "A darky's a brickel thing to put your trust in. Suppose one of them's loyal enough to his master to warn him what's coming?"

"If I can keep half the white men in this country scared to split on me," said Murrell blandly, "don't you think I can nail the black mouths shut as well? They keep the secret partly because of the grand things they expect to gain from this. They're looking forward to having their liberty, owning their own land, re-creating Africa right here, being biggity as white folks . . ."

Stewart had some difficulty in swallowing the bile that kept rising to the back of his throat.

"That's the carrot out in front of the donkey," Murrell went on, "but I've got a goad at the tail end as well. Oh, we throw the fear of the devil into these Nigras, Brother Hughes! We make it downright plain what will happen if they leak any of our plans."

Brother Hughes threw out one more objection. "This country out here may be kind of unsettled and insecure, but it's still a piece of the United States. Do you reckon Jackson's just going to sit still while you raise jesse with it?"

"Jackson!" Murrell said contemptuously. "My Mystic Confederacy is not a bunch of swamp-rat Seminoles. Or British lobsterbacks, to march against his 'Dirty Shirts' by rank and file. When we strike, it will be at a sign—an attack on a score of fronts, as near simultaneous as possible. Memphis, Natchez, Vicksburg—the whole Mississippi valley at a stroke. By the time word gets to Washington City, Jackson will have an accomplished defeat to consider. A war, Brother Hughes, declared, fought and finished before he can stir. Mark you"—he took a final drag on his cigar and tossed it into the fire—"Jackson won't be *fighting* me, my lad, he'll be negotiating *treaties* with me! Just as he does with England or Spain or any other empire."

Stewart slowly, sadly shook his head. He picked up a couple of nearby branches to stoke the dwindling fire.

"Does all this sound to you like a madman's ranting, Brother Adam?" Murrell asked, kneeling again and regarding him closely.

"No," Stewart admitted. "It sounds well thought out."

"Right!" Murrell clapped a hand on Stewart's knee. "A lot of planning and hard work has gone into it. There's still a lot to be done. Let slip the dogs of war . . . but not tomorrow or the next day. This has to be done right; there'll be only the one chance. That's why I've set the date nearly two whole years from now. Christmas Day, eighteen thirty-five—how about that for patience, Adam?"

"You couldn't pick a better time for taking folks by surprise."

"For everything there is a season, and a time for every purpose under heaven." Murrell looked expectantly into Stewart's face. "Well, then, what say you?"

"What say I to what?"

"Why, to joining us, of course. Adam, my boy, I'm offering you a place right alongside me, right up there in my inner circle." He smiled. "Bet you've never had such another opportunity come down the pike, eh?"

No, Stewart hadn't. He fumbled for a reply. This was discon-certingly like being invited home for dinner by a cannibal.

Murrell apparently took his speechlessness for astonishment. He said, "Some of the other top boys may grumble a bit at this impetuosity, but they've got to admit I'm a good picker of men. I picked *them*, didn't I?"

Stewart had never been one to credit omens or portents, but he could see now that this encounter had been ordained from that moment he had stumbled on the dying Negro last summer. Everything since then had been prelude to this. It was all part of the piling-up storm cloud he had mentioned to Naomi. On the weight of evidence, he was destined to be here. But now what?

"Adam. Adam." Murrell savored the name. "Almost pro-phetic. How would you like to rise up like your namesake—one of the first lords of this new Eden?"

Stewart thought faster than he ever had in his life. As far as Henning's original scheme was concerned, he had certainly absorbed enough Murrell-damaging information today. But Stewart himself had by now developed a personal interest in this business, a personal horror of this man's intentions, and an even more horrifying attraction to his mesmeric will. On the one hand, it was no longer a matter of a couple of missing slaves; it was a menace to himself, to his whole country and fellow whites. On the other hand, Murrell was more of a *man* than he could remember ever having met in his life.

Stewart stared at his own two hands. He had no ambition to play hero—or martyr either. But damnation, a man owed a duty to something, a man had to take a stand once in a while. It was no good reminding himself that Murrell was unarmed; that he could shoot the villain and just ride off. Somehow, even dead, Murrell would have ways to make sure he didn't get far with what he knew. The alternative was to embrace Murrell's offer and play the cards as they fell. This promised about as much personal ease and enjoyment as sitting down on a scor-pion.

But maybe, just maybe, he could influence Murrell; make him drop the notion of a wholesale uprising, without having to harm the man he had come to like. Hell, if he could get Murrell off this revolution idea, the man had the brains and personality to get himself legitimately elected President! Stewart almost had to laugh at this line of thinking; it put him so in mind of those obnoxious boy heroes in the storybooks who were always reforming the hardest-hearted blackguards and showing them the error of their ways. But this was no laughing matter. He sighed instead. What the hell, he'd see it out to the end. Probably his own.

"Poor whirly weathercock," he muttered, not meaning to say it aloud.

"How's that?" said Murrell.

"I said I'm your man."

Jubilantly Murrell pummeled his shoulder. "Ah, Adam! Adam! I want you there beside me the night we turn the terror loose on New Orleans. The city the whole British Empire couldn't take, *we* will—you and I and our clansmen! By the eternal, you won't regret this, Brother Hughes!"

"I'm grateful for the opportunity," Stewart managed to say.

"I'm headed for my meeting ground over in the Arkansas Territory—you come right along," Murrell said excitedly. "You can send word back to your wife not to expect you for a while. And Adam—Adam, when we get there, I promise there's a new horse bespoke for you that's the twin to my own Tempest!" He rubbed his hands briskly. "Damme, but I can't help thinking it was a good day's work meeting up with you!"

"I just hope I prove out."

"Had I thought you wouldn't, you wouldn't be sitting there this minute," said Murrell. "I told you about my kid brother, and how good he was to me. I still won't tell you what happened to him; you might not sleep all night. But when I came around that bend past the toll bridge, I thought: *by God, he's alive again somehow.*" He plucked a spotless linen handkerchief from his coat sleeve and blew his nose. "You remind me of him, Adam. If you didn't, you'd be as dead as he is."

He dug in his pocket again as if to produce some more cigars in celebration of Stewart's still being among the living. But this time his hand came out with brass in it. He pointed the toylike pistol at a tree—a closer one this time—and ripped off four quick-fire shots. Stewart looked, rather abashed, at Murrell and at the gun. Then he got out from under his blanket, walked over and examined the tree. As he had more or less expected, the four holes were within a hand's span.

"A four-barrel Darling pepperbox," said Murrell casually. "Very popular with gamblers. Well, what do you say we go to bed now, partner?"

"I'd just as soon," said Stewart, grateful that he wasn't scheduled to sleep somewhat deeper.

Murrell banked some clods over the fire to keep a spark for morning. Then he unbuttoned the loops of his trousers and kicked off his boots. He rolled himself into his blanket, yawned cavernously and said softly, ". . . Yet a little sleep . . . a little slumber . . . a little folding of the hands to sleep . . ." And, as if it had been an enchantment he recited, he was asleep on the instant. Not babies nor angels slept more swiftly or sweetly.

Stewart gave the man a good head start, forcing himself to stay awake. When he was certain Murrell was not shamming, he crawled quietly over to the dim glow of the banked fire, pulled out Parson Henning's memorandum book and, with a stick of bullet lead whittled to a point, began to write.

•

When he rode into Memphis at Murrell's side, Stewart was beset by minor misgivings. He had had dealings in this city before, and was known by name to a number of commission merchants, wholesalers and outfitters. It would be worse than embarrassing to have someone hail him as Virgil or Stewart in Murrell's hearing. But their ride through the eastern "liberties" of town and into the busy central streets was uneventful, and their destination, the seamy riverfront section called the Pinchgut, was not one which Stewart had heretofore frequented.

They had been on the trail for four days since the night of Stewart's reluctant recruitment. On the morning after that, Stewart had stopped a traveling tinker and prevailed on him to drop off a message when he got to "the Hughes place, just two days on your way." If there really was a Mrs. Marybeth Hughes somewhere in Tennessee, she was probably still puzzling over the note he'd sent.

The nights since then, they had put up in wayside inns, at

Murrell's insistence and expense. The expense was doubtless nil—Stewart assumed that the man was spending what he called the queer—but the accommodations were not worth much more. The various frontier doggeries were distinguishable only by their geographical location. In matters of bed and board and degree of filth they were depressingly alike. Their shilling-plate supper was regularly a clot of unlovely and unrecognizable pieces of pig (the ears and trotters, Murrell opined) congealed in cold grease. And sleeping on the corn-shuck, rope-sprung beds was as backbreaking as an all-night ride on a new saddle.

During all this time, Stewart played the role of a perambulating ear. While he rode mute and attentive, assuming alternate expressions of awe and admiration, sometimes genuine, Murrell kept up a running disquisition on his and his Clan's past triumphs, present eminence and future plans.

"We've even set up our own mint, would you believe it? Solid as the Biddle Bank. Turning out bushels of queer money—government notes, Planter's Bank notes, even railroad money when that began to come in. I sell it at half its face value to my various gangs and gamblers, and they spend it at face, in their own territories."

"But," Stewart pointed out, "every storekeeper now has a copy of the Bank Note Detector."

"If we can print the rinctum-rhino, we can print a detector, too, can't we?" Murrell was almost gleeful with pride. "Lord knows how many of our bogus books are in use, but they sanctify our own money and condemn some of the real stuff. Confusion? That's probably our heaviest artillery."

On another occasion: "We have our own marts for trading stolen slaves, our own yards for stolen horses and cattle. Besides making all of us passably rich, we use a portion of the money that comes in to oil the various wheels of the legal machinery. When one of my outfits pulls a job, law officers usually find it profitable to go snuffing off along false trails. Or if the culprits do get hauled in, witnesses are bribed to testify for them and plaintiffs are scared to testify against. Sometimes, just for a lark, I do the pleading for the defense. Hell, I'm a sight better learned in the law than any of these back-country stump judges. All they know is what they can read in the Justice's Form Book."

Blithely, Murrell recounted the killings that bestrewed the trails of yesterday; the thefts, kidnapings and robberies; and enlarged zestfully on those he already had lined up for forthcoming profit and pleasure. He named names and dates. He bragged of his connections in high places, some of which—"Old Judge Awdward, now, he owes me quite a few favors"—Stewart recognized with hard-to-conceal surprise.

When Murrell again brought up the projected Black Insurrection of 1835, Stewart couldn't help asking, "What's to stop the blacks from plowing you under—all of the Clan—along with the rest of the whites?"

Murrell made a careless gesture. "They need me to lead this thing, and afterward they'll cry for my leadership more than before. Once the deed is done, they'll be like so many lost lambs. While they stare in horror at the blood crusting on their hands, I simply pluck the weapons from their numb fingers and shackle them more tightly than before." He smiled a wicked smile.

"Of course, they don't know this yet. There are a thousand already committed, but I don't keep them under mobilization. No, I don't want them talking among themselves and maybe making plans contrary to mine. They go on working for their masters, do a little recruiting among the other Nigras in their neighborhoods, and just sneak away to our Clan meetings at intervals. To all appearances, they are their usual woolly-headed, simple selves. Their owners wouldn't believe it, to see them on those nights when we call them to meeting—to see them dancing fierce African war dances and singing bloodthirsty war songs about what they're going to do to Ole Massa's private parts when the time comes."

Stewart confined his utterances to occasional naïve questions and exclamations of "Is that a fact?" But at night, when he could get a separate room or was sure Murrell slept, he set down in his memorandum book all he could recall of the day's colloquy. After four days of this, the book was bulging with notes.

And so Stewart, weary of riding and of listening, was glad

enough when they came to Memphis. It was true that he was open to at least a possibility of exposure. It was equally true that any comer to the Pinchgut had a good chance of being knocked on the head for his purse, or fractured in a fracas, or merely poisoned by bad whiskey. But Stewart had resigned himself to taking his chances with the former possibility, and he figured that Murrell's aegis would exempt him from any of the latter.

When they turned their horses into Smoky Row, the Pinchgut's principal thoroughfare, they were immediately surrounded by grimy and tattered urchins of all ages, who loudly advertised the various local landmarks and the attractions to be found thereat.

"The Bull 'n' Bottle, mister! Fancy lady in ev'ry room!"

"Nah! Nah! The City House! Not a bug in ary bed!"

"My sister——"

"The Jackson! The Jackson, mister! Fi'-cent whiskey and four-bit women!"

"My sister——"

Murrell rode through them as if the crowd of children had been a swarm of gnats. Stewart had to swipe away three or four of them who were yanking at his bridle and dragging along at his stirrups.

Smoky Row was a broad but twisty street of red clay mud, deep and mucky in the driest weather. It sucked at their horses' hooves and spattered liberally over the accompanying crowd of young pimps, who seemed as indifferent to it as did the numerous hogs that ambled about. These roving herds of swine were Memphis's established garbage collectors, operating even in the best residential areas. They all seemed to have congregated in the Pinchgut at the moment, not because the provender here was of better quality, but because it was more abundant.

Both sides of the street were jammed with crazed, jerry-built structures of two or three stories, shouldering each other and sometimes leaning together. Even the ones with a frontage barely wide enough to accommodate a door carried the signboards of "hotel" or "saloon." These signs displayed rebuses of their names instead of words—a crude picture of bull and bottle, for instance—to identify them to the illiterate. Why a man should seek out one of these sties in preference to another was not apparent. From the open doors, as Stewart and Murrell rode past, came bellows of sound and billows of stink. From the upper windows, heavily painted women leaned out, waggled their breasts and squealed invitations.

The street paralleled the Mississippi, and on one side the buildings backed against it; many of them were built out over the river on precarious log stilts. The riders could catch glimpses of the oily brown water through the crevices between hotels. The rotting trash, dead rats, cats and dogs floating in it added more effluvium to the Pinchgut's ripe atmosphere.

The few inhabitants who were not making merry inside the cribs seemed to have no urgent reason for being outside. Only the still-clamoring ragamuffins showed any sign of ambition or enterprise. Their elders either leaned against building fronts and hitching racks, moodily chewing and eyeing the newcomers, or lay drunk and snoring in the mud, oblivious to the swine, garbage and dung. Three hogs were nosing at one of these unconscious men as if investigating his edibility. One of them rooted in a pocket, found the man's quid of tobacco and trotted off, chewing contentedly. Except that he wasn't drunk and couldn't spit, the hog might have been a Pinchgut citizen in good standing.

It was impossible to gauge a man's occupation or station in life by his individual attire or demeanor. All those in evidence were unwashed and unkempt, hard-eyed and grim-lipped. Every man of them appeared to have a pistol somewhere on his person, either in a belt or shoulder holster or stuffed into waistband or boot top.

The crowd of young entrepreneurs trooped along after Murrell and Stewart and, when Murrell drew rein outside one particular building, they all abandoned their shouted touting and now hollered for a fee to "watch the hosses." Murrell dismounted and threw a handful of pennies into the throng. Stewart did the same. They had stopped before a saloon, distinctive only in that it was considerably larger, louder and smellier than the others on the Row, and dangled a huge brass steamboat bell above its double doors in lieu of a sign.

"Paddy Meagher's place," said Murrell. "The Bell Tavern. Come along in and meet some of my boys."

"Maybe you better break the news to them kind of easy," Stewart suggested. He was being prudent, not timid. He figured he could hold his own against the unwelcome he might expect from Murrell's fellow rogues. But if someone in there recognized him and heard his new name spoken . . .

"Tut tut," said Murrell. "Let us approach with sincere hearts in the full assurance of faith. I'm here to meet a couple of the men of my inner circle. You'll be one of them soon or later; might as well be now."

Stewart shrugged and started for the swinging doors, wishing he had a hand gun. Or a company of militia. Or good sense.

"Wait," said Murrell. "Here." He took a wad of paper money from one of his pockets. "From now on, Adam, you're working for me, so the outlay is on account." Stewart resisted, but the dark man thrust the wad into his hand. "You'll need spending money. And it's not charity; I'll charge it up against the first divvying. You'll earn it."

Stewart devoutly hoped he wouldn't have to, but he stowed the money away and followed Murrell into the Bell Tavern. The noise that had been noise outside the doors was bedlam inside. The interior was one big room with a few small, dirty windows. It was mainly illuminated by a multitude of cheap candles stuck on the rims of three wagon wheels that hung horizontally on ropes from the high ceiling. The candles dropped gobs of hot tallow liberally and continually onto the hats and heads of the customers, and occasionally one of them would fall entire and set fire to somebody's hair or clothing. In the unventilated room, the tobacco smoke and the steamy, sweaty miasma of the crowd were so thick as to obscure the little light the candles shed.

Most of the available floor space was occupied by tables and chairs. All the chairs were occupied by drinkers and card-players, and whatever standing room was left was occupied by drinkers and kibitzers. A long, crowded puncheon bar ran along one side of the room. Bottles and kegs were stacked on shelves behind the bar. Spittoons were scattered here and there around the floor, most of them overturned. A railed-off balcony, almost invisible in the gloom, hung on the back wall. There a perspiring musician hammered viciously at the keys of an old-fashioned square piano, and it responded with appropriate agony.

A number of females circulated through the throng of men, risking and enduring pinch bruises. They wore gay-colored sateen dresses, modestly full and long in the skirt but daringly low-cut on top, the bodices shaped to form a sort of scoop between the breasts, inviting the patrons to toss coins. Many of them did, but some of the drunker ones tried the same trick with squirts of tobacco juice. The gowns were also tobacco stained from the hems halfway up to knee height, from having dragged around in the glop on the floor for maybe weeks between washings.

Most of the girls were young, and some of them pretty despite their heavy cosmetic masks and the unnatural colors of their hair. One or two of them puffed elegantly on small cigars, and all of them were determinedly vivacious. Their function seemed to be to urge on the drinking frequency of the table sitters, and to fetch tray loads from the bar. But once in a while, a girl would pry a man loose from his card game and lead him upstairs, through a door off the piano player's balcony.

Of the fifty or sixty villains teeming in the sulphurous murk of this noisy, noisome arena, none looked worthier than an assassin and several managed to look worse. A number of the patrons nearest the door turned to inspect the newcomers. Some glanced over with only mild interest, some with quick recognition, some with squinting calculation, and a few with apprehension. In his dandified clerical ensemble and in the company of the farmer-boyish Stewart, Murrell gave a highly misleading first impression.

"Not another one o' them goddamn Temperance blueskins!" was the disgusted growl of someone who didn't recognize him.

"Give us a hymn, preacher!" shouted someone who probably did.

"Black John!" roared a thug at the bar, and sprang over to feint a friendly punch at Murrell, who parried it, grinning.

"It's Murrell!" bellowed another at his side, flinging his mug up in a welcoming toast. As the mug passed his nose, Murrell twitched it out of the man's hand and drained it at a gulp.

"Murrell, by damn!" "It's John Murrell!" "Murrell's in town!"

With an occasional "Who's 'at with him?" it went up and down the room, in hollered greetings and cautious whispers. Many recognized the man and almost everyone seemed to recognize the name. Most of the merely inquisitive faces tactfully turned to other interests. The dark man wove his way through the crowd at the bar, shaking hands, slapping a back here, stealing a drink there, cuffing shoulders, leaning over to kiss a beaming orange-haired girl behind the bar, yanking the beard of an old-timer. Stewart threaded along in Murrell's wake, eliciting only an occasional ambiguous nod from those he passed.

When Murrell had pummeled his way to the back of the room, he bounded onto an empty chair, waved his arms for a measure of quiet, and shouted: "Paddy! Paddy! For a welcome back to old John—set 'em up for the house!" The room shook to a wild cheer, the piano player thundered into "General Andrew Jackson's Triumphant Presidential Grand March" (unheard); there was a trampling rush to the bar, leaving most of the tables empty and a few overturned.

Murrell was toppled off his chair. Grinning, he grabbed Stewart's arm and plowed a way for them out of the jostling mob. Panting with exertion and pleasure, he led the way along the back wall under the balcony. In a far corner were three men who apparently had been unexcited by the offer of free whiskey. They gazed contemptuously at the struggling throng at the bar. At Murrell's approach, they shifted inquiring faces to him and his companion.

"Well, boys!" said Murrell jovially. "Good to see you again!" He put a paternal hand on Stewart's shoulder. "Three of my oldest friends—meet one of my newest."

·

If these were the Mystic Confederacy's "high priests," they could have given cards and spades in balefulness to any sampling of Hottentot witch doctors. In their individual and aggregate air of corruption, malevolence and misanthropy, they made the other inhabitants of the Pinchgut look as genteel and demure as countinghouse clerks. Although Stewart nodded hello coolly enough, he was privately damning Parson Henning's notions and his own recklessness in getting into this company.

"Brother Adam Hughes," Murrell introduced him. "Brother Yancey, Doctor Cotton—and my personal body servant, Big Tip."

"Howdy," said Stewart.

He got a surly grunt from Brother Yancey. This was a broad-shouldered, thickset, black-haired man. His face might have been ruggedly handsome, except that he seemed to have frowned once in infancy, and the expression had frozen on him. Now the lines and furrows were permanently engraved and, even when he leered or raised his eyebrows or looked surprised, puzzled, whatever, it turned out to be just another kind of frown. In his hand, Yancey was stroking, flipping, fondling a thing that looked to be the foot of a deer. At one end of a brown-haired shank was the little black cleft hoof; the other end was capped with a piece of brass. Whatever the thing was, Brother Yancey handled it constantly and lovingly.

"Hello, Hughes," muttered Dr. Cotton in his turn, but the greeting seemed incongruous with his cadaverous aspect. "Good-by" would have been a more natural remark for a man who looked so near death. His head was almost fleshless, and as hairless and gray as a skull. His eyes would have been colorless blobs of jelly, had they not been spectacularly bloodshot. The hat he idly fanned himself with (perhaps it was the only one he'd ever been able to find to fit his little bone head) was a dead-colored cocked beaver tricorn of Revolutionary vintage. For a doctor, he seemed curiously heedless of the numerous vermin that were crawling around in his hat's patchy fur.

The third party, leaning against the wall, merely made a gesture toward his forelock. It was unusual that a Negro should be inside a white man's drinking house; this one seemed to appreciate the toleration and made himself as unobtrusive as possible by lurking in the shadows. But it would have been a brave man who decided to try to throw him out. He was black as the inside of a chimney, ugly as a gorilla, and stood at least seven inches over six feet, with corresponding breadth. A preposterous black stovepipe hat added another foot and a half to his stature. Standing there against the wall, Big Tip might have been a crudely carved ebony column holding up the balcony that rested on his hat.

"Met Brother Hughes on the trail," said Murrell, dragging over two more chairs. "He got the drop on me, would you believe it? I was so impressed I offered him a job."

Yancey scowled at the stranger even more fiercely. "To hell with all this Brother crap," he growled. He squinted at the empty mugs on the table and then, with a sweep of his arm, sent them bouncing and smashing across the floor. "Let's get some more o' that forty-rod whiskey out here."

The four clansmen looked at Stewart. He took the hint and made his way to the bar, knowing that they had all put their heads together the moment he left. The crowd was thinning out now and drifting back to the tables; Stewart managed to wedge his way up to the puncheon counter and catch the eye of the orange-haired girl.

"Whiskey," he demanded, in his deepest voice, and jerked a thumb toward Murrell's table.

She smiled, nodded, put two quart-size crockery bottles and five mugs on a tin tray. Stewart thought this a little lavish, but the girl must know the boys' capacities. He scrounged in a pocket, untangled one of the bills Murrell had given him and handed it across to her. She took it, glanced at it and then at him, with blue-steel eyes. He gazed back, puzzled, and suddenly she grinned understandingly. She picked up the tray, came around the end of the bar and took him by one arm. He let himself be led back to the table, where she set down the tray and yanked Murrell's hat down over his face. Yancey guffawed, Cotton snickered, Big Tip rumbled.

"Hoy!" said Murrell, struggling out from under the hat.

"Is this boy new with you, John?" she asked sternly.

"Why—yes, Sally."

"Then how about you tell him we don't take your rhino here?" she said, shoving the bill into Murrell's open mouth. He spat it out, looked at it and chuckled.

"Guess I should have mentioned, Adam," he said to the uncomfortable Stewart. "We don't use these shinplasters among friends. Sally Meagher can spot one a rifle shot away. And when she does, it's wise to be out of rifle shot."

"Now, no need to scold him, John," said Sally, smiling.

"He's sweet. *Ow!*" She turned to slap Yancey's hand out from under her skirts.

Murrell reached in his pocket and danced a handful of silver on the table. "There's Mexican dollars, Sally. They do?"

"Do fine," she said, taking one. She squeezed Stewart's arm. "You're forgiven," she said, and went away.

Stewart sat down, feeling a mite resentful and absorbing whiskey, while Murrell, Yancey and Cotton carried on a cryptic conversation about the incomprehensible activities of unidentifiable people in unnamed places. Stewart wasn't especially eager to ingratiate himself with this horde, but it graveled him that so far he was giving an imitation of a feebleminded clod. So, when Murrell and the doctor got into a clinical discussion of the interesting shotgun wounds of some clansman named Ivy, Stewart turned to the now silent Yancey and ventured, "What is that thing you're fooling with?"

Yancey favored him with a look of undisguised disdain. "Any goddam fool can tell it's a deer foot." He tapped a little rhythm with it on the table edge, flipped and caught it—and then with a sudden lunge leaned across the table and pushed his face close to Stewart's. "See," he hissed, "once I was a-laying in this here thicket, waiting for a stage to come by. It was a tejus wait and I was getting tired o' nothing to do. See?"

Stewart nodded, leaning a little back from the frown.

"So, whaddaya know, I was so quiet, this purty young buck deer comes a-tiptoeing along. Never seen me, never smelt me, walked past just a yard or so away." Holding the foot by its brass end, Yancey walked it along the table among the whiskey mugs.

"So," he went on, in his conspiratorial whisper, "I gathered myself"—he let go of the foot for an instant, drew his arm back while it stood balanced—"then I *jumped!*" He darted his hand forward again and caught his toy before it fell over. "I had him! With my hand clamped on his right forefoot!" He leaned even closer, squinched his eyes up and said emphatically, "That's how *quick* I am."

"I'll say," Stewart said faintly.

"Well, he bucked around like crazy." Yancey waggled the piece of leg. "Kicking me in the head and all with them sharp li'l hoofs. But I hung on." Again he leaned close and blew his whiskey breath at Stewart. "That's how *tough* I am. Wellsir, I knowed I couldn't wrassle him all day. So I took a firm holt of that foot . . . and I twisted my wrist . . . so . . . like this . . ." Clenching the thing, he slowly rotated his wrist "And *crack!* Broke the bone. Right there where you see that brass cap." Again the confidential lunge toward Stewart. "That's how *strong* I am."

Stewart drank a quick shot of whiskey.

"The deer fell over, still a-kicking, nearly braining me. Well, I couldn't shoot him, afeared the stage might be coming and hear the noise. So I whupped out my knife, sawed through the skin and tendons, and the foot come off in my hand. I let the buck get up then and he limped off on three legs." Stewart braced himself for another lunge. "That's how *mean* I am."

"We'll have a drink to that!" Stewart said hurriedly. They lifted glasses to each other and drank, Yancey eyeing Stewart half humorously, half contemptuously over the rim.

"Anyhow," Yancey said, smacking his lips, "the job come off so well that I've kept this here trinket every since, as a lucky piece." He abruptly abandoned Stewart, reached out to grab a passing wench and hauled her down onto his lap. She squealed and wiggled delightedly as he tickled her with the little deer hoof. Stewart turned to the skeletal Dr. Cotton, to try him for possibly less lunatic conversation.

"Reckon you're the surgical department of the organization, Doctor," he said. "Right smart idea to have a full-time doctor in attendance . . . I reckon . . ." He trailed off, quailing before the red eyes that turned flaming on him.

"Shit," Dr. Cotton said succinctly.

Murrell snorted a laugh. "I'll tell you about Doctor Cotton, Adam. It's only right you should know. Your life may be in his hands someday."

"I got to go out back," rasped the doctor, arranging his skeleton upright and clattering off across the room.

Murrell laughed silently. "Yes, the good doctor does ride with us, to attend our occasional little illnesses and plug up a bullet hole once and again. But, as you may have gathered, he doesn't do it willingly. It's just that since he was defrocked—or disbarred, or whatever it is they do to derelict doctors—ours is the only practice he can hold. With us it doesn't matter too much if he loses a patient once in a while."

"Hell, every doctor loses a patient now and then," said Stewart tolerantly.

"But not quite so, er, dramatically as our Doctor Cotton. It happened while he was in practice in New Orleans. By the way, he's not one of your fashionable leech-and-calomel men. He believes in Thomsonian medicine. You know, steam doctoring."

"There's lots believe in it," said Stewart. "Why'd they kick him out for that?"

"Well, there's steam and steam," said Murrell reflectively. "Steam inhalers. Steam tents. One of Cotton's refinements was a steam cabinet—to sweat the evil biles and rheums out of a body. I understand it was especially popular among the plumper ladies down there, who fancied that it restored their girlish figures. Cotton prospered prodigiously. His income soared— from buying him one quart a day to three and four."

"Oh," said Stewart.

"Yes. Well, one day he locked the governor's wife or somebody into his steam contraption. A prominent woman, anyway, in more ways than one. He stoked up a slow-burning fire under the boiler, so as not to have to tend to it every little while. Then he went off to the docks to sample a new shipment of Demerara rum that had just come in. Somebody found the lady on about the third day. She'd lost a few pounds, all right. And tender . . ." Murrell licked his chops. "They say you could have cut her with a fork. I've heard they buried her with two boiled potatoes and a carrot, and planted parsley on the grave, but I won't vouch for that part of it." He roared with laughter. Stewart reached for the bottle and took a large helping.

"Anyway," Murrell went on, "Doctor Cotton sobered up in one hell of a hurry and managed to get out of Orleans Parish before the tar kettle came to a boil. He wound up in Natchez-under-the-Hill. He was barely earning a quart a week, patching up after saloon brawls, when we took him on."

He looked up and smiled as Dr. Cotton shambled back to the table and disintegrated into his chair. "Now we give the good

Hippocrates all he wants to drink, occasional food, the pleasure of our companionship, a chance to see the whole country . . ."

"Oh, go to hell, John," muttered the doctor, tossing down a formidable draft of whiskey.

". . . And as long as he manages to keep two out of three of us alive, we won't run him back to Orleans Parish," Murrell concluded.

Stewart glanced at Cotton with a measure of sympathy.

"One thing this son of a bitch won't tell you, boy," Cotton said suddenly to Stewart. "And that is that I *do* tend to his passel of scum as best I can. Maybe I'm not a stand-up-and-be-counted doctor any more, but by Jesus I'm still faithful to the healing oath. Now you'll admit, John, that I could have let that bastard Ivy bleed to death, with half his face shot off. I fixed him, didn't I? He's a sight to make a buzzard retch, sure, but he's up and around, isn't he?"

Murrell leaned over and patted a hand on Cotton's spiky knee. "Just ragging you, Doctor. I don't know what we'd do without you," he said, without sarcasm.

The old doctor said softly into his mug, "Maybe I'm a besotted disgrace to the profession of Galen and Aesculapius. But damn all, I *save* lives while you *take* them. At least I try— and I can hope that when it comes to weighing out in the last balances . . ."

Murrell ignored him, to say to Stewart, "Adam, it's getting on for dark and this place will be getting crowded." Stewart looked around at the already intolerable crush. "The other boys have taken rooms at Sam Stodgen's. Why don't you trot over and lay on rooms for you and me, as well? We owe ourselves a soft night's rest after this trip, and we'll most likely be traveling again in the morning."

"Sure thing," said Stewart, standing up a little unsteadily. "Where do I find it?"

"It's the Pedraza Hotel. Take Tip along. He'll show you, and he can see to our horses."

Stewart was glad enough to go. He'd had more than his fill of the whiskey and the company both. As he weaved away, Murrell called after him a warning not to try his paper money on

Sam Stodgen either, and Sally Meagher laughed from over by the bar. He left the Bell Tavern feeling like a midget alongside the floor-creaking bulk of the giant Negro. He wondered muzzily if Big Tip's real function was not to stable the horses, but to make sure that Brother Hughes didn't bolt. They made the short trip to the Pedraza in silence. After what he had learned from and about the others back there, Stewart wasn't eager to inquire into this Clan member's past. Ten to one, the big black would haul out a trophy collection of shrunken heads and reminisce and gloat over them.

•

Yancey and Cotton plumped for a steamboat ride down the river to the Clan headquarters, shipping the horses separately, but Murrell said he was damned if he'd entrust his beloved stallion Tempest to the care of any broadhorn crew of "thugs and thieves." Nobody laughed.

"But tarnation, John," said Cotton. "This is still January. A steamboat would be nice and comfortable."

"You're the real patron saint of steam, ain't you, Doctor?" said Murrell sarcastically. "Never mind. It'll get warmer as we get south." And that was as far as he would let the argument go.

The result was that they booked passage on a string of lashed-together shanty boats, a sort of floating island that was already carrying everything but topsoil and trees. The homemade boats were as ungainly as scows, not much better than rafts. Two farmers were emigrating downriver from Illinois, in search of milder climate, and had brought with them a team of plow horses, two milk cows, numerous pigs, uncountable chickens in crates, farm machinery, household furniture, wives, invalid grandfolks and what sometimes seemed to be about two hundred children.

"And both the hen hussies are pregnant," grumbled Dr. Cotton. "Probably throw quadruplets apiece. For Christ's sake, don't let them know I'm a medico."

The two harried captains of the conglomerate craft were only too happy to take on the travelers for cash fare, and only too willing to rearrange their portable barnyard to make room for them. The farmers would no doubt have an interesting and instructive time trying to spend the money at the end of their voyage, but, for now, it bought Murrell and his companions as comfortable quarters as the flatboats could provide. He, Stewart, Cotton and Yancey had one boat for themselves; Big Tip and the five horses shared another.

Left to his own devices while these arrangements were being concluded, Stewart wandered uptown to the stage and post office, where he composed and dispatched two letters. One, to Ed Clanton in Tuscahoma, pleaded urgent personal business as an excuse for his lateness in returning to work. The other was to Parson Henning. It contained a brief report on what had already transpired, promised details and further revelations whenever possible, and closed with fond regards to Naomi. Stewart was uncertain just how the good pastor was likely to take the news that his soon-to-be son-in-law was now a bona fide bandit. He was unhappily aware how Naomi would take it.

They shoved off that very day, after laying in supplies for the trip and a list of necessaries for the headquarters—and a good stock of Paddy Meagher's whiskey against the rigors of river travel. They needed it. The trip was monotonous and wearisome, the scenery was bleak, the farmers' children were a pestilence to vindicate Herod. A bone-chilling wind blew nonstop from the North Pole during the few hours it wasn't raining. The river current was sluggish and seemed to take them nowhere, except at night, when the river brisked up enough to wash over the low decks of the boats, flood the living quarters and playfully float the cursing men around among their baggage.

As Stewart learned later from a map, Murrell's headquarters lay only 140 miles from Memphis in a straight line. The river's curves, bends, doublings back, kinks and hairpins made that 230 miles, but the two farmer-captains' inept navigation probably doubled even that distance. They knew nothing about handling their lumbering ark, and less about the eccentricities of the Mississippi. The fact that the two of them piloted simultaneously, and often to contradictory purpose, didn't help. They were forever running aground on sandbars, and ramming sawyers, and hanging up on snags and, sometimes, actually running into the riverbanks. When it came to choosing which side of an island to run around, it was a good bet they'd take the channel that petered out in an inland swamp.

Even when the good ship *Barnyard* made time down the river without hitting anything, it might be careering down sideways or backward as often as prow first. Sometimes the two captains would stand side by side on their "pilot deck," staunchly fronting southward, their proud chins jutting into the breeze. And sometimes it would be the stern boat pointing the way, with Big Tip's gorilla grimace and stovepipe hat poking above the horses' rear ends for a kind of figurehead; a sight to astonish people passing on other boats.

Among the traveling clansmen the only entertainment was cardplaying and chuck-a-luck. Stewart was exempted from the games, as he supposedly had nothing but Murrell's funny money to gamble with; and Big Tip, as he had nothing but his hat. The play soon palled for the other three when it became evident that they were all about evenly matched at cheating. For a while they made bets about the time and place of the next grounding, but that happened so frequently and money changed hands so often that this game, too, evened out disappointingly.

There were no books to read. There was nothing of interest to look at, bar the infrequent passing steamboat. There were Paddy's jugs, true; they got plenty of exercise. The only other diversions consisted of occasionally fishing for a child or two that had fallen overboard; helping to pole the ark off submerged sandbars two or three times a day and nine or ten times a night; and one particularly memorable episode when the boat lashings somehow parted, and an acre or so of the *Barnyard* went bucketing off downriver on its own, bearing a cargo of assorted cheering children and screeching women.

As might have been expected, one of the wives and one of the cows each came to her accouchement during the voyage. Both times Dr. Cotton sat huddled in his tent with a blanket over his head, drinking toward oblivion as fast as he could swallow, and trying not to hear the commotion from the farm boats. And both times he surrendered and staggered off to preside over the blessed event. Stewart reflected that it must have been a treat for the woman—or the cow, for that matter—to have that tricorn-hatted death's-head looming over her miseries.

One bundle from heaven was a bull calf and the second was a girl child. "An extraordinary facial resemblance between the two," Dr. Cotton remarked sourly. He was in bad humor because the farmer-captains had insisted on paying him—overriding his insincere remonstrances—and then had given him some of their Murrell money. He did have one compensation; they named the baby girl after him: "Doctor."

The trip went on and on, seemingly interminable and eventually unendurable. For a while the clansmen wanly looked forward to the prospect of going ashore for a while at Helena, on the Arkansas shore. It had facilities for raising sufficient hell to revivify their damp spirits. But, as chance would have it, they raised Helena in the middle of the night and the middle of a storm, when the river was being especially rambunctious. The captains jointly apologized to their passengers, and pointed out that it would be folly to attempt a landing. The clansmen could only concur, having witnessed the captains' seamanship in bright day and dead calm. There were some critical mutterings, meant for Murrell's hearing, about the folly of having embarked on this goddamned expedition in the first goddamned place. Then the unhappy mariners sat and watched the seductive lights of Helena, the imagined music and laughter and rouged lips, fade behind them into the blackness of the storm.

Occasionally they passed a waterside Indian village on the western bank, no grander and no meaner than the whites' shanty hamlets on the eastern. Once in a while, a flat-headed Choctaw trapper in a canoe, or a fishing party in several of them, would pull alongside and try to dicker for powder and lead in exchange for pelts or smoked fish. The furs smelled about as high as the fish and the fish looked about as delicious as the pelts. These nuisances shied off in a hurry when they caught a glimpse of the fearsome Big Tip looming among his horses' rumps.

Time passed and tempers raveled and frayed. If Stewart, Murrell and several farm women hadn't intervened, Yancey would have brained one of the tormenting youngsters whom he had caught sneaking off with his deer foot. It was probably only coincidence that that same child should have been the single casualty of the voyage, lost overboard unnoticed during a windstorm the next night. When Murrell called a Clan meeting and aired some suspicions, Yancey's defense was that he didn't even believe one of the little bastards was missing. *He* couldn't notice any diminution of the number of brats still resident, and defied anybody to count them twice over and get the same total. Anyway, after the accident, the remaining multitudes were never afterward let to annoy or play near any of the Murrell men.

Another salubrious auspice, now, was that they were floating into springtime at about the same rate that spring was moving north. Day by day the weather got warmer, the banks' vegetation greener. The trees leaved out almost perceptibly, each one thicker than the last, like a conjuring trick. Brilliant parakeets flickered flame from grove to grove. The river became more beautiful than all the songs about it. But this did little to dispel the fuggy atmosphere of the Murrell boats; it was just one more evidence of what a chunk this voyage was whittling out of the year. It would be difficult to reckon the actual time the whole trip took, except to estimate that they reached their destination a slim fraction before they reached their limit of endurance. Another day, another few miles, and Murrell would have had a mutiny to put down.

He directed the captains to set them ashore at a deserted bend on the west side of the river. Fortunate it was that they had arrived here in daylight and calm weather. Had they slipped just a few miles past it, Murrell would have had to set up new headquarters in Louisiana. To Stewart the landing place was indistinguishable from any other piece of the many weary miles they had come. All he knew was that he was farther west than he had ever been before, and that it was Arkansas Territory over there.

The captains cooperated with a will, and with their usual ineptitude. They swung the *Barnyard* in a grand, flourishing arc toward the western bank, and were still forty yards off when the whole flotilla came to a jarring, grinding halt. Every passenger and animal aboard fell down. The captains came sheepishly to ask the men to lend a hand with the poles to push them adrift again. Yancey told them exactly where they could each push a pole, preferably a pointy one.

"Don't fret, friends," said Murrell. "We'll all swim ashore with our horses. Without that load, you'll float right off again."

The five men bundled up their baggage and distributed the packs among the animals. They were so eager to be away that not even Yancey thought to steal anything from their hosts. When they had loaded everything, they led the horses to the edge of the deck and pointed them shoreward. The horses had been as miserable about the trip as everybody else, but this they cared for even less. They balked at having to swim, fully loaded, and refused to disembark so undignifiedly. Finally, while Stewart and the Illinoisians gawked in amazement, and Murrell swelled with seigneurial pride, Big Tip simply picked up the horses one by one and threw them overboard.

As each one hit the water, his owner plunged in after and grabbed the saddle pommel or the animal's tail. The horses immediately and efficiently swam for shore. In a few minutes the whole gang had clambered dripping onto the bank. They sat down for a minute to catch their breath and to watch the fate of their late farm home. As Murrell had predicted, it was already slipping away downstream, with a vague air of relief about it.

Then they pushed into the riverside brush to round up their horses, which were trying to bump off their packs against the trees. After a short but spirited chase, each man claimed his mount and Murrell led the way down an almost invisible trail that snaked inland, into thick woods.

•

By the time they had ridden two miles through the warm forest, their clothes were dry again. And here they were, once more looking out over a body of water. "Oh, no," groaned Stewart. "We've come right around in a loop to the river again."

"Not quite," said Murrell. "This *used* to be the river. But the old Miss' shifted her bed, about a million years back, and left this. It's a long oxbow lake—and that land you see yonder is an island. Our castle surrounded by a moat."

Yancey and Big Tip each fired a rifle into the air. A few

minutes later, two men on horseback appeared on the far shore. They waved and a halloo came thinly over the water. A minute more and they poled a big ferry raft out from the greenery there.

"Dean. Boyd." Murrell greeted them genially when they grounded the ferry on the gravel right at his horse's feet.

"Hi, John," said Boyd, squirting tobacco amber.

"Good to see you home, Murrell," said Dean.

There was some commotion in loading aboard the raft, so Stewart didn't have much time to size up the two newest clansmen. He noticed only that Boyd was a shrunken old man, older than Dr. Cotton, enshrubbed in a wilderness of long gray hair and long gray, tobacco-stained beard. Dean was about Stewart's own age, height and build, except that his arms hung oddly almost to his knees. Both he and the old man regarded the newcomer in silence, Boyd with a sort of amused speculation, Dean with a chilly half smirk and a glitter in his eyes.

They made the crossing in two shifts, then mounted again; it was another half mile down the island to the headquarters. Murrell put spurs to his stallion and quickly outdistanced the others. Stewart brought up the extreme rear in some embarrassment, at a shambling and uncertain canter. His old mare glanced back at him from time to time out of her good eye, as with reproach for his goading her to this unladylike activity. He arrived in a clearing just as Murrell brought his Tempest to a skidding cloud-of-dust halt some distance ahead, reared the horse dramatically, and then vaulted into the pummeling, shouting, blaspheming welcome of a group of several men.

The tumult of the horses' arrival was compounded by the roaring of half a dozen wild-eyed, wild-tongued hounds—just about the biggest, most vicious-looking dogs Stewart had ever seen—chained to the wall of a ramshackle doghouse at the entrance to the camp. They howled, snarled, slavered, chomped their teeth and lunged against their collars as if the arriving men were a long-awaited feast of meat.

Stewart reined in a short distance from the others, and his mare stood spraddle-legged and wheezing. He sat his saddle and looked around. The stump-studded clearing appeared to occupy the entire width of the narrow island, leaving a thin screen of camouflaging trees and brush along either shore. It extended maybe half a mile to another wall of forest. At this end of the clearing was a very long, narrow, one-story log building, with a door in the near short-width wall and a few one-log-deep window holes cut at intervals along its length. A clay pipe chimney trailed a thin thread of smoke up into the clear Arkansas air. A flock of scrawny chickens and a number of half-wild razorback hogs appeared to have the run of the island. Farther down the clearing was a rudely fenced corral, where a sizable herd of horses peered interestedly over the rails to see what all the hubbub was about. And farther beyond that was another, very small log cabin with no discernible door or windows at all.

Stewart looked again at the men, some thirty feet away, between him and the headquarters building. They were all afoot now, standing in a clump and staring silently over at him. Murrell stepped out from among them, flung an arm at Stewart and shouted, "Boys, I want you to make the acquaintance of the newest soul to come to damnation"—someone laughed coarsely —"Brother Adam Hughes."

The men gave a ragged, undecided sort of cheer, and someone imitated a trumpet fanfare. Stewart started to swing off his horse.

"No, no, sit right there!" Murrell shouted. "I've got something for you, Adam!"

Stewart sat back on the leather, petrified with astonishment, while John Murrell slowly drew the pistol called Jonathan from its holster. The sound of the hammer cocking carried across the clearing as he raised his arm high and at full length. Stewart had hardly time to wonder if there was any use at all in reaching for his rifle. Murrell's arm came remorselessly down and the black hole of the muzzle leveled deliberately on Stewart. The pistol went "whoom!"—not loud in all this open space.

Stewart felt his horse flinch under him at the report, and experienced a momentary surprise at not feeling the smack of the .54 bullet against his body. Then his mare quivered from stem to stern, like a wet dog shaking, and fell from under him. Stewart flailed in the air for an instant and came down heavily on his behind, to an explosion of laughter from the gang of men. He scrambled to his feet and looked down at the fallen animal. Murrell's ball had put a neat puncture in the near side of her head, and made a bloody ruin of the other side, where it emerged. Stewart swung angrily toward Murrell.

The man grinned mischievously, then turned away from him and called, "You, Tip! Run down and fetch me Israel!" The giant Negro showed a blinding expanse of white teeth and went off toward the corral at a lope.

So that was it. Stewart unclenched his fists. He hadn't given that promise another thought since Murrell had made it, way back yonder in Tennessee. Now here the man was honoring it before he'd even sat down in his own headquarters. But what a hell of a way to spring his surprise! Stewart rubbed his aching butt and took one last look at his old mare. No denying he felt bereaved, but he determined not to show it. He swallowed once, squared his shoulders, gingerly dusted the seat of his trousers and sauntered over to the group.

"Don't know which I care for less," he said. "Looking down that tunnel gun of yours or busting my ass."

"Looking a gift horse in the mouth of a gun, hey?" said Murrell, and chuckled at himself. He pounded Stewart's shoulder. "Wait'll you see Israel. You'll forgive me. Here, let me sprinkle some introductions around." He pointed and named off a barrage of names; only a few of them stuck immediately in Stewart's mind. Albe Dean and Andrew Boyd: those were the two from the ferry raft, the mean-favored young one and the gnarled oldster. And John Ivy: the shot-up one Dr. Cotton had talked about back in Memphis. God knows he *was* awful to look at. There were eight more altogether, but their names didn't register.

"Never mind if you don't remember everybody's handle," Murrell said. "Half of them change their names with their underwear anyhow."

One at a time, the clansmen stepped up and shook hands. In the case of young Albe Dean, his arm was so long that he seemed to be bringing a paw up from underground to do it. Nobody actually crushed Stewart's hand, but they all made a quick test of his grip, and hung onto him long enough to run their eyes up and down, measure his shoulders, girth and reach, and take a deep look into his eyes. Stewart took no offense; it was a frontiersman's way, to appraise a stranger so. It was evident that all these men were wondering about him—how he had got in here, and how he would fit in—and equally evident that Murrell was damn well going to wait his own pleasure before satisfying any curiosity.

Then Big Tip clumped up leading a horse on a halter, and Stewart forgot everybody and everything else.

"Now," said Murrell, with a flourish, "meet Israel."

In everything but color, Israel was indeed the twin of Murrell's stallion. Israel was lighter, a honey-touched sorrel. Deep in the chest, neck held high and proudly arched, sleek muscular flanks, sturdy fine-boned legs that would never stumble and never get tired. His coat was impeccably curried and brushed, his heavy mane and tail combed out fine.

"This is mine?" Stewart choked out.

"You don't have any other," said Murrell, smiling with the pride of benefaction. "You'd have a hell of a time keeping up with us on foot."

Stewart moved around to look Israel in the eye. The horse looked forthrightly back; the deep brown eyes were unafraid but not unfriendly. His head was small, fine, with flaring nostrils. After a moment, Israel condescended to lower his muzzle and give Stewart an inspection of his own.

"There's Arab in him," Murrell said, enjoying himself fully as much as Stewart.

"He could be part camelopard and I wouldn't care," said Stewart, still overwhelmed. "Any special significance to his name?"

"Just one of my scriptural jokes, Brother Hughes. He's out of my dam Egypt Sand by Meadow Farms' Blue Moses."

Stewart laughed. Out of Egypt by Moses—by Christ, by jingo, this was a horse to take a man's breath away.

"Well, put him back, Tip," said Murrell, still smiling indulgently. "Right now, Adam, let's get unpacked and see have the boys got some beans for us."

Big Tip turned and led the horse away. Stewart gazed after him, admiring Israel's light, proud way of walking. That was a rich man's horse—a seven- or eight-hundred-dollar blood—and here Murrell had handed him over as casual as a chew of tobacco.

Suddenly Stewart's conscience stabbed him with a reminder of why he was here, what Murrell really was, and what he, Stewart, was going to have to do to him. That magnificent horse had been given to Adam Hughes. For a moment Virgil Stewart despised himself. He turned away from watching Israel.

Murrell, still grinning, was waiting for him. So was somebody else, not grinning. All the other men had drifted into the building. Only Albe Dean waited and looked on, his face set hard.

"You mean," he said to Murrell, "you mean you're *giving* Israel to this—this—to *him?*" He jabbed a contemptuous thumb at Stewart, from about knee level.

"Yep," Murrell said.

Dean exploded, "I've been after you to *sell* me that horse for a whole goddamn year!"

"I never said I would." Murrell's white-scarred eyebrow ticked up, a danger signal.

"You never told me no, neither!" For a supposedly hardened desperado, this one seemed remarkably near tears.

"Now, Albe, Israel's too short a horse for you," Murrell said cruelly. "Your arms would drag."

"Goddammit, here I've been currying, combing, trimming that animal all winter long, like he belonged to me!"

"Well, he doesn't. Israel is Adam's, my boy, and that's all you need to know about it!"

He brushed the younger man aside with a sweep of his hand and stalked into a long building. Dean stood quivering, his eyes radiating hatred so hot Stewart could almost feel it.

"If'n you want to keep Israel in your fambly," Dean said, in a tight voice, "you better write out a will. You don't bequeath him to some kin, *I* aim to inherit him when you're dead. And right soon!" He spun on his heel and followed Murrell.

So here was trouble. It was kind of a relief to have it show at last; things had been disquietingly easy up to now. It had to come soon or later, with one or another of them. Stewart shrugged, blew out his breath in a long whoosh, and went to unharness his dead mare.

•

Stewart came in carrying his saddle, bridle, blanket, rifle, pack roll and the bundle of supplies from the *Barnyard,* and dumped them inside the door.

The building had one enormous room that ran the full length, like an auditorium. Along one side, door openings in a plank wall led into about a dozen separate cubicles, apparently the men's sleeping quarters. Some of these rooms had sagging wooden doors on leather hinges, some were screened only with a scrap of deerskin, some scorned privacy and had nothing over the opening. There were no beds in the rooms, just pallets of straw or shucks, with mangy bearskins and ragged blankets for coverings.

The main room contained some rude furniture: several deal tables scattered up and down its length, a multitude of backless puncheon benches and up-ended log butts for stools. On pegs along the walls hung saddles, harness, bags, holsters and an assortment of weapons. From one peg, on rawhide strings, hung two boards smeared with molasses and covered with flies that had got stuck there; every so often somebody would slap the two boards together to stop the buzzing. The resident chickens wandered in and out of the building at will, and an occasional hog would have to be ousted.

The whiskered Andy Boyd seemed to be camp cook. He was stirring up a midday meal of what looked to be fried side meat and beans, on a large, nondescript stove about a third of the way down the room. The stove was not much more than a shell of itself, having burned and rusted through a long, long time ago. Some of the fire was inside and some spilled out in heaps of embers and ashes around and under it; Boyd had to stand about a yard away and lean perilously over the bed of coals to stir his bucket of coffee. This situation boded no danger of fire (unless to Boyd's beard), as the entire building was floored only with hard-tromped earth.

"What about that dead hoss out there?" someone asked Murrell, as Stewart entered. "If you're just gonna let it lay, you might of shot it a little further downwind of the house."

"Turn the dogs loose on it," Murrell said. "When they're done, there'll be less of it to haul away."

The man went out and, a moment later, a cacophony of

roars and snarls rushed past the building in the direction of the horse's carcass, and then abruptly silenced. Stewart swallowed hard.

The horrible-faced man named Ivy was sitting at the table across from Murrell, busily recounting the headquarters' recent activities. ". . . And that was a good haul. But then *I* brought in three more, day before yesterday," he said proudly. "Took 'em from a dinky li'l place over the Ouachita. Wouldn't think such a place'd have three niggers. But me and my boys, we fetched 'em all."

"I've lost count. How many is that altogether?"

"Thirteen. Not bad, huh? Yessir, even with half a face and one eye, I don't do bad, huh, John?" He seemed pathetically anxious to establish that he was still worth his keep.

Murrell smiled at him and said, "Not bad at all, Ivy."

"Yessir, old Doc Cotton fixed me up good as ever. Not much he could do about the filigree work, but the foundation's still solid. Hey, Doc?" He turned and smiled a frightful smile at Cotton. The doctor was propped on a stool in the corner, vigorously nursing the remainder of Paddy Meagher's whiskey. He waved his jug in mute acknowledgment.

"And Murrell," another man put in, "there's still Tucker and Barney and Anderson out foraging. They oughta be back any day. You want to wait for their contributions?"

"I don't know," said Murrell. "Thirteen already. The other boys might be a while getting back."

"Yeah," said Boyd, from over by the stove. "I ain't looked in on 'em, but I 'spect them niggers is getting a mite restless, a baker's dozen of 'em jammed into that coop down yonder."

"They giving any trouble?" Murrell asked Ivy.

"One of mine is tol'able sassy. Big light-tan buck. Fit us all the way home from the Ouachita, and been jumping up and down like a muley saw ever since. Talks a blue streak, but all nonsense. I think maybe he's tetched."

"Tetched or not," Murrell said thoughtfully. "I wouldn't want him stirring up the other dozen."

"Another thing," said one of the men. "We ain't had nothing to spare 'em 'cept corn bread and commons. Likely they're getting hongry, too."

"The dogs won't finish that horse," said Murrell. "Carve them some of that for supper."

Ivy looked mildly scandalized. "Them niggers is used to better'n that! They won't set still for horse meat!"

Murrell said absently to tell them it was buffalo.

"Well, John," Boyd called over again, "if you want to convince this batch they're p'inted for heaven on earth, as usual, you better get Tip down thar and get it over with and get 'em started for thar new homes."

Murrell said, "I'll go down and look at them after we eat. If they look too miserable, we won't wait for the other boys. We'll start arrangements to get them down to the market."

That appeared to settle things for the time being. The men distributed themselves around various tables. Boyd slid a mug of turbid coffee in front of each of them, and a shingle heaped with his indescribable fried concoction. The men produced knives and fell to as if it were edible.

"Being's this is the first time you've et my cooking," Boyd said, as he served Stewart, "I best tell you that to hear complaining grieves me bad." He put a hand to his heart. "Any griping and I just take straight to my bed with the vaporous fantods—and then I can't cook atall."

"I'll bear that in mind, Mister Boyd," said Stewart, mock solemnly. "I wouldn't want the job handed on to me."

He could have done better at it though, he decided, as he choked down his first knifeful of the greasy, slippery victuals. He wryly considered the notion of throwing the food away and eating the shingle. But hell, he had to get used to it sometime; he bucked on bravely through the meal. As each man finished, he tossed his shingle and whatever was left crusted on it to the ground at his feet. A line of dark shadows slipped in through the open door, like the ghosts of wolves. The giant hounds, already gorged, sniffed and sampled rather daintily at the dregs of the men's meal.

The man on Stewart's left said, "Nemmine them dawgs. They'll get used to you. Anyhow, they full o' your hoss right now. They ain't hongry fer *you* yet." He laughed heartily. Stewart noted that Dr. Cotton was not eating at all. He was still tilting the jug and wedging his old bones more and more firmly into the corner. Albe Dean, too, was consulting a bottle oftener than his shingle. When Stewart glanced at Dean, he discovered that the man's eyes were fixed malevolently on him. Any time now, he thought.

He was right. A minute or two later, Dean had stoked up to the pressure level that steamed him into action. He hitched at his belt and came to stand menacingly over Stewart's bench. "Hey, you," he said in a thick voice. "I'm gonna fight you for that stallion."

Stewart chewed deliberately on his last mouthful, swallowed it and said, "Stallion's already mine. You'll have to fight me for something else."

Dean smoldered at him and said, "Awright. What?"

"You'll think of something," Stewart said. He tossed his shingle to the ground, stood up and turned his back on Dean. Every man in the room had caught this brief exchange. Their eyes glinted at Stewart's casual dismissal, and then swung to fasten impellingly on Albe Dean. Stewart went to Murrell's table, indicated his gear by the door and said, "You want to tell me where I stow away and doss down?"

Murrell made a lazy gesture. "Just pick a cubbyhole and fling it in. Long as nobody else objects."

"Hey," said Albe Dean. His big paw swung Stewart around. "I object. Feller can't just stroll in here and squat, don't he prove he's worth living with."

"Figures."

"Awright then, where you aiming to move in at? All them cubbyholes aweady got one–two men bunking in 'em. Whose you gonna try and crowd into?"

"Just so I won't make any mistake, which one's yours?"

Dean hesitated, then pointed to a door covered by a flap of rat-nibbled hide. Stewart went unhurriedly over to his pile of gear, picked it up, carried it across the room and dumped it into that cubicle. There was an expectant silence in the room; even the dogs were watching.

"Now," said Stewart, coming back to Dean. "You want to throw my goods out? Or me?"

Dean hit him low in the stomach, bringing an arm like a leg up from the floor. Stewart barely had time to tense his belly muscles against the blow. Even so, the wind was knocked out of him. He let the punch throw him far enough away to get a breath into himself before Dean could catch up.

"You made your will yet?" Dean shrilled happily, showing all his teeth in a ferocious grin. Then he charged, his extraordinary arms windmilling.

At the ends of those ape limbs, his fists were like iron maces slung on chains. Stewart had to stay inside them or be knocked silly. He stayed, for a minute, and pummeled away ineffectually at Dean's midsection. But one of the arms seemed to reach from somewhere behind him, around from in back of his head. The fingers clawed into his face and wrenched him backward. As he went, Dean's knee came up viciously for his groin. Had it landed, Israel would have had a new owner. But Dean was a little off balance himself; the kick caught the inside of Stewart's thigh. Stewart went down and landed rolling away, naturally expecting a kick aimed at his head. But Albe Dean wasn't going to resort to anything puny like hobnail boots while he still had his sledge hammers. Stewart rolled right into one of his fists whistling along at floor level.

The blow was so explosive that Stewart hardly had to make any effort in getting himself to his feet. Dean's fist came up from the ground in a long arc with Stewart dangling on the tangent. Stewart separated from the fist and crashed into the wall behind him. Just to complicate things, a mess of harness jarred loose from a peg somewhere above him and came down in a tangle over his head and shoulders. For that moment, he was stunned from the blow and enmeshed in the leather trappings. He was helpless and wide open for the finishing punch. But Dean misjudged his distance when he threw it, and the heavy fist looped in to smack the wall beside Stewart's ear. Before Dean could swing again, Stewart was out of the harness and free to dodge, long enough to clear his head.

This couldn't go on for long, Stewart told himself. He had landed only two or three futile punches on Dean's uncaring belt buckle. And here he was already half groggy from the other's unbelievably crippling hooks. His face was streaming blood from the fingernail gashes. And now he was foolishly dancing around out of range, like a yappy terrier dog. He heard a rustling stir from the audience, meaning this was no show at all, and why didn't Albe get it over with?

Stewart managed to ward off two more of Dean's looping swings, nearly breaking his own arm when he caught them, but still unable to get close enough to do anything for himself. Think, dammit, think! Those lullabyers were sure enough lethal, Stewart calculated desperately, but they had one weakness. Like a man swinging an ax, Dean had to get his arm way back to start a fist around in that whistling arc. And, like the axman, he had to be planted foursquare for the necessary leverage. Get him off balance, maybe, at that split second at the top of his windup . . .

At that moment Stewart got his chance. Dean's left hand was up in front of Stewart's face, to keep him in just the right target spot, and the other arm was going backward in its orbit. Dean was grinning again, as he measured for the knockout blow. Stewart ducked under the prop hand and dived recklessly forward, head first. The top of his head rammed Dean in the center of his chest and he tottered back. Like Stewart's theoretical axman, Dean, off balance, found that his back-swung arm was so much dead weight. He didn't fall, but for an instant he had to shuffle backward for balance, and in that now-or-never instant, Stewart slammed his fist as hard as he could into Dean's throat, right under the chin.

Stewart knew the several simultaneous effects of this blow to the larynx. You go blind for a moment; the pain is more intense than that from any blow to the face; you stop breathing, seemingly forever; the paralyzed carotid sinus and jolted vertebrae just give up and resign all responsibility for your well-being. Dean reeled, and his grin was gone. Summoning what control he could, he blindly swung both his arms backward at once, as if to squash Stewart between them when he brought them together. But Stewart was hurt and exhausted himself; he wanted to end it. While Dean stood there wide open before him, he drove his fist with all his force into the sick man's midriff, boring it up under his breastbone into the solar plexus.

Dean's face cramped in agony. Abandoning all hope of the fight, he doubled over and wrapped his ape arms across his stomach.

Stewart stepped close, clasped his hands together into a knotted club and raised it high over his head. He crashed it down on the exposed nape of Dean's neck at the same instant his knee bashed up into the downturned face. The effect was like that on a pebble caught between two millstones. At the shock of collision, Albe Dean was simply squirted out from between, spraying a red mist and fragments of teeth. He crossed the room in a series of clumsy cartwheels and fetched up against the table where Murrell sat, then collapsed into a clutter of used shingles and dirty knives, and lay there groaning feebly.

"Reckon the doctor ought to take a look at what's left?" someone suggested.

"Aw, hell, Cotton's having hisself a nice peaceable drunk. Don't wake him up."

"A right pretty piece of work, Brother Adam," Murrell said approvingly. Stewart realized that Murrell would have been rather stickily embarrassed before his lieutenants, had his newest protégé lost this first encounter. Stewart felt a small pride at having vindicated the chief's faith in him. Then it occurred to him that the newest protégé could very well have been dead by now, and he felt glad for more personal reasons. The other men in the room made gruff noises of congratulation, and set about their various businesses. Big Tip gathered up the discarded shingles from the floor and stood in the doorway scaling them high over the far treetops. Boyd and Yancey cleared a table, unfolded a checkerboard and sat down to play.

"Adam, we'll go down and have a look at the Nigras," said Murrell. "But first you'd better wash the badge of battle off your face. There's a bucket and soap down yonder at the back of the room."

Stewart was bent over the bucket, soapsuds dripping from his face and hands, when he heard *"Hughes!"* shouted from the other end of the chamber. He turned and blinked. Back there, Albe Dean had got onto his feet again. His face was black and blue, where it wasn't encrusted with blood, and he was wavering on his feet. But he had picked up a long knife from the floor and was balancing it in his hand.

"You make your will yet?" the man shrieked, in a sort of

sob, through his injured larynx. Then he took the knife blade between his fingers and drew back his unhuman arm. If his eye was still any good, that arm of his could drive the knife not only through Stewart but through the log wall behind him as well. Stewart stood helpless, swiping away the soap from his eyes and tensing himself against the throw. Dean's upper body pivoted slowly, the knife hand lifting above his shoulder. This was not going to be just a gesture of frustrated rage; he was taking careful aim to kill.

But Murrell, standing behind him, reached up indolently and took gentle hold of the knife's handle. He bore down on it —hard—as Dean whipped his long arm forward in the throw. Dean let out a whinny of surprise and pain when his hand lashed out. It flung a flying arc of bright blood that spattered as far as where Stewart stood, and the man's thumb fell onto the ground at his feet.

Albe Dean stared unbelievingly at the jet of red pumping out of his mangled hand, then at the peculiar sight of his thumb lying there on the dirt. He clasped his left hand tightly around his right wrist and whirled on Murrell, who stood dangling the knife by the handle, blood dripping from its point.

"*Jesus Christ, Murrell!*" the man screamed. "Look what you've done to me!"

"Here," said Murrell, and tossed the knife to Dean, who jumped aside as if it had been a meteor. "Cut the other one off. You're lopsided."

Dean's whitened lips twisted and twitched without words; his eyes were panicky. He ran to the corner where Dr. Cotton was still propped, and shook him, shouting for help. The doctor rattled off his stool and fell sideways onto the ground, snoring. Dean cursed him in a strangled voice, then rushed off into his bedroom, leaving a trail of blood soaking into the dirt floor.

Stewart toweled his face with a piece of sacking and came back up the room. "You can let me look out for myself," he told Murrell quietly. "I've faced down knife slingers before. You didn't have to do that to him."

"You licked the damned chimpanzee once," Murrell said. "He didn't deserve any second try."

Dean came loping out of his room again. He had wrapped the injured hand in a wad of filthy rags; a rope was twisted around his forearm for a tourniquet. Breathing heavily, he followed his own blood trail back to the spot where the knife had landed, and began to scrabble around on the ground. His frantic search brought him among the legs of the checkers players.

"Hey, you down there!" Yancey snarled at the kneeling man. "You're jiggling the goddam board!"

"Where'd it go?" Dean babbled. "Where'd it fall? What's become of it?"

Without looking up from his checker pieces, old Boyd waved a hand over his shoulder. "Seen one o' the dogs carrying it out the door."

Dean leaped to his feet. "And you just *sit* there, you damned old fart?!" he shrieked. Boyd imperturbably crowned a king for Yancey. "I gotta find it," Dean quavered. "Maybe Doc Cotton can sew it back on or somethin'!" He ran whimpering out the door.

•

Murrell, Tip, Stewart, Ivy and half a dozen others went off down the island, trailed by a few optimistic chickens, to visit the slave quarters at the far end of the long clearing. It was a pleasant springtime walk. The air was clear and warm, the grass a bright new green, the trees waving a gentle breeze around. The sky was making early arrangements for a spectacular sunset.

The slaves' cabin stood in the shadow of the trees, and was perhaps a sixth the size of the main building. Big Tip lighted a candle lantern before he opened the heavy padlock on the oaken door. The lantern was necessary; there was only one tiny, barred window in the single room. It let in less light than air, but not much less. The room was fetid, hot and moist. The log walls crawled with slime.

Murrell went in first and held up the lantern; the others crowded in behind him. Stewart couldn't see very well, come in from the bright outdoors, but he could tell that the thirteen blacks each sat on a straw pallet, among a litter of tin pans, wooden pipkins and scraps of food. Each man's right ankle was attached to the wall by a metal circlet and a length of chain that gave him some little freedom of movement. Over by the window stood two buckets that exuded an almost visible effluvium. Stewart put a hand over his nose.

At their entrance, there was a slight stir among the captives, and a battery of staring white eyeballs turned on them. The Negroes all greeted them in soft gutturals and made motions to rise. All except one; he sprang to his feet as if to attack, and flung himself toward them to the length of his chain. He was a big, tawny man—young, but as bald-headed as Dr. Cotton. His eyes were luminous with anger and outrage. He waved his arms wildly and spouted a stream of high-pitched gibberish.

"That's the one I told you 'bout," Ivy giggled. "Sounds like he's got the gift of tongues, don't he?"

Murrell held the lantern to shine on the man, then backed out of the cabin as if he had barged in on Old Scratch himself. The other men looked at him in surprise and followed.

"Shut the door, Tip," said Murrell, in a grim voice. With a curse, he dashed the lantern to the ground and, in the same movement, whirled and seized John Ivy by the throat.

"You goddamned one-eyed imbecile!" he raged, flapping the man like a blanket. "Can't you see well enough to tell a son-of-a-bitching *Indian* when you grab one?"

Ivy managed to get loose and staggered away, stammering, "H-he—he ain't nothing but another mulatter . . ."

"Mulatto! You've carried off a red goddamned Indian, you dickless reprobate, and you've had him locked up with a dozen blacks for two days! You'd have insulted him less to shut him up with the dogs! You pus-faced bastard—we're lucky we all still have our hair!"

"But he was in the slave shanty with the other two," Ivy wailed. "We tooken all three of 'em together."

"Probably there to steal one for himself!" Murrell railed on. "And you have to go and steal *him!*" Then, with an effort, he controlled his temper and said, almost softly, "Don't you see? He wouldn't have been raiding alone. There must have been others with him. They're bound to have missed him and started trailing him."

All the men, Stewart included, looked uneasily about them. The day was fading fast and shadows were gathering in the woods not far away. Ivy trembled and whined, "You—you want him fetched out of there?"

"No! Wait. Yes. Bring him out." Big Tip picked up the lantern and started for the door. "No, not you, Tip. He's probably had his fill of Nigras. Smith, you go in and get him. But in God's name keep the gyves on and keep a tight hold."

Smith emerged after a minute with the prisoner still doing his St. Vitus dance at the end of his leg chain. He seemed to sense immediately that the dark, handsomely dressed man was in charge here, and directed an impassioned speech at him. The language was incomprehensible, but the import was plain. He also recognized the half-faced Ivy as his captor, and grimaced and spat at him.

"Take a good look with that one eye of yours!" Murrell grated at the unfortunate Ivy. "Where'd you ever see a Nigra with a nose like that?"

John Ivy withdrew to the fringe of the group, as far from Murrell as he could get without actually disappearing among the trees, and distractedly picked at his scars with trembling fingers.

"Tip," said Murrell. "You run like the wind and fetch Andy Boyd down here. He can palaver some of these redskin lingoes."

The Indian was either repeating himself over and over, or he had saved up an impressive list of grievances. His harangue was unflagging; he punctuated it by pointing at the sun, waving his arms, making chopping and twisting gestures in Ivy's direction, squatting down to drum his fists on the ground. The men all watched him uneasily. "Can't we just turn him loose, John?" suggested Smith, who held the chain.

"No," growled Murrell. "We've humiliated him as bad as if we'd gelded him. He's mad enough that he let himself get caught at all. And then the way he's been treated—the Indians look down on Nigras worse than we do."

"Maybe if we loaded him up with goodies," said another man. "Give him a hoss, a rifle maybe . . ."

Murrell shook his head. "That's not going to square him with his ancestors, or his war god, whatever the damn heathen worships. He feels lower than a squaw by now, and a few trinkets aren't going to make him feel any better."

"Well, there's one other way," said another man. He made a discreet slicing motion across his abdomen.

"Don't you suppose I thought of that, first thing? I've got no love for redskins. But it's like I said. A slave-raiding party would have meant more than one man. He's got friends somewhere and they're wondering what's become of him. Wouldn't surprise me if the island isn't surrounded by war canoes right this minute." The men bunched closer together and again inspected the shadowy depths of the forest around the clearing.

Andy Boyd came at a limping run, his lank hair and whiskers waving in the breeze. "What's up?" he panted. "I couldn't make out what Tip——" He caught sight of the captive, now out of breath and quiet, but still heaving his arms around. "Oh, Jesus." Boyd turned to Murrell. "Where'd you get *him?*"

Murrell made a face and pointed at the cabin. Boyd looked at it blankly. "Pretty-Boy Ivy brought him in," Murrell explained, "for us to convert." Boyd turned horrified eyes on Ivy, who slunk nearer the woods.

"Crank him up again," Murrell said to the man with the chain, "and let Boyd have a listen."

Smith hauled the Indian over to the whiskered old man and pointed back and forth between the two of them. The Indian took a deep breath and began at the beginning again. Boyd flicked a look at Murrell and said, "Cherokee." Murrell clenched his fists and began to pace up and down. "That's fine," he muttered bitterly. "That's just fine. The Cherokees *love* the white man, they do."

Boyd listened and watched as the Indian went through his whole performance, occasionally tossing in a word of his own. The Indian seemed to be a little nearer appeasement at having somebody to talk to. He strung his woes out to epic length, but finally Boyd switched him off with a gesture and a few words, and turned to Murrell.

"Well, I can't pertend to grasp it all, John. But he's considerably riled."

"God damn it to hell, Andy, I didn't think he was singing the Doxology at you! Where'd he come from? Who and what is he?"

"Well . . ." Boyd scratched reflectively in his beard. "Lemme put it this way. Where he comes from, he's—uh—John Murrell."

Murrell breathed deeply and looked up at heaven for a minute. Then he squared his shoulders and said wearily, "Let's have the rest of it."

Boyd looked sincerely troubled. "Well, he heads a dog-eating bunch of outcasts—Cherokees, Chickasaws, breeds—prob'ly a lot of no-goods booted out of their tribes. Hangs out around the headwaters of the Ouachita somewheres. He was out with a couple of his red brothers, looking to liberate a black brother or two from his white brothers, when the half-headed brother over yonder snuck up on him unawares . . ."

During this speech, Boyd had sidled over to Murrell. Now he took the chief's arm and, still translating, led him a distance across the clearing, out of earshot of the others. They all looked at each other, avoiding Ivy's piteous eye. Boyd and Murrell talked for several minutes. Then Murrell led the way back to the group, his head bowed, his hands deep in his pants pockets and an unhappy frown on his face. He came directly to Ivy and said gently, "We're in trouble."

"Jesus, I'm sorry, John," the man said, in a voice close to breaking. "You know I wouldn't never——"

Murrell silenced him with a pat on the shoulder. "The Clan has enjoyed unperturbed immunity here on this island for near five years . . ."

"I don't know what all that means, exactly," said Ivy, "but I'll do anything I can to set things right."

"Will you go back with that Indian when we turn him loose?" Ivy's one eye widened. "He wants to take you the way you took him. Spoils of war."

Ivy's ragged mouth opened and shut. A small creak came out.

"He led a raiding party," Murrell went on patiently. "He's got nothing to show for it. And he's suffered gross indignity at your hands. Nothing will answer for it but he takes you prisoner."

Ivy found words at last. They came out in a rush. "Go back with him? You know what that'll mean, John? You know what him and his bunch will do to me? I'll be handed over to the squaws! I'll be thankful if I end up *dead!*" Murrell and all the others looked tactfully at the ground and said nothing. Ivy turned desperately from one to another. "Murrell," he whispered in abject terror. "You wouldn't side with no dirty redskin ag'inst one o' your own men?"

"I've got more than one man to think of here. Turn that Indian loose—or sink him in the lake—and it won't be long before we're raided by his brother braves. We'll *all* end up being sport for the squaws."

"Haven't I suffered enough?" sobbed Ivy. "Look at me, fellers. I warn't a bad-looking man, once. It was working with you- all I got these scars. My own mother couldn' look at me now 'thout getting sick. But did I ever complain? Did I ever accuse or blame, or say it wouldn't of happened if I hadn't been so all-fired faithful to the Clan . . . ?"

The Indian stared haughtily and impatiently at Murrell and then at Ivy, implacable as an eagle.

"In the name of mercy!" Ivy burst out. "Ain't there any other way, John?"

"Well, yes," Murrell said finally. "I guess there's one."

"Whatever it is—let me take it instead! Tell me!"

"I'll show you," said Murrell. "Look yonder."

John Ivy had to turn around to aim his one eye in the direction indicated, and Murrell shot him in the back. At that point-blank range, David's massive bullet took him like a battering-ram between the shoulder blades, and hurled him some twelve feet before he flopped to the ground.

Murrell said to Smith, "Unchain the redskin."

The Indian immediately came to stick his face into Murrell's and begin another tirade.

"What now?" Murrell asked Boyd.

"He's aggravated that you cheated him out o' his pleasure."

"The stinking coyote is getting what he wanted," said Murrell. "Tell him to shut his goddamned mouth or I'll show him some tricks his squaws never learned."

Boyd spoke a few words to the Cherokee and then, to Stewart's surprise, handed him a long knife from his belt. The

Indian took it with a sniff and grunt. Ignoring everyone else present, he stepped over to the fallen Ivy and began to saw professionally at his neck. Stewart turned away, sickened, but the decapitation took some time, and he couldn't stop the sound of it.

"I don't reckon we'll have much to worry about now," Boyd said to the group at large. "He won't bring any war party. It'd mean admitting he'd been something less than heroic. Instead, he'll carry *that* back with him and spread hisself around bragging how he fit to get it and what all he done to Ivy afore he killed him. Them scars ought to bolster his story."

"I hope his fambly's got strong stomachs," said someone. "I thought a heap of Ivy, but I wouldn't want *that* hanging over my bed."

Carrying his trophy, the Cherokee accompanied the clansmen back to the headquarters building, but he wouldn't deign to come in. He waited outside, while the men brought out a jug of whiskey for him, a battered rifle and some ammunition, and a saddle that was worn down to the wooden frame. Tip went to the corral and cut out an expendable horse for him. The Indian accepted all this without a flicker of acknowledgment, as if it was no more than his due. He never spoke again, even to Boyd. Only after they had added an iron skillet and a wool blanket to the plunder did the Cherokee grunt to signify that his honor had been restored.

The sun had finally set, in a cosmic glory of red and orange, and misty lavender twilight was stealing over the island when Smith and Yancey ferried the ex-prisoner and his horse back across the lake. They said he rode off without so much as a glance backward, Ivy's dripping head tied by its hair to his saddle cantle.

•

The men poked morosely at the repellent supper Boyd set before them, and gave most of their attention to a couple of whiskey jugs that circulated. Boyd's victuals were hard enough to cope with when a man was in the best of spirits. The memory of Ivy's dissolution was a dampener; they talked little, ate less, and drank a lot.

The injured Albe Dean was no inspiration to appetite,

either. He crouched in a corner, aloof and broody, hiding his battered face in the shadows and mourning over a chewed and unrecognizable piece of gristle. Dr. Cotton had been resurrected long enough to stop his bleeding with an application of turpentine and castor oil, and to bind up the hand with a dressing of cobwebs. But he frankly admitted his inability to replace the thumb, especially now that the dogs had already enjoyed it.

Big Tip was absent. He had attended to burying Ivy's leftovers, and then remained with the slaves down at the cabin, to begin their indoctrination into the precepts of the Mystic Confederacy.

"He has several excellent attributes for the work," Murrell told Stewart. "Big Tip is not only one of them; he overawes them with his sheer size and with his obvious importance in the hierarchy. They can look up to him and aspire to be like him."

"What exactly does he tell them?" asked Stewart, twiddling his knife around in the mess on his shingle.

"Why, that they've got to come in with us. That they're now initiated into the Clan and, from this night forth, wherever they go, they've got to obey the Clan's orders and do the Clan's bidding. Or suffer for it if they don't. Tip can make it sound more convincing than any of us whites can do. Besides, he speaks several of the African tongues. When he sprinkles some Dahomey or Senegal or Aradas words into his speechifying, it really sounds straight from the horse's mouth."

"So the darkies buy it?"

Murrell smiled. "Naturally, they all say so, because they don't get loose until they do. There'll be some backsliders, sure. But Tip does make the prospect attractive—that they'll all be free men on their own land, upstanding citizens of their own piece of this continent, maybe even have a vote in the running of it. Yes, most of them will buy it."

"Then what?"

"We cart them down to the Yazoo Market and put them on the block. We make a right smart piece of money. They get a smidgen of it, and new homes. But we warn them that they're constantly under our eye. They are, too. It's rare that they'll be bought by some plantation that doesn't already have one or two of our trained Nigras. They're instructed to go about their work, and keep their mouths shut. Once a month or so, one of our local men will call a Clan meeting for them to sneak off to, and give them a refresher dose of Great Days a-coming."

Stewart shook his head. "I just don't see what use they are to you right now. Why you're going to so much trouble with them, so far ahead of time."

"Oh, for one thing, we'll have made some money out of them. And we'll make more, stealing them again eventually and selling them somewhere else. In the meantime, we give them an occasional job to do. Count the master's weapons, or poison his best mount, or something like that. Just to give them the feeling of belonging, and bind them closer to us. And they'll be plenty useful, Brother Adam, when the time *does* come!"

•

Stewart leaned on the corral fence. He had come out for a breath of air and a respite from Murrell's enthusiasm. He was not eager to go back into the smoke and stink of the building. Out here the night air was soft and clean, the night noises soothing as the sound of a spinning wheel, and the moonlight gave an illusion of peace and perfection to the whole world. The horses in the corral were glazed with blue-white in this light, glowing, and flashing little glints when they moved, like articulated statues of some luminous metal.

"When you're sick to death of your feller human beings," said a voice, "there ain't nothing quite so comforting as the company of hosses."

Stewart looked around, surprised to discover that old Andy Boyd was standing a few feet away, his elbows and whiskers draped over the top rail.

"That's a fact," Stewart said amiably.

"Don't know what a man'll do for philosophical company, someday when all the hosses is gone," Boyd ruminated. "Steamboats beginning to crowd onto the river yonder. Railroads a-building back East. I've took me a look at 'em both. A steamboat's a purty thing to see, and a steam locomotive's a scary thing. Good in their way, I reckon. But I can't see a man getting comfort out of just being nigh 'em, when he's tired of everything and everybody else."

"You tired of everybody, Andy Boyd?" Stewart asked.

Boyd shrugged, sighed, and said he had overheard Murrell and Hughes talking over the forthcoming Negro uprising. He'd heard it all many a time before, of course, but every time he did he got sort of a bad taste in his mouth.

"You don't go for his idea?"

"What I think makes no never-mind. But John's already got all the rhino he can ever spend in his life, and more power than's good for one man. Why can't he be satisfied?"

Stewart wondered if he might just have discovered an ally.

"John thinks when he turns them blacks loose on this country he can command 'em like troops. Not likely! Once they get the blood fever up, they won't listen to no bugles. They'll strike out at anything that ain't as black as them. It'll be Katy-bar-the-door!"

"Now, Andy—them poor dauncy field hands and levee workers? They'll hit one lick, maybe, and then stop dead in fright at what they've done."

"Huh! Son, I reckon you been brung up amongst the nice old uncles and mammies, stomped down to where they won't raise a hand 'cept to tug at their wool and say yassuh. But I've seen 'em when they first come off the slave ships at Charleston. I've seen 'em tear off their own hand or a foot to get loose of their chains. I've seen a white dockhand get too close to 'em and get tore all to pieces afore the whips could beat 'em off. No, if Murrell gives 'em weapons and says go to it, and they rise up, you're going to see something worse'n Black Hawk's piddling massacrees."

Stewart meditated on this for a while. It was disturbingly close to what he had been thinking.

"If he sparks off them savages, Murrell'd be well advised to turn tail and head for Mexico or China. Him, you, me, everybody that's lighter complected than tobaccy juice. Just three years ago, mebbe you recall, there was that Southampton Insurrection back in Virginny. That crazy Nat Turner and his feller blacks butchered fifty-five white men, women and children in less'n one day! And our uprising—who's to say how far it's liable to spread? It might go on until the last white man's been shoved off the Atlantic sea wall or into the Gulf, and the cont'nent swept clean of us."

"Well." Stewart shifted uncomfortably. "It's not set to go off for nearly two years yet. Anything can happen in two years."

"I dunno why I should feel especial bad about it," Boyd said, almost to himself. "Damn'f I do. What's this country ever been to me but a lot of acreage for the law to chase me around on? God knows it don't make much diff'rence to me whether I get cut down at last by a black or a white man."

He subsided into a mumble for a while, and then swung suddenly toward Stewart as if the younger man had put up an argument.

"I'll tell you why I care. And you can laugh if you want to. I was borned afore the Declaration of Independence was. My pappy was one of Marion's Raiders. Yessir, he fit the British 'longside the old Swawmp Fox hisself. I figger that gives me some kind of stake in this goddamn country . . ." He sighed. "Even if I ain't been much of a credit to it nor my pappy neither one."

"You mean you don't want to see the whites lose it?"

"No, that ain't it. This is a helluva big, wide, sprawling nation, boy. Lookahere—you just now come down a goodly length of the Missassip. Maybe you reckon you seen a sizable stretch of country."

Stewart nodded bleakly, remembering.

"You seen about that meechy-much of it," said Boyd, marking off a half inch of his thumb. "There's more goddamn *country* in this country than any man can imagine. I been caving around in it for a good sixty years, and *I* ain't looked into a tenth of the closets and bedrooms and dogtrots and back porches it's got. There's room here for us *and* the niggers *and* the Injuns *and* the Mexicans. No, I ain't wishing that Murrell'd leave things alone for the sake of me and mine. I'm just wishing he'd leave things alone."

He brought out a plug and bit at it viciously.

"Look at it from your own view, Adam. Here you've gone and j'ined the Clan, hoping you'll stand to gain from it, right?"

Stewart squirmed slightly.

But, said the old man, supposing Murrell's big scheme did come off as planned. The country would be in such a fix—so raked over, burned down, torn up—that it wouldn't be worth a fippenny bit to anybody, the honest folk *or* the Mystic Confederacy. Who would there be to rob when there were no people working and building and making money and hiving it away? Or, he went on, suppose Murrell's scheme should fizzle in the pan. The way things were right now, the Clan took a little here, a little there. Nobody lost too much at one time, so nobody got riled enough to rise up in force against the Mystic Confederacy. But if Murrell should make his big play and lose, there'd *be* no more Clan. The name of John Murrell would be dirtier in the mouth than Benedict Arnold's or Simon Girty's. He'd be hunted down like a killer dog, and every single one of his followers with him.

"Well, if you feel that way," Stewart said hesitantly. "If you don't like John Murrell—why do you stick?"

Andy Boyd stared at him in amazement. "Not *like* him! Why, how you talk!"

"Well, I got the impression——"

"Never met a man I cottoned to more," said Boyd positively. "He's got an air about him—I dunno—you just can't help liking him. I can't think of but a few people what ever didn't, and they're mostly dead." The old man shook his head, evidently overwhelmed at the thought of anyone not adoring the chief. "If John had ever really took to preaching, instead of playing at it the way he does, he'd of riz a sight above men like Finney and Beecher. If he'd of chose to go into politicking, he'd be in Congress right now with Davy Crockett and Dan'l Webster. Or if he'd gone sojering——"

"He'd make a soldier, all right," said Stewart. "He sure is handy with a gun." He told Boyd how Murrell had put both his bullets into the one hole in the pine tree.

The old man laughed delightedly and slapped his leg. "By hokey day, that's John all right! Just the kind o' trick he'd pull. Son, didn't you ever hear of putting two balls in one bar'l?"

"Hey?"

"Reckon anybody can hit a tree with one gun, so it wouldn't matter where t'other was p'inted. And if that one pistol had two balls in it they'd fetch up together, wouldn't they?"

Stewart scratched his head, thought about it, and grinned.

"There's no denying," Boyd continued, "that Murrell is about as shifty as quicksand. He's slick enough to talk a mother out of her first-born. And God knows he can be fractious, sneaky, cold as a snake, cross as two sticks. But not when he likes you, not when you live up to what he expects from you."

"He wasn't very considerate of Ivy," said Stewart.

"How now?" retorted Boyd. "He was just pertecting *you*— and all the rest of us. Would you ruther of seen him hand over Ivy to that buzzard Injun, to have fun with at the stake? I opine he gave Ivy an easy way out." Boyd spat juicily. "He gives more'n he takes, does John Murrell. Look at me, for instance. Old man like me, I wouldn't be no use to myself alone. What'd I be doing now to keep buckle and tongue together? Swawmping out some Pinchgut saloon, most likely. This-away, I don't have to work too hard. I only ride out with the Clan on easy jobs, where there's some li'l bit of it I can handle. And still I come in for a fair share of the booty, same as any other."

"Well . . ." murmured Stewart.

"It's like that with everybody in the Clan. Not a man amongst us but wouldn't of hung a long time ago, wasn't for Murrell leading us and pertecting us. Some o' the fellers cleave to him on account of his brains. The way he plans and pulls off jobs that none of them could think up. Some are beholden because he keeps 'em out of jeopardy—like the doctor. And some of 'em, I reckon, just plain love him like a pappy— a body to look up to and try to please. But you know what's John Murrell's biggest secret?"

The question was rhetorical. Boyd tapped a finger on Stewart's arm to underscore each word of the answer: "He gives a man just what that man hankers for. Now, what can you say ag'inst a man like that?"

Stewart couldn't say anything.

"Take them niggers," Boyd went on. "I dunno how many hunderds of 'em he's filled up with his great-day-in-the-morning notion. But don't you reckon they take comfort from it? They never had nothing to look forward to before, 'cept to die in the traces when their time come. They maybe won't never see this heaven on earth he's promised 'em, but for a time they've got something they didn't have before—a dream to dream about—and they're that much happier on account of it."

This argument was getting into metaphysical byways where Stewart was lost and bemazed.

"You just ain't been with him long enough," said Boyd, "to know how John Murrell can win a body over. But he 'pears to favor *you* a lot. Giving you that fine hoss. Yanking that Arkansas toothpick out of Albe's hand to save you swallering steel."

"Yes," said Stewart unhappily. "I reckon I am beholden to him considerable, already."

The old man gave him a penetrating stare from out of his thicket. "What is it, Adam?" he asked at last. "Don't *you* like John?"

Stewart gave a little start. "Why—why, yes. And not just because I'm beholden. I like the man." He surprised himself. It was true, and he'd known it for quite a while. But this was the first time he had really honestly admitted it, even to himself.

"Well, then, you got nothing to trouble about," said Boyd complacently. "Murrell can make you a big man, a rich man, high-low-jack-and-the-game. Just do like he tells you, bear up your end of things, and don't do nothing to cross him."

They both left the corral and moseyed up the clearing toward the headquarters.

"What would he do," Stewart asked offhandedly, "if one of the Clan did cross him?"

"I wouldn't know," said Boyd, with a frosty chuckle. "Nobody ever has."

•

Stewart was startled awake very early the next morning by a gunshot that brought him bolt upright on his straw pallet. No one else in the building seemed to have heard it. On the other pallet in the cubby, Albe Dean lay snoring, his face flushed with fever from his wound. Stewart untangled his legs from his blanket and pulled on his boots. There came another gunshot; it sounded far away, but the clap of it racketed up and down the silent lake. Now he heard a rustling stir from the main room and ducked out under the flap of deerskin that covered his door. Yancey was there, looking sleepy behind his usual frown, and yanking on his own boots.

"Two shots," he said, keeping his voice low. "That's the signal for the ferry. Fetch your saddle."

Stewart reached back into the bedroom and lifted his saddle from where he'd been using it for a pillow. He followed Yancey out the door. The big dogs came stretching and yawning out of their kennel and looked at them curiously, but did not go into their usual roaring frenzy.

"Must be Barney and the others come back," Yancey said, as he led the way down to the corral. "They been foraging in Loosiana."

Stewart expected some natural distrust and antagonism from Israel on this occasion of the first ride. The handsome horse did register a mild surprise at being accosted by a stranger, but he stood still and obedient while he was saddled, not even puffing up his belly against the cinch.

It was like riding a well-upholstered rocking chair. Stewart's seat was untaught, and had necessarily been practiced to the jolting of his stiff-legged old mare. But he hadn't ridden a hundred yards before he adjusted to Israel's smooth gait, and man and horse became a centaur. Stewart found that he was really happy to be up so early and cantering through this bright morning.

"That's funny," said Yancey, when they reined in at the water's edge. "There's only one man." He lifted a hand to his brow and squinted out under it. "Tom Anderson."

They slid the big raft out from its concealing willows and poled across. Even from midwater, Stewart could tell that something was wrong with the waiting man. When they grounded on the gravel bank in front of him, Tom Anderson looked down from his horse with burning eyes in a clay-gray face. He moved his mouth to make words, but they didn't come out. He was bare-chested; he had wound his shirt into a sling that supported his left arm, and the sling was soaked and caked with blood. The rifle that he had struggled to fire and reload and fire again now lay on the ground between his horse's feet. Anderson swayed giddily in his saddle; Yancey and Stewart leaped ashore to help him down. His legs buckled when he touched the ground.

"I'll take him," Yancey said to Stewart. "You lead the hoss aboard."

Yancey held the injured man wavering on his feet all the way across the lake, not laying him down in case they couldn't get him up and mounted again. Stewart poled the raft by himself, wobbling all over the water. When they finally made the island, Yancey and Stewart got Anderson into Israel's saddle, and Stewart climbed up behind to ride pillion and hold him on. They rode slowly and carefully back to the headquarters clearing, Yancey towing the extra horse. There was still no sign of life in the big building. Yelling for Dr. Cotton, they eased Anderson down once more. Andy Boyd's head popped out of the open door, all spiky, uncombed hair and whiskers, and popped back in again. When they half carried, half led the injured man into the building, Boyd was dragging Cotton out of one of the cubicles.

The doctor wore his tricorn hat and a rumpled and dirty woolen union suit. He clattered over and peered at the man dangling from Stewart's shoulder. Blinking and sniffling, he said, "Stretch him out on that table yonder."

"What's the story?" someone asked Stewart, when he had put down his burden. It was Murrell, who had appeared suddenly and silently. He was wide awake and as nattily dressed as if he were off for church.

"Heard a signal from the ferry," Stewart told him. "Yancey said something about Barney and the others. But there was only this one when we got there. That's all I know. He ain't been able to talk."

Dr. Cotton stripped off the man's makeshift bandage and began swabbing away the crust of blood, lint and dirt to find the wound. Boyd had propped up Anderson's head and was gently trickling a mug of water into his mouth. "He's feeling mighty dauncy," said Boyd to the doctor. "Can I give him some whiskey?"

Cotton nodded curtly. "Then take that goddamn pistol belt off him. And his boots. Loosen his clothes as much as you can."

The application of whiskey appeared to lubricate the man's talking apparatus. He managed to ask, "It look very bad, doc?"

"Can't tell till I get this trail dirt off. You just rest easy."

Murrell stepped close to the table, patted the man tenderly on his good shoulder and said, "Can you tell us what happened, Tom?"

Anderson began painfully and haltingly to talk, wincing occasionally as Dr. Cotton probed into the hole in his body. It had happened at a one-horse settlement called Providence, just over the border in Louisiana. He, Jehu Barney and Jim Tucker had been flushed by a citizens' committee while they were herding off the contents of somebody's slave quarters. The attack was so sudden that both Tucker and Barney had been captured immediately and unharmed. Anderson had escaped with this wound in his shoulder and chest. Though unable to stanch the blood, and suffering excruciating pain, he had hung around close enough and long enough to watch the disposition of his partners. Barney and Tucker were now lodged in jail under guard, awaiting the visit of the circuit judge.

"Hell, you know I'll get them off," said Murrell. "You didn't have to kill yourself getting here to tell me that."

"But that ain't all," gasped Anderson. He clutched at Murrel's sleeve with his free hand. "The sheriff's got 'em locked up, but he won't keep 'em. Because the townies ain't figgering to leave this to no stump court. They're aiming to lay lynch law on Jehu and Jimmy."

Boyd gave him another sip of spirits and he went into a fit of coughing. When he finished there was blood in the whiskey mug. Dr. Cotton barely glanced up; he was sponging the gaping wound with turpentine, and looking solemn.

Murrell roused himself from deep thought. "Well, if it's hanging they had in mind, Tom, likely it's all over by now. You still didn't have to——"

"No, it ain't," panted Anderson. "That's why I pushed myself to get here. You mebbe can still get 'em loose. There's a camp meeting on. A big one. People there from all over. It's going on now, through Sunday. What day is this?"

"Saturday," someone said.

"Going to last through tomorrer, and they won't do no hanging till the meeting breaks up. It's a two-days' ride from here. You can mebbe still get there in time."

"Let's get you taken care of first."

Cotton was hardly the picture of the fashionable doctor. But, despite the whiskey tremor in his hands, his movements were dexterous, sure and gentle. He finished poulticing and bandaging the wound, and directed a couple of the bystanders to carry the man carefully to his cubbyhole and make him easy. Then, with a look, he beckoned Murrell out of Anderson's hearing.

"If you want to go after Barney and Tucker," said Cotton, "go ahead. You won't do this man any good to hang around and watch over him. You said it yourself—he killed himself to get here."

"That bad, eh?"

"Looks to me like they must have got him with a cannon full of scrap iron. If he'd holed up where he was until the bleeding eased—or if he'd ridden slow and careful coming back here —he might have saved himself. But now I can't probe for the pellets. Some of 'em have worked into his lungs, the way he's hemorrhaging from the mouth. If they don't kill him, inflammation will. He's got everything but lizards crawling in that hole, and he's lost too much blood to fight off the poisoning. I don't know how much time he's got left, but he won't need a calendar to count it."

"Hell," Murrell murmured. "I guess I owe it to him then, to go after Jehu and Jimmy."

"If you don't, you write off *three* men," said the doctor.

"All right. I'll leave Tip to help you with him. Do what you can, will you, Doc?"

Cotton said stiffly, "I always have."

Murrell smiled affectionately at him, then banged a table for attention. Everybody was awake and dressed now. Most of them were clustered around the stove, dipping up mugs of bitter lukewarm coffee left over from the night before.

"You all heard Tom Anderson's story," Murrell said loudly. "You all know where we're heading, so start packing gear and rations for two days' hard riding. Andy, how about you scrape together some breakfast for us? Tip, you see to the horses. Everybody, make sure your guns are cleaned and loaded."

Stewart watched the men's faces. The wrinkled masks of sleep became expressions of joyous, ugly anticipation. Only Albe Dean frowned. "Jesus, Murrell. I ain't no portsider. I can't handle a gun with this—this fish flipper."

Murrell looked at him coldly and said, "You'd better learn in one hell of a hurry." Then, to the rest, "All right, boys, hop to it. We're going to spring Barney and Tucker."

•

Stewart was uncommonly glad he wasn't making this expedition on his old horse. It was canter and walk, canter and walk, pushing hard and fast. They rested their mounts and behinds only when they stopped to boil coffee and choke down an otherwise cold meal of jerky and biscuits. The trail southward was open and clear, but this was empty country and there were no wayside inns or other comforts or diversions. There were a dozen men altogether; only the doctor and the big Negro had stayed behind. At their night's camping, Stewart made a careful list of the party in his memorandum book. Besides himself, there were those with whom he was already fairly well acquainted: Murrell, Yancey, Andy Boyd, Albe Dean, Lee Smith. And the lesser-known Ruel Blake, Bill Sanders, John Rogers, Angus Donovan, and the Earle brothers, John and William.

All of them were eager for the adventure. The stealing and herding of slaves had become a rather monotonous business. This was different: a liberation of their own fellows, from under guard, out of a town swarming with enemies. They looked forward to it exuberantly, talking excitedly among themselves and repeatedly checking over their weapons for readiness. Murrell regretted only that he had had to leave his newly recruited slaves on the island. Before the gang departed, he had instructed Tip and Cotton to explain the circumstances to the prisoners, and assure them that they would be carted to the Yazoo Market—and ultimately to new homes —just as soon as this mission was completed. "Give them the run of the island," he had told the doctor. "They'll be too afraid of the dogs to make a break. Give them plenty to eat and some of that horse-medicine whiskey. Maybe that'll keep them happy."

Now he gathered his men around him, explained his intended tactics for the morrow's raid on Providence, and gave each of them personal and explicit instructions. Stewart was secretly happy to learn that the plan minimized the likelihood of killing, but some of the others grumbled as if they were being sorely deprived.

"It would suit me fine," Murrell replied to the objections, "to shoot up the goddamned place and then burn it to the sod. But this town is too close to headquarters. We don't want to make them so mad they'll trail us back home. We should be able to get Barney and Tucker out without firing a shot."

At dusk on Sunday they breasted a low hill and looked down on their destination. At the foot of the hill was the town of Providence, almost deserted and showing just a scattering of window lights. Beyond it was a forest, and in there among the trees the camp meeting's bonfires were beginning to blaze up against the night.

"Hughes and Yancey with me," said Murrell. "The rest of you circle around and filter into the camp through the trees, not all in a bunch. Take your time; we've got all night. Go in unarmed; leave your hardware on your horses, but tether them handy. Try to look like you've been around since the meeting opened." There was an all-around nod of understanding. The greater part of the party wheeled their horses off the road and vanished.

"Let us go down after the Philistines by night," Murrell said to nobody in particular, "and take spoil among them until the morning light." Then he buttoned his coat to hide his guns Jonathan and David, kneed Tempest to a walk and, with Stewart and Yancey behind him, went down the hill.

Providence, Louisiana, was about as metropolitan, Stewart observed, as his own Tuscahoma, Mississippi. At the bottom of the hill the road became Main Street. At this nearer end of it, a little shanty stood like a sentry box. When they approached, a heavy-faced man stepped out of it and stood in the middle of the street, a double-barreled shotgun held at port arms. Murrell reined in and Yancey and Stewart stopped on either side of him, a pace or two behind.

"A good evening to you, Brother," said Murrell, in his most melodious voice. "Be this the city where the souls are gathered to praise Almighty God?"

"This is Providence, yessir," said the man. "And the meeting's going on out beyond." He jerked his head up the street. "You all come to jine in?"

"Indeed we have," Murrell said heartily. "I, my good man, am a wayfaring preacher. These are my two acolytes."

The man looked at them uncertainly. He surely had no more idea what an acolyte was than the two acolytes did, but he may have decided that they were lost souls that the preacher took around to show off as bad examples.

"Well, you're right welcome," he said at last. "Excuse the scattergun, Reverend. It's just we aim to discourage rowdyism. If your friends'll be good 'nuff to leave their weepons here with me?"

"Certainly." Murrell gestured. Stewart leaned his old rifle down to the sentry, and Yancey unbuckled his pistol belt.

"Y'all can pick 'em up as you leave." The man set aside his own gun and said, "Don't know as you're going to find much employment down yonder, Reverend. 'Pears to me they got more preachers than sinners. Cumberlanders, Scotch Covenanters, Missionary Baptists, Primitive Baptists . . ."

"Never too many voices to cry unto the Lord," Murrell said piously. "Tell me one thing about the meeting, Brother. No-hellers, or hell-redemptionists?"

"I reckon they've preached everything short of popery, Reverend. But mostly hell-redemption."

"Thankee, Brother, and God bless you."

The sentry waved affably as they trotted on past him and up the lonesome street. They passed not more than two or three other people. The few shops along the street were shuttered and dark. Only an occasional house showed a gleam of firelight or candlelight. Murrell flashed a glance backward to catch the attention of his acolytes, when they rode past a one-story, solid-looking log house with a barred window and a heavy door. On its front steps sat two men with shotguns across their knees. That was obviously the jail where Jehu Barney and Jim Tucker waited for the judge. Or the lynch mob. Or Murrell.

•

Stewart was not unacquainted with camp meetings but, being somewhat less than religiously inclined, he had attended them only infrequently and briefly, as a half-amused, half-skeptical onlooker. His involvement in this one prodded him to take a closer interest in the goings on.

The focus of the meeting was a cleared area in the middle of the wood. The clearing was filled with plank and puncheon benches and seat-height log butts set parallel in several score long rows. The men sat on one side of a central aisle and the women on the other. At either end of this arena was a high stand ascended by a staircase, bearing a crude lectern and lighted from below by bonfires. Any preacher who felt the call could leap upon one of the stands and unburden himself to the congregation. (There was a waiting line of would-be un-burderers.) When he tired, another preacher would mount the stand at the other end of the clearing and pitch in to spell him, the audience turning in their seats to face the new exhorter.

Other bonfires burned here and there around the clearing, and occasionally someone would throw metal shavings on them to make them burn blue or green for a while. Likewise for decoration, an uncountable multitude of tallow candles had been fixed in the branches of all the trees roundabout. A crew of small boys climbed about like monkeys, replacing them as they burned out. The candles flickered prettily, like a million fireflies in the forest, and gave the scene a carnival air. Un-fortunately, they attracted a myriad of flying insects, while hundreds of birds, displaced from their nests, flew around squawking and demonstrating their displeasure.

"Goddammit, something just shit on me!" blurted Yancey, and Murrell shushed him.

At a distance around the outskirts of the arena were bivouacked all the people who had come from far away to attend. Their pinebough pallets, canvas tents and covered wagons populated an area of several dozen acres. Beyond them was another concentric circle of the tethered horses, mules and oxen. The lanterns, lamps and cooking fires of this vast encampment gave the shallow valley the semblance of a big and bustling settlement. Only in two places in this infinity of light, noise and activity was there a measure of quiet and darkness. A clump of woods abutting on either side of the clearing had been set aside for a necessary purpose. As the prospectus of "The Providence, La. Protracted Camping Meeting" put it, "a grove of timber on the north side for the retirement of the females, and a grove of timber on the south side for the retirement of the men." The meeting having been going on for four days and three nights now, these two pieces of property were beginning to make themselves olfactorily obtrusive.

In its first day or two the convocation—like all protracted camp meetings—had been conducted with almost military punctilio. Trumpets awakened the people in the morning, signaled the call to meals, the call to prayers, the lights-out at night. Services were held at scheduled times, with scheduled preachers. Plaques were set up on the stands designating the scriptural text for the sermon and the numbers of the hymns to be sung, as indexed in the Watts Hymnal that nearly everybody carried. A prescribed area was laid out for the community kitchen, and the women took turns cooking and serving the whole population. Relays of men were detailed to care for the animals, lug wood for the fires, and attend to any other hard labor. A hospital tent was set up and manned by one senile doctor, two no-nonsense midwives, and a gaggle of busybodies. The traffic here was considerable, comprising a continuous stream of women who had gone into the vapors or the jerks in an excess of religious ecstasy, children who had fallen out of trees, and those gravid females who had endured the discomfort of a long journey deliberately to birth their babies with a maximum of publicity, and would inevitably name them, boys and girls alike, "Providence." The village booby drove a garbage wagon. The youngsters were conscripted to police the area of litter. Squads of vigilant chaperones trooped the woods to rout spooning couples.

But as time went on, more and more newcomers had poured in from all directions. Besides the genuine pilgrims, there came the men with portable saloons and gambling layouts, these only slightly outnumbered by men of the cloth: circuit preachers, defrocked preachers, self-ordained preachers, fanatics with axes to grind, and gentle lunatics clad in burlap robes and rope sandals and carrying shepherd's crooks. Discipline rapidly fell apart, but the general fervor rose and rose. The trumpets soon despaired of trying to regularize the proceedings. People ate where and when they felt like it, and let the garbage fall where it would. The hospital tent began to get a new kind of patronage, of men with broken jaws and knife wounds.

Preaching went on incessantly in the central arena, sometimes at both stands at once, to a fluid but usually overflowing congregation. Consecutive sermons and simultaneous sermons were unrelated and often contradictory. The hymns were lined out on the spur of the moment, by the preacher of the moment. And when a preacher couldn't wrangle his way onto one of the platforms, he would like as not gather himself a splinter congregation off among the trees. Many of the women and girls in the audiences were inflamed by religious rapture into amatory vulnerability: fair game for any man who wanted to lead them into the bushes. The roving chaperones threw up their hands and left the woods to the lovers.

Now a battery of enterprising taverners occupied a far corner of the encampment, dispensing popskull whiskey from barrels set up on sawhorses, and making their fortunes at an exorbitant fifteen cents a mug. Nearby, there were the thimbleriggers and the sharpers dealing monte and faro, tossing chuck-a-luck, spinning roulette wheels, and shattering all the laws of mathematical probability. The camp meeting was a prickly place for a man with money in his pocket; what the hat-passing preachers and the gamblers didn't get their hands on, the pickpockets did.

There were tents tactfully labeled "Men's Physician," dispensing specifics for the "diseases of bad company": Minerva Pills and The Unfortunate's Friend. There were the doctors of "female disorders," advertising easements for the discomforts of the monthly, but doing their biggest business in patent abortifacients like Dr. Rolfe's Aromatic Pills. There were more innocent enterprises, too, in abundance. There were stands selling gingerbread, cookies, fried catfish, pork cracklings, hot coffee and cold lemonade. There were hucksters of "Yankee notions": tortoise-shell combs, pomatums, picture puzzles, rouge papers, amboyna lotion, books, suspenders, reading spectacles of guaranteed genuine glass. There were the business stands of cobblers, barbers, dentists and barber-dentists.

Murrell, Stewart and Yancey meandered through all this in

the deepening dusk, like yokels at a county fair. Here and there, they could see the other clansmen doing the same, singly and in couples, being resolutely unaware of each other. Murrell caught a signal from Lee Smith, and they went through an act of meeting unexpectedly.

"Why, bless me, it's Brother Smith!"

"Well, if it ain't the preacher!"

"How's Tildy and all the younguns?"

"Middling good, Parson. How's your old woman and the tads?"

"Just prime, Brother Smith. Ask after you many a time." And, under his breath, "What's up?"

Smith threw a look around and muttered, "I've had at least three of these jakes invite me to stick around after the meeting. It's folding at midnight. Then they shuck their hypocrite halos and give Tucker and Barney a chance to wear some for real."

Murrell rejoined Yancey and Stewart. They stood at the edge of the clearing and stared at the congregation. The benches were nowhere near filled at the moment, the greater population of the camp being busy over their supper fires. The present sparse and shifting congregation was being rather desultorily addressed by a sandy-bearded, rusty-suited little man. He appeared to be drawing out his argument into a filibuster, to hold the platform until the aftersupper crowd came along.

"You ready to go into your pitch, John?" Yancey asked.

"Not just yet. I'll wait till the people are full and the benches too."

It was Murrell's plan to make himself known as a traveling preacher to all the people gathered there. But Stewart suspected that this was only partly to abet the jailbreak. From what he knew of Murrell, he was quite sure that the man simply could not resist an opportunity to be the center of attraction.

"What're you gonna give 'em?" Yancey asked. "Do unto others? Or God so loved the world?"

"No-o . . ." mused Murrell. "I've always found that *lust* goes over best with a big crowd at the tail end of a meeting. Yes. I'll shove good old Second Peter."

Finally it was full dark, and the bonfires and the candles

in the trees shone out in all their glory. The families began to drift back through the forest to the clearing, the men contentedly picking their teeth and the women fanning their aprons at their fire-flushed faces.

"Time I stirred them up," said Murrell happily. He unbuckled his gun belt and handed it to Stewart. "Adam, you watch over David and Jonathan until I'm through."

Yancey and Stewart faded back into the trees beside the clearing and settled down expectantly. Murrell climbed quietly to the unoccupied stand at the other end of the arena and just stood there, his legs spread and his arms akimbo, the white expanse of his shirt shining in the darkness. The working preacher couldn't help noticing; his discourse faltered, garbled and then stopped; he stared quizzically at the tall, silent man confronting him. His listeners noticed his gaze; one or two heads swiveled around. Others followed the line of sight. In a moment, as though imperiously bidden, they were swinging their feet over the benches. More and more of them, then all of them, turned their attention to Murrell, though he hadn't said a word. The prevailing preacher realized suddenly that he was losing his audience. Confusedly he tried to pick up the thread of his sermon, but fumbled through only a few hesitant sentences before he gave up.

Still Murrell stood, sweeping his pale, inscrutable eyes back and forth over the rows of benches. The murmur of sound in the arena dwindled to comparative silence. The people lounging in the fringe of trees, digesting their meal, began to emerge and slip onto the benches. At last, as calm and folksy as if he'd already been talking to each man and woman over the supper fire, Murrell began to speak.

"Dearly beloved . . ."

•

His rich voice filled the clearing, speaking the easy idiom of the country.

"I just got here tonight, Brethren and Sistern. That's becuz I had to come a tejus far piece for the li'l time I'll get to spend with you-all. But I heared the Lord say to me, 'Preacher, there's a conventicle of souls down in Providence that's a-striving to hear the good word.' Said, 'They already got a passel of pious and godly men to talk to 'em, but there's allus work for one more. So you hump yourse'f and get on down there.' "

The displaced preacher resignedly left his platform and sat down on a bench to listen like everyone else.

"Y'all are a sight to gladden the heart," Murrell went on. "All you hunderds of hard-working Brethren and Sistern come to sing hosannahs unto the Lord. I see many a fambly what's endured a long and arduous journey. I see folks gathered together in friendship and brotherliness. There's only one thing I don't see here. One thing that grieves me cuz it's missing."

He suddenly dropped his arms and his relaxed stance and stood hard and upright.

"The Lord ain't here!" A surprised and anxious stir went through the congregation. "Yes, you may well jump and look around. You won't see Him nowhere here." He let them fidget and mumble for a moment. "You come here to praise the Lord, did you? No, you Sistern are here to gossip and run down each other's flour gravy and pick at each other's reppitations. You Brethren are here to sneak off and nip at the whiskey bar'ls and go caving round the woods after easy women. *Aha!* Mebbe the Lord *ain't* showed up here yet—but He's up yonder watching and shaking His head in pity and sorrer."

Murrell leaned negligently on the lectern. "Now I'm not blaming the good and righteous men what've already exhorted you-all. A whole swad of you come up here to the anxious seat and you fall on your faces and embrace Jesus, and cry crocodile tears and beg forgiveness for your sins. Then the poor preacher you've deluded goes off sweating and thinking, 'Well, I've done had so and so many convictions. That's so and so many sinners I've turned back to Our Lord.' He don't see you slink away the minute his back's turned, and go off and sin some more."

His dark hand suddenly shot out at an inoffensive-looking farmer in the fifth or sixth row back. "You there!" The man recoiled. His neighbors on either side shied a little apart from him. "How many times you been up here to the mourners' bench? How many times you done declared for Jesus?"

The man appeared to have swallowed his tobacco. "Why . . . four."

"Four! And how many times you been to the whiskey bar'l since your *last* conviction, Brother?"

"Why—I dunno—mebbe thricet, I reckon."

The audience tittered nervously.

"I'm not a-gonna ask any of the rest of you what you been up to in between the services here. Becuz even if *you* ain't done nothing sinful—lately, I mean—you're guilty of standing idle by and letting your neighbors damn theirselves to perdition."

At this point, a couple of helpful men came out of the woods and laid fresh fuel on the fires that flanked Murrell's platform.

"Mebbe there's been other pastors afore me what's preached on Second Peter's during this meeting." He lifted a slim, black-bound volume from one of his big side pockets. "But it bears repeating—and it has partic'lar meaning tonight." He flicked the book open and tapped a finger against the outspread pages. Stewart had been present when Murrell bought it from a book peddler's stall; it was a volume of Shelley's poetry.

"Peter asks, just like I been asking, how you-all expect to get away with sinning, when even the angels don't. God spared not the angels that sinned, but cast them down to Hell! That was *Lucifer,* Brethren. He was the first poor sinner what thought he could get away with it behind God's back. Then Peter goes on to tell how God spared not the ancient world, but presarved only Noah when He brought a flood upon the ungodly. Lemme tell you, that ancient world was better than this one. It was just brimful of prophets and wise men. But did that cut any figger with God? Nosirree! God looked down and said, 'It's no good. Let's start over.' "

"Amen!" from out of the darkness.

"Noah gets the world all cranked up ag'in, and the people prosper and multiply, but does this new crop turn out any better? Huh! The people all got together and said, 'Well, that old fool God has done give us another chance. Let's build Sodom and Gomorrah and have some fun.' You all know what happened then. The Lord turned the cities of Sodom and Gomorrah into ashes, condemned them with an overthrow. Now, how many more calamities does the Lord have to whomp up afore y'all catch on He means bizness?"

"Amen!"

"Peter calls the sinners creatures without reason—born mere animals to be taken and destroyed. But Peter ain't talking about the beasts of the field. You don't see your hosses skulking round in the woods back there, waiting for some loose filly to roll in the weeds with. You won't catch the oxen waiting till the preacher ain't looking, so they can swill from the whiskey spile."

"Lay it out, Brother!" screeched a woman's voice.

"Shore, our Lord put whiskey and faro on this here earth. He put high clifts and swift waters here, too. But you don't go ambling off a clift or try to swim in the millrace, do you? Better if you did, Brethren and Sistern, than to indulge in the sins of the flesh. You walk off a high bluff, it don't matter, cuz a crippled man will walk upright into Heaven. But when you heed the temptation of the whiskey bar'l, or when you cast covetous eyes on t'other Sister's flowered bonnet, you're crippling your *souls!* Oh, I can hear you out there, moaning oh woe and forgive me. I wonder how many times you've pulled that hypocrite stunt afore now. The Lord says in this here Second Epistle of Peter—them that escape the defilements of the world through knowing our Lord, and then sink back into sin, the last state is worse than the first!"

Murrell passed an arm across his face as if he was suddenly very weary.

"Brethren. Sistern. Don't think that I'm harsh, or that I'm just pleasuring myse'f to talk sharp at you. I feel sorry for you-all and want to he'p. I think how proud Jesus'd be if He could say to His angels, 'Take a good look at them folks down there at the Providence Protracted Camp Meeting—so's you can greet 'em by name when they get up here.' Wouldn't it just make your hearts sing, Brethren, if you could hear Him a-saying that?"

"Let me come, Jesus!"

"*But what do I see?* I see the woods a-humping with lust and fornication and adultery! I see the whiskey flowing like God's tears! I see the Sistern counting each other's bangles and bijous with envy in their eyes! I see the Brethren throwing away their feed and seed money on Satan's cards and dice!"

The congregation was momentarily distracted. One of the Sistern, carried away, had stripped off and broken a string of tawdry beads and was scattering them by handfuls, broadcast to the crowd. Gentle hands restrained her and the commotion subsided.

"Oh, mebbe this camp meeting is a lark for you, Brethren and Sistern. I hope, when you're sizzling down there in the hell-fires, you can say, 'Well, damnation don't matter. I had a good time drinking and whoring and gambling and gossiping at the Providence Camp Meeting.' Yessir, I hope that'll gratify you. Becuz you know how many times you'll get to say that over and over in an eternity? You know how long eternity is laid out to be?"

Murrell leaned his elbows on the lectern and waited until the moans and groans had faded into an expectant silence.

"There's a rock a few miles out yonder in the middle of the Missassip. A big, hard rock, big as a steamboat. And there's a li'l bird, called the Eternity Bird, no bigger'n a bee bird, what flies up from the Caribbees just one time each year. He comes for to sharpen his li'l bitty beak on that big, hard rock. And then he goes home and don't come again for another whole year." He looked solemnly around. "Now, you want to count how long eternity is? Well, when that teensy li'l bird has been wearing away that whole tremenjus rock—just by honing his delicate li'l beak on it once a year—and when that whole steamboat rock has been wore away to powder and washed down the Missassip . . ." Another awesome pause. Every soul in the clearing was holding his breath. ". . . *That, Brethren and Sistern, will be ONE DAY of etarnity!*"

In the silence his baleful voice seemed to reverberate from hills miles away. The listeners expelled their breath in a groan of abject misery. Somehow, Murrell's magnetism had spread through the whole encampment, and people were leaving their tents all around, drawn to the clearing. He had collected the prime crowd of the meeting; there must have been between four and five hundred people sitting, standing and squatting in the area. The stalls, the sawhorse saloons and the gambling tents were deserted; even their proprietors had come, to see what the competition was. At this suspenseful moment, two men stood up in the congregation and began to belt out a hymn.

My thoughts on awful subjects roll,
Damnation and the dead . . .

Stewart recognized them. They were Ruel Blake and John Earle, playing the claque. For a line or two they sang alone; then, here and there, other men stood up and horned in—Albe Dean, Angus Donovan and the others. In a moment the whole congregation was wailing:

What horrors seize the guilty soul
Upon a dying bed!

It went on for four or five more stanzas, each more lugubrious than the last, and trailed off in mournful howls and brays. Murrell was right there.

"Ever burn your hand on a stove lid? You know how quick you jumped away. Now s'pose your whole body was just laid over with red-hot stove lids. You can't jump away now. Reckon you can stand it all through etarnity? Well, you'll have to. You'll have to lay there and burn and burn again and burn still more."

The weeping and wailing had risen to a loud orchestration behind his impassioned harangue. Murrell opened his book of poetry again and waved "Queen Mab" at them.

"Rightchere, the apostle Peter says the day of the Lord will come as a thief in the night—in the which the heavens shall pass away with a great noise! The noise of all the thunders that ever was, the light of all the lightnings in the skies—churn 'em all together—they'd be puny 'longside that last great irruption. And afore we've got our senses back, the archangels will be amongst us, cutting out the sheep from the goats. We won't have no chance then to say, 'Just a minute, Gabriel. I really meant to be a lamb of God, not no hairy old goat, but the Judgment Day tooken me unawares.'"

There was the beginning of hysteria in the crowd. One man began clumsily to coon up a tree, shrieking in tongues. Several women had fainted and were being fanned by neighbors.

"Now, the Lord ain't never showed me no painted panorammer of Hell. But I can see in my head what it's like, and oh! I wish I could wipe it away! Them poor souls wallering in what looks like mud—but it ain't mud, it's b'iling-hot molten brimstone—and them with the flesh peeling off 'em, layer by layer, like an onion." A wave of agonized moaning came from the congregation. "And the adulterers, clasped together like they was in their lustful life, but each one's skin is hotter than t'other, hotter than Bengal fire, and oh! they wish they could let go of each other, but they never will!" Five more women fainted. One went into the jerks, every part of her body twitching and thrashing, her teeth grinding together, her long hair coming undone and cracking like a whip. "And the drunkards —with Satan's imps pouring drink down their thirsty throats. Only it ain't whiskey. It's blistering hot sand! Scorching their innards out, but they got to go on swallering and swallering throughout etarnity."

Now he was almost drowned out by the ocean of sound from the crowd. Some of them were running in circles. Others were crawling purposelessly over each other on the benches. Some hung together in clusters, anchored against the tides of darkness, weeping down each other's necks.

"Oh, ain't there no way we can get off?" Murrell thundered over the noise. "Ain't there no other road 'cept that one that plunges to Hell? Ah, there is, Brethren and Sistern!" Several faces lighted a little in hope of reprieve. "We don't desarve it, not a one of us. But the sweet Lord Jesus has gone on ahead, and hacked a way for us through the horns of temptation and iniquity! Yonder's the path, Brethren—what's holding your feet?" The people stood rooted, puzzled. "I'll tell you what's holding you! You're snarled in your own briers of wickedness and lust! Once you give in to 'em, them li'l lusts gets stronger. They grow taunting eyes and grasping hands!" The people gazed around with burning eyes, looking for the lurking lusts. "Yonder they come! Grabbing at you! Can't you feel 'em? The hungry lusts!"

The people screeched and squealed. They flailed out with their hands, fending off the encroaching invisibles. Two men began, unseeing, to beat each other. Women fainted right and left. A young girl ran stumbling down the aisle to fall on the ground before Murrell. "The lusts!" she shrieked. "The lusts got my body!"

"You got to kick 'em off you!" bellowed Murrell, kicking out powerfully at the air. The crowd began to kick—mostly each other's shins, but nobody felt it. "Stomp 'em down!" roared Murrell, stamping until the platform rocked. "If you stand still, they can catch holt of your feet!" People began to stagger around as if hobbled. They fell over one another and rose to fall again.

"Look out, Sister!" Murrell called to the girl writhing on the ground before him. "There's a fiendish li'l lust a-clinging round your ankle now!" She screamed and rolled around. "Look, he's beginning to climb up! Up your legs!" The wretched girl was out of her mind with terror; her eyes rolled up into her head. With frantic hands, she peeled off her skirt. "Now there's another'n climbing over *him!* That's the way they do. There's one a-sneaking farther up. He's ducked under! He's in amongst your petticoats!"

With a cry of awful anguish, the young girl tore off all her clothes in rags and shreds. She gave another insane cry and, clad only in shoes and stockings, fled at a blind run into the woods. Most of the other men and women were shucking garments, to shed the demon things Murrell had stuck onto them.

Murrell kept on, pitilessly, hypnotically. "They're all over you! They're inside your clothes! They're tickling and caressing like your lover's hot fingers!" The crowd noise was of bestial baying. People clutched and clasped at one another. Stewart was dimly aware that Yancey, on the ground at his feet, was grappling with a bare-breasted girl too young to have much of a breast.

"They're crawling all over your skin, making your skin twitch, making you feel all excited. Oh, *ain't* it just the most glorious feeling you've ever had?" The expression on Murrell's face could have been one of transcendent religious joy, or Satan's own evil. "It's like being drunk and happy and making love all at once, ain't it?" The mob swarmed and writhed and clutched and groaned ever more feverishly. "Never think of Hell now, do you? This is *such* a sweet feeling!" But then Murrell roared, *"All of a sudden—BANG!"* the loudest noise that ever was. It acted on the people like the signal for climax.

Men and women together poured out a vasty sigh, compounded of grunts and sobs and the exploding breath of orgasm.

"*All of a sudden it's Judgment Day!*" Murrell shouted. The people began to pick themselves up from the ground and away from their partners. "And here you stand, feeling foolish, wondering what got into you." The people looked bewilderedly around. With little gasps, they began to rearrange their clothing and stared with unbelieving stupefaction at the strangers next to them. "It's done come Judgment Day, and here are the archangels to mark you with a big, cold spot." Many of them there could feel the damning spot inside their clothes. Just about every man and woman in the encampment was crying.

"But wait!" said Murrell suddenly, his face lighting and turning skyward. "Wait—Brethren—hesh a minute." The hidden faces began to lift, the sobbing subsided into sniffles. Murrell waited, his arms raised, while the hopeless and dejected eyes fixed on him.

"Could you speak up a li'l, Lord? Some of the poor lost Brethren are a-weeping down here and I can't quite . . ." Women stuffed handkerchiefs into their mouths. "What's that? Oh, Lord—*thank* you, Lord!" Murrell smiled a sunrise of rapture. Stunned and not daring to hope, the people began one by one to fall to their knees. "Yes, Lord, I'll do that. And thank you again, Lord."

He lowered his head to look out over the clearing, and he wore a smile of vast benediction.

"Ah, Brethren, do you know what thrilling and wonderful words the Lord said to me, just this minute?" Hesitant voices began to cheer and pray. "He said, 'Preacher, don't scold them poor children no more. Don't hold 'em off from my mercy. Let 'em come to the anxious seat! *Let them come to SALVATION!*'"

Even before he had finished the invitation, John Rogers and Bill Earle were on the move. Then Bill Sanders and Angus Donovan. Then, in one great wave, the hundreds surged forward, climbing over each other, falling down, beating their way to the mourners' bench. The people crushed forward to the foot of the platform, and it almost turned over. The few other preachers who had regained their own sobriety and objectivity stood off at one side of the arena, green with envy.

The scattered clansmen, their work over for the moment, coolly withdrew into the woods, all but old Andy Boyd. With tears pouring down into his whiskers, he was in the thick of the mob at the anxious seat, shouting hallelujahs as loud as anybody. A number of men and women clambered up the platform stairs and began to paw affectionately at Murrell.

"Let Saint Peter have the last word!" he cried. The crowd quieted. In his most melodious and gentle voice, Murrell recited, "Wherefore, beloved, be diligent that ye may be found in peace, without spot and blameless." He raised his arms. "Grow in the grace and knowledge of our Lord and Savior Jesus Christ. Amen."

The congregation, glowing happily and adoringly up at him, roared *"Amen!"* and then burst into a hymn, singing in parts to the "Hallelujah Meter." The very trees rocked to the basso bellow of the men:

Thanks be to God the Lord!

And the sky rang to the sweet soprano of the women:

The victory is ours!

Then, voices commingled in ecstasy:

And Hell is overcome
By Christ's triumphant powers!

While they were engaged in trying to shout loose the stars, Murrell made his way swiftly down from the platform and threaded through the crush to where Stewart stood. His eyes were twinkling with mischievous satisfaction and his face was wet with sweat. Stewart mumbled something about "good show."

"Yep," panted the preacher. "Couldn't have played them better if they were trained circus monkeys."

•

Somebody sang out, "Take up a c'lection!" It was enthusiastically seconded by several voices: "An off'ring for the preacher!"

About a dozen men began to hand their hats around, and Murrell winked at Stewart. Someone else roared, "Le's clean out the camp!" He was joined by a score of the huskiest and rowdiest of the younger men. They conferred for a moment, then all ran into the woods, shouting a war cry, "Clean sweep for the Lord!"

Murrell was again surrounded by men and women, crying, laughing, mooing, bleating their worshipful affection. They elbowed their way up to him and clasped his hands or threw their arms around his neck and dripped salt water down his collar.

"I done seed the light, Preacher, and it was all your doing!"

"Praise the Lord," Murrell murmured sanctimoniously.

"I'll be a better woman for your preaching!" exclaimed a gaudily gowned and rouged fat lady. "Bless you, Parson!"

"Go with Jesus, Sister."

"Fell down flat on the ground, I did," a man avowed, "and I smelt the stench of Hell right below!" Murrell backed away from this one's embrace; the man had too obviously fallen in one of the "groves of retirement" and he smelled like hell sure enough.

Stewart edged his way out of the throng. He discovered Andy Boyd sitting under a candle-filled tree, still sniffling, and wringing tears and drool out of his whiskers.

"I really oughtn't to come to these whoop-ups," the old man admitted sheepishly. "He *allus* gets to me like this."

Stewart snorted as he sat down. "You must be simple if you got any religion out of that. It wasn't any holier than hog calling."

"The Lord works in mysterious ways . . ." Boyd mumbled vaguely.

"He was playing the whole crowd for fools," Stewart growled. "I never saw such a shameful shivaree even amongst the Indians."

"Listen at you!" said Andy Boyd with asperity. "Who're you to say where and how folks should get their religion?"

"Well, damn all! Can't get it from a man that ain't got any!"

"They tell me," mused Boyd, "that the papists get their religion from fingering a string of little hard beads, and from colloguing with statchers. Who's to say that Murrell is any less a vessel of the Lord than a hunk of painted wood?"

Stewart glowered and said nothing.

"What it is," Boyd concluded, "you just can't get used to the idee that there might be some white wool even on a black sheep."

In the middle of the clearing, one of the organizers of the meeting jumped onto a bench and launched into a speech full of hyperbolic homage and laudation to Murrell. The congregation stood in a respectful circle, and the object of their affections stood with head bowed. Then Murrell was presented with a peck basket, half filled with money. He hefted the basket appreciatively but, before he could speak, the leader of the "clean sweep" movement came running out of the woods with a lumpy croker sack over his shoulder.

"This here is the devil's money," he panted, as he dumped the sack on top of the basket. "But we-all hope you won't balk at accepting it, Preacher, and putting it to the Lord's purposes . . ."

Murrell expressed heartfelt thanks, and opined that the Lord likely wouldn't inquire too scrupulously into the source of such a benefaction. Then he excused himself for a few minutes, and carried the sack and basket over to where Stewart and Boyd sat. The crowd smiled after him, and tactfully kept their distance while the three men counted the money. A group of disheveled men came to the edge of the woods on the other side of the clearing and glared lively hatred. They were the firewater and cold-deck purveyors, the thimbleriggers and pill pushers, a goodly portion of whose receipts Murrell was now clucking delightedly over.

The money was in bank notes, silver, some gold and a sprinkling of railroad scrip. Not more than a hundred dollars or so was recognizable as the contribution of the Clan's counterfeiters. Happily humming "Bringing in the Sheaves," Murrell stacked it all neatly, by specie, on the ground. And then he did some adroit manipulation and substitution. Those voluminous coat pockets did lend themselves to a variety of uses.

Carrying the bulky sack, Murrell went back to the arena and stood on a bench. "Friends!" he called, in his carrying voice.

"They say when the preacher comes, the chickens weep." (Laughter.) "Mebbe you thought it typical of me to run right off and count the collection." (Murmurs of "No, no.") "You see, I'm a wayfaring preacher, without a congregation of my own, and a man what lives in Spartan ways. That means I get along fine with a little. And that's why I went off and counted the amount of your generous offertory. Becuz I wanted to be able to say"—he waved the sack in the air—"here's one thousand, three hundred and forty-seven dollars *and* fourteen cents what I'm donating to the furtherance of the Providence Protracted Camp Meeting Association!"

His last words were drowned out in a tumultuous cheer, and hats and bonnets flew into the air like a snowstorm back-end-to. Stewart stood slowly shaking his head in genuine wonder. This man had given these people a bogus sermon that was just so much hot wind, and a laving of erotic hysteria that passed for religious exaltation. Now he had pocketed what would be a fortune for any one of them, and substituted a croker sack that was worth about as much as a croker sack—and they looked ready to elect him mayor on the spot.

Was it, Stewart wondered, that Murrell worked some kind of subtle magic that was his alone? Was it that this sampling of humanity was spectacularly simple and gullible—or only that it was human? Maybe Andy Boyd had said it best: "He gives a man just what that man hankers for."

•

The clearing began to empty, as the congregation broke up into families and individuals. They all started to collect belongings and children, preparatory to packing their wagons and grabbing some sleep against an early start homeward. This work, it appeared, had been delegated to the womenfolk. Most of the men still present stood idly about and looked suspiciously innocent, or clustered in groups that talked low and conspiratorially. Now Murrell came over to Stewart and retrieved his Jonathan and David. "You know your part, Adam," he said, as he buttoned his coat to conceal the guns. "Just stick with the mob." And then he was gone.

Stewart stood undecided, wondering if this might not be a

good time to make a break. Go and mount Israel and clear for Tuscahoma, and the hell with all this business. He was a little disturbed because he wasn't sure exactly what the jail-break attempt was going to involve. True, Murrell had ex-pressed his intention to get Tucker and Barney free without bloodshed. He, Stewart, was unarmed, and his instructions were to act the spectator rather than a participant. But if the other clansmen decided to indulge in a little plain or fancy mayhem, he would be adjudged as guilty as they.

"Stick around, bud," whispered a voice in his ear. Stewart turned and raised his eyebrows at the stranger. "Gonna be some fun in a li'l while."

"Like what?"

"Couple nigger thieves locked up in jail in town," grinned the man. He put a fist under his right ear, cocked his head to one side and let his tongue loll out. Then he went away chuckling.

Virgil Stewart had witnessed mob action before. As a young-ster back in Georgia, he had watched his father and uncle, among several hundred other white men, run an entire tribe of Cherokees off their land. In that case, the mob had been ever so righteous and legal. They had armed themselves with a spurious court order signed by a rum-pot judge. It declared the Indian property to be in public domain and the Indians to be a public nuisance. What the unoffending Cherokees were actually guilty of was living peaceably and farming prosper-ously on top of a "gold mine." The gold was no more than a skimpy trace that would have provided employment and a marginal living for three or four miners at the most. But the white mob overran the tribal grounds, half drowned the wiz-ened old chief in a rain barrel when he protested, beat into bloody unconsciousness the dozen or so young bucks who showed indignant fight, and put the torch to the Cherokees' neat little townsite. Three small Indian children burned to death in the schoolhouse. By nightfall, the whole tribe was trickling forlornly westward, in wagons, on horseback and on foot, carrying what few possessions they had managed to snatch up in their panicky flight. The white men had been efficient, and continued to be so: they wrung the land dry of its scanty gold supply within a fortnight. That land was probably still lying fallow and forgotten now, a dismal wilderness of diggings and ditches and doleful ghosts.

Right here and now, men were comparing their expertise in tying lariats into hangman's knots. Others were loading pistols and borrowing powder and caps from one another. Flasks, bottles and jugs were being freely circulated. Stewart could think of no explanation for the men's having gone from the extreme of abject religious prostration to the extreme of playing God themselves; all he knew was that he felt a little sick. He untied Israel from the tree where he had left him, back among the campers' wagons. The horse whinnied his delight at seeing a friend again. Stewart brought him conveniently near the edge of the clearing and sat down on a stump beside him to wait for the eruption.

The men were beginning to feel their liquor and getting increasingly eager and rumbustious. They shouted impatiently at the women still hanging about, to hurry up with their frittering and get off to the wagons. The preachers had already prudently disappeared. An *ad hoc* committee solemnly judged the rope-tying contest and selected two braided rawhide nooses with knots as thick and long as a man's forearm. At last the women, tight-lipped, unprotesting, had all taken themselves and their young ones out of sight. This left about a hundred and fifty men gathered in the clearing. A big, black-bearded man jumped onto one of the benches and waved his arms for attention.

"Men!" he shouted importantly. "We got a job to do. I reckon you all know what it is. And I reckon it's time we was getting on with it. Now—anybody wants to drop out, let him do it and go on back to keep the women comp'ny. We don't want nobody turning yeller at the last minute!" He swept glittering blackberry eyes over the gathering. "Awright. Now here's the way we'll do. The deppities know we're coming, so there oughtn't be no fuss atall. Try to keep the pris'ners quiet, but don't bung 'em up none. This ain't gonna be no free-for-all. It's a nice, quiet, desarving act of justice. We'll lead 'em down to Chaffee's stable. He's got two sets of block 'n' tackle rigged up on the barn, up by the hayloft door. We'll h'ist 'em up to that."

Stewart winced. They planned to haul the men up on pulleys from the ground, not pitch them through a trap or whip a horse out from under them. This would mean no quick and merciful broken neck, but a slow, grisly strangulation, with the victims contorting and dancing on empty air.

"You all ready?" the man shouted, and the pack growled a concerted affirmative. "Let's git on with it, then."

Every third or fourth man picked up a torch from one of the bonfires, and they all began to march silently out of the clearing through the wood toward the road that led to town. Stewart delivered himself of a large sigh and a small prayer, and climbed into his saddle. Israel perked up happily, as if he would have liked to stretch out in a lickety-split gallop, but Stewart held him in. So Israel contented himself with a stately minuet of a walk, lifting his legs high and dainty, like the improbable steeds that General Jackson was always riding in the pictures of him.

The greater part of the mob was on foot, though some of them were riding bareback on their unhitched wagon horses and mules. Most of the other clansmen seemed to be present on horseback. In the shifting torchlight, Stewart couldn't count them, but he was sure that Murrell was not among them. The procession moved slowly but with relentless purpose. They came out of the woods and into a magnificence of moonlight. The town sat silent and silver ahead of them. The amorphous mob had to funnel down into a shuffling, shouldering column as it squeezed into the main street between the first of the town's buildings. Stewart and all the other riders dismounted and led their horses. There was not another person to be seen in Providence. Inside the houses, invisible hands quickly jerked down blinds to darken the few lamplit windows as the procession came abreast of them. There was no demonstrativeness in the mob, no chanting or hurroaring; there was only the shuffle of boots, the occasional nervous snort of a horse, and the clinking of harness metal and weapons.

They could not see the jailhouse until they rounded a slight bend, where Main Street dog-legged around the community pump. When the van of the mob turned the corner, the men in the lead stopped abruptly; those behind trod on each other's heels and piled up with oofs of surprise. "What is it?" the men in the rear said to one another as they milled and jostled. "What's happened?" "Why're we stopping?"

Stewart was near the front of the crowd and he saw at once what had brought the column to a halt. There was the jail building, a squat and gloomy darkness even in the moonlight. The two guards had vanished, as expected, from in front of its heavy door. But another man stood firm and forbidding before the portal, with his arms folded, a black rigidity like an exclamation mark. This one time, at least, Stewart felt his heart surge in exhilaration, pride, confidence—and downright gladsomeness—at coming face to face with John Murrell.

•

"I'm ashamed of you, Brethren. Here I cripple my lungs begging the Lord to bring you to salvation, and your good behavior lasts about as long as a love affair in a whorehouse."

The mob of men stayed a respectful distance from Murrell, but there was a crowd on either side of him, and a line of them against the houses across the street, a semicircle ringing the jailhouse. No one spoke except their black-bearded leader.

"Preacher, we got the greatest admiration for you, and all that," he said. "And we're godly men—at the right time and place. Come next Sunday or next meeting, we'll be glad to listen to you ag'in. But right now you're jamming the wheels of justice."

He went on to explain, patiently and logically, that it would be another three weeks before the circuit court sat, and it wouldn't be sitting fifteen minutes before the two thieves now in that jail would be sentenced to swing. But in the meantime they were costing East Carrol Parish good tax money to feed and house. He and the fellows here were just anticipating the court's desires. And it would benefit the malefactors, too, in that they'd be spared the long drawn-out suspense of contemplating their certain doom. When he finished, the whole crowd was nodding and murmuring that yessir, nobody, not even a preacher, could quibble with that line of reasoning.

Blackbeard and all his followers took a step forward. Murrell unfolded his arms and propped his hands on his hips. This flipped back the long coat, and the silvered ivory hafts of David and Jonathan shone out stark in the moonlight. The entire assemblage took the same step back again, as if they'd just been absentmindedly practicing the first movement of a quadrille.

"Some preacher!" sneered the leader. "Packing guns like a land pirate!"

"Sometimes, Brother," Murrell said, "the Lord has to speak a little louder than I'm able to. You come at me again and you're going to hear Him roar."

"Preacher, I'd enj'y standing here and talking you out of your misapprehensions. But it's late at night. We're tard and sleepy. Let's get this over with and stop wasting time."

"You'll be wasting more than time, friend," said Murrell. He pointed to the jailhouse roof. A low parapet of pointed log butts ran around it, like the top of a stockade. From between the log butts, one at each side of the building, protruded the snouts of shotguns. "I know," said Murrell, "the deputies were supposed to crawfish out and leave the field to you. But they listened to me and the Lord, and decided to stay."

"You bastard Henry!" the leader shouted at the roof. "And you, Steptoe! You side with this outlander, you better be ready to leave town with him!"

No response from the roof.

"Well, if this don't damn damnation!" Blackbeard blustered. "But it won't hinder *us*, will it, boys? Maybe we'll just have to string up a couple more to keep them nigger thieves comp'ny."

The shotguns didn't waver.

The leader said angrily, "You want trouble, Preacher, you're gonna get it!" He turned his back on Murrell. "You men there. You cut around behind the building. Circle the whole place. When I yell *Go!*, some of you make for the roof and collar them two runagates up there. The rest of you bust in through the back door. We're gonna get this job done yet, you bet!"

Some forty of the men did as he directed, and vanished down alleys on Murrell's side of the street.

"Awright, now, the rest of you men. Them deppities ain't got but one shot apiece, and this son of a bitch has only got two. It's my hunch that Steptoe and Henry won't shoot atall, and anybody knows a preacher couldn't piss at his own foot and hit it."

"The apostles John and James," said Murrell casually,

"once lit into a situation like this. They said, 'Lord, wilt thou that we bid fire to come down from heaven and consume them?' "

The mob leader paid him no heed. "When I yell, hit him from the sides, not in front. He can't aim them pistols both ways at once. What's the matter?"

He had just noticed that he had lost the attention of his audience. Almost all the men were looking curiously back down the street, along the road they had traveled from the camp. He looked too, and grunted. It was midnight, but here was the sun coming up—and in the south, to compound the peculiarity. The whole sky down there was glowing orange and rose. The mob's mumble of wonderment was cut short by a racket of horses' hooves. Two men galloped into view and reined in at the edge of the crowd. "Fire!" the two men shouted. "The wagons—the camp—*fire!* The women can't hold it. Get buckets and get back to help!" Without waiting to judge the response, they wheeled their mounts and galloped back again.

The men churned in dismay and confusion, looking to Blackbeard for guidance. He simply stood staring with his mouth open. The men he had sent around the jailhouse had rejoined those in the street. Murrell watched with an ironic smile. Stewart realized that not all the clansmen had marched with the mob. Those two (he had recognized the Earle brothers) and some of the rest had evidently stayed behind to set fire to the encampment. From the light in the sky, they had done a good job; it must be an inferno. The crowd's loyalties were not long divided. "My kids!" one man shouted suddenly, and began to run. The rest looked anxiously from him to the jail, and then a number of them pelted after. "We can do the hanging later!" someone shouted, and led another contingent off toward the camp.

"Wait a minute, you men!" their leader bawled. The undecided remnant of the mob quieted for a moment. "This is some kind of a trick. No damn *God* didn't set that fire just cuz this stump preacher asked for it!"

Murrell smiled smugly up at heaven and said, "Thankee, Lord."

"That son of a bitch had friends to set that fire! Just to

buck us out of here! You listen to me! Here's one of the preacher's pups—I seen 'em with their heads together!" He reached out and seized Stewart's arm. "He's got other pards, too, down there putting the torch to them tents! You gonna let him get away with that?"

Stewart saw nothing happen that would account for it, but the black-bearded man suddenly let go of him, drew himself up very tall and took a deep breath, as if he was going to blow the fire out—and toppled on his face. There appeared to be a deer's hoof growing out of his back, but Stewart had no opportunity to examine this oddity. He had to leap aside to get out of the way of the mob. As if the dead man had been the dropped handkerchief to start a foot race, everybody else sprinted off toward the camp. Not one of them paused to inquire what had so mysteriously pacified their leader.

The dust cloud of their departure settled around what was left of the lynching bee: Stewart and the clansmen who had ridden out from the camp with him, Murrell, and the dead man prone in the street. There was another pounding of hooves as Albe Dean and the two Earle brothers rode down the street to join them.

"Good work, boys!" said Murrell. "The Lord lent a hand right on time."

"We know," said one of the incendiaries. "We just now got out of the way of the whole kit and kaboodle running like mad."

"Let's have the keys," Murrell called up to the roof. The men behind the steadfast shotguns stood up, and turned out to be Smith and Rogers. One of them unlooped a big ring of keys from around his neck and dropped it over the parapet. While Murrell was trying the keys in the door, Smith dropped two more objects that thumped heavily into the dust of the street—the two guards, limp and unconscious—and Rogers threw their shotguns after them.

"Get the horses ready," Murrell called, as the door opened and he ducked inside the jail.

Andy Boyd rode out of the shadows of an alley, leading Tempest and two extra mounts, doubtless liberated from the camp. Murrell was out again in a moment, with two men running after him. He had got them out of their cells with no trouble, but none of the keys on the ring fitted their shackles, so each of them still wore handcuffs with a foot of chain jingling between his wrists.

The horses had been unnerved by all the excitement. Mounting up was accomplished only after most of the men, cursing, had hopped around their circling animals, with one foot in the stirrup and the other pedaling. In the commotion, no one noticed one of the battered deputies stir and reach a cautious hand for the shotgun that lay nearby.

Murrell reared his stallion, waved his black hat and sang out cheerfully:

> Through all the dangers of the day,
> Sweet Providence attends our way!

"B-lam!" added the shotgun, and John Rogers was lifted half out of his saddle. He reeled and his horse staggered, but he managed to grab leather and hang on. Before the sound of the shot had got to the end of the street and echoed back, Murrell and three others had their pistols leveled on the imprudent guard and let fly together. The man, from lying propped on his elbows, did a neat backward somersault and didn't move again. The rest of the clansmen, outraged, pumped bullets into the other still-senseless deputy and into the corpse of the black-bearded man.

"That shooting is going to fetch the mob back here!" Murrell warned. "Rogers, can you ride?" The wounded man, his face screwed up like a chalk scrawl on the darkness, nodded curtly.

"Let's hit for home, then!" Murrell commanded. The Clan thundered out of town and up the hill like a cavalry charge. There was no sign of the sentry they'd encountered on the way in. Stewart didn't even think, as they flashed past the shack, of the trusty old brass-bound rifle he was leaving there. Israel and Tempest set the pace, and a hot one it was. The road whipped backward beneath them like a stair-runner carpet being jerked from under their feet. Some of the men rode in a bunch, clustered protectively around the horse of the injured Rogers. The road narrowed down into a trail, and now the riders had to string out in single file, dodging and yelping and cursing as twigs clawed at their faces. They rode on for half an hour at this breakneck gallop. Then Murrell sawed his horse down to a walk, when he heard Andy Boyd calling, "Stop! Whoa! Dammit, Murrell, slow up!"

The rest of the column clattered to a halt, the men and horses panting gratefully. Boyd made his way to Murrell's side and said, "We gotta take an easier pace, John, or we're gonna lose Rogers. He's bad off."

Murrell swore and looked anxiously at the sky. "I figured to ride on till daylight before we holed up," he said. "Let's have a look at him."

Rogers had ridden the whole way with both his hands clenched tight around the saddle horn and a companion holding his horse's reins. He sat weaving with fatigue and bent with pain, his breath coming in great rasping gasps. The whole near side of his mount was covered with blood, most of it the rider's, but the horse had taken a few pellets, too. The center of the shot pattern, luckily, had been stopped by Rogers' wide leather belt, or he would have been blown open like a mushmelon. But the rest of the shot had torn away most of his haberdashery and a hunk of skin and flesh from his left side. When Murrell wiped away the slowly welling blood, three of the man's ribs could be seen, shining out naked and white.

Murrell shook his head sympathetically. "I don't like to say it, Rogers, but it was your own fault. You tossed the shotgun where that beef-witted hellfry could reach it."

Rogers gritted an acid oath from between his teeth, and added, "That don't make me feel no better."

"Well, look. If we stop to rig a litter between horses, and then have to plod along with it, we needn't worry about the townsmen running us down. They can send their women to do it. Do you think you can go on a while longer?"

"Do the best I can," the man mumbled.

"We've got no more than three hours yet to sunup. Then we'll pull off in the woods to camp and make you as easy as we can. But there's not really any help for you till we get back to Doc Cotton."

"Awright," the man gasped impatiently. "Druther ride than talk-talk-talk."

Murrell held them to the trails that ran close beside the big river; this put them in danger of an easy pursuit, but it was the shortest way back to headquarters. Like the trip down, this one was now canter and walk, but a damned sight more cantering than walking. This, despite the fact that the moon had set, and riding in the pitch dark was dangerous, and Rogers was having a harder and harder time sticking his saddle.

Finally the sky began to pale in the east, and the Mississippi showed itself as a steely gleam through the trees to their right. It was about then that a shout came from the rear guard and brought the whole column to another halt. Rogers had at last quit fighting the pain and slipped unconscious onto the ground.

"Lay him across his horse, Bill, and lead it," instructed Murrell. "The rest of you ride on and strike off to the left, one by one, at separate places about fifty yards apart. We don't want to leave a sign like a stampede turned off the trail. Keep bearing west until one of you hits a clearing. That man make a smoke and the rest of us'll find it soon or later."

It was Stewart who came upon a campsite, a grassy glade beside a clear spring, about a mile inland from the river. Quickly he lit a fire and piled dew-wet grass on it. A thick pillar of inky smoke climbed unshredded into the windless dawn air, hard to see against the dark blue sky until it reached an altitude where it met the oncoming sunlight and turned to a plume of gold.

The others straggled in by ones and twos, Murrell and Bill Earle accompanying the horse with John Rogers draped across the saddle. When all were accounted for, Stewart kicked his smudge fire apart and rebuilt it with smokeless dead windfall branches. They stretched the wounded man out beside it and Andy Boyd put a canteen of water on the fire to heat. Rogers was half awake again, so somebody started dosing him from a flask of the Clan's universal anodyne. The others unsaddled the horses and turned them loose to blow and graze. Murrell took the ex-prisoners, Jim Tucker and Jehu Barney, to one side. Stewart overheard the conversation, without paying close attention.

"You mean we gotta ride a hunderd miles sporting these bracelets?" one of them protested.

"There's none of us here that can pry them off you,"

snapped Murrell. "Be glad they didn't chain you both together."

"But why can't we come——?"

"No," Murrell interrupted firmly. "I don't want or need you at headquarters. The hue and cry will be out for you all over this territory, and that'll make you both worthless to me for a long while to come. Do as I tell you. As soon as you've had a snooze, head across the Miss' and up the Trace. Sherrill and Robbins are operating somewhere in the area around McIntoshville. They'll be glad to take on two extra hands."

"If we got any hands left by the time we get there," grumbled Tucker.

"I told you. Stop at Bill Vess's in Tuscahoma." Stewart stiffened and listened. "Vess has got a forge and tools to peel those gyves off you, and he'll give you fresh horses. Now, no more argument. You know what to do."

He left them abruptly and strode over to share some coffee that Dean and Blake were boiling over the fire. Barney and Tucker obviously didn't like their instructions. They bitched and groused for a while, then, having cussed themselves into resignation, lay down clanking for a nap.

Stewart lighted a pipe and sat brooding in a cloud of tobacco smoke. He hearkened back to his first conversation with William Vess and remembered how, way back then, he had got the impression that the man was a not-too-secret admirer of John Murrell. But Stewart didn't get much gratification from recalling his own perspicacity. It troubled him that Vess should turn out to be just one more of the Clan's "respectable" hirelings. But why should that trouble him? Because he was wondering: was Hester in on it, too? He had to assume that yes, she must share or at least be winking at her husband's perfidy. A man couldn't be one of Murrell's hangers-on and keep it from his wife for long.

But Christ, he thought, am I any better than Hester—*or* William? If the infuriated citizens of Providence did catch up and capture this bunch, could he prove that none of the dozen or so bullets in the bodies in the street were his? Even taking the brightest possible view of things, and supposing that the whole crew wasn't summarily hanged, could he ever make a judge and jury understand why he was among them? Stewart unhappily compiled a mental list of the crimes in which he was, as of now, guilty by association—slave stealing, horse theft, inciting to riot, passing counterfeit money, jailbreak, arson, murder. There were doubtless more, but he recoiled from extending the inventory.

He couldn't keep on like this. His moral guilt in these atrocities was a matter for conjecture. But the time would come, inevitably, when to protect himself he would have to go for a gun—against somebody, somewhere, who was on the right side of the law. And if that happened, he might as well reconcile himself to riding with the Clan for the rest of his life. There'd be no turning back after that. No, it were best he washed his hands now of Murrell and the Mystic Confederacy. The Almighty knew that he had already risked enough, physically and otherwise, in the course of this inside-the-ranks investigation. And he had collected enough in the way of eyewitness testimony to let the duly appointed lawmen finish the job.

There was one more thing: his unexpected liking and admiration of Murrell, for the very swagger and dash of his roguery. Stick with him much longer, and he might get so fond of the villain that he couldn't make himself betray him. Already the thought of it made Stewart feel unclean and unmanly. Considering everything, it was high time he abdicated from the Clan, allied himself again with his own people, and put this episode firmly behind him.

While a couple of other men held Rogers down, Andy Boyd sponged out his wound with scalding water and then poured raw whiskey in it—and Rogers screamed almost loudly enough to be heard back in Providence. Now that Rogers was all but professionally embalmed, what with the liberal applications of alcohol internally and externally, he drifted off into another coma and Boyd bandaged him with what was left of his shirt. When all the men had had a few swigs of alkali coffee, a bricklike biscuit and a smoke or a chew, Murrell reminded them that they had another night's hard riding ahead, and they disposed themselves around the glade to sleep.

There was a chilly wind blowing up from the river. As the day wore on and the sun was damped by an overcast of cloud, the unblanketed men huddled together for warmth. Stewart, finding himself beside the wounded man, who was half undressed and shivering in his sleep, sympathetically lay close against him to lend his body heat. The shivering stopped, but Stewart himself got colder and colder. This was curious; Rogers was so saturated with forty-rod whiskey that he should have radiated like a Franklin stove. At sundown, when the bunch roused to ride again, Stewart leaned over his bedfellow and murmured solicitously, "How you feeling, Rogers?"—to find that Rogers was feeling nothing at all, and that he had been bundling with a cadaver all the livelong day.

.

They came back to the headquarters in midmorning the next day, bringing Rogers' body lashed across his saddle. There had been no sign of pursuit. Evidently the camp conflagration and the aborted execution had effected confusion and delay enough to give them a clean getaway. Tucker and Barney had left the main force, as directed, at the beginning of the second night's ride. Angus Donovan went off with them, on an errand to Greenville, across the river, that no one bothered to explain to Stewart.

Dr. Cotton and Big Tip responded to their rifle signal, and put the crew of slaves to work ferrying them across to the island. The Negroes had been given the run of the place and appeared to be enjoying it. The returned clansmen were too tired to stand and too sore to sit, but somehow they managed to stay awake while they tied into the big bucket of coffee and the gross of vulcanized eggs the doctor set before them.

Cotton informed Murrell that Tom Anderson had died the day before, and asked, "How'd the expedition pan out?"

Murrell gestured with an egg on the point of a knife and said, "Well, we got Jehu and Jimmy loose, and we turned a monetary profit. But considering that we've lost Anderson and Rogers, we just barely broke even."

"I observed that Rogers seemed to have less appetite than the rest of you," said Cotton drily. Tip had removed the dead man from his horse and brought him into the building. The body had stiffened into a right angle, and sat propped against the wall as if snugly comfortable there. "What'd you bring him back for?"

"We was a little curious," said Ruel Blake. "His wound ought not of been mortal. It didn't seem nat'ral that he should of kicked off so sudden like he did. We thought you might take a look at him and tell us why."

"I don't have to look," said Cotton. "I can tell from here. He smells like a vat of sour mash. Who diagnosed that he was suffering from a deficiency of our creosote whiskey?"

Boyd waved an egg. "Reckon I'm to blame. But whiskey never killed nobody, Doc, or we'd all be worm fodder by now."

"We've all got alimentary tracts like canal locks, I expect," said the doctor. "But you poured it into the hole in his side, didn't you? Well, let me just say that they don't call it rotgut for nothing. You might as well have dumped in privy lye."

All but Stewart stumbled bleary-eyed off to their cubicles. He picked up his mug of coffee and walked down to Murrell's room, at the far end of the building.

"Can I have a word with you?" he asked.

"Help yourself, Adam," Murrell said, kicking off his boots. "But I may be asleep before I can fire any words back."

"It's only that when I wrote my wife, I said not to expect me for a *little* while. I've still got a farm to think about—and the trip down here took so ungodly long. You know the old saying: plant cotton when the cottonwood blooms. I'm late with my spring plowing already. If I'm going to join the Clan permanent, I have to get back and make some kind of arrangement about cropping my holding."

Murrell flopped back on his pallet and grinned up at Stewart. "Your missus likely to rag you to know where you've been? Is she the naggy sort?"

"No. She keeps her own counsel and lets me keep mine."

Murrell sighed and said appreciatively, "A quiet wife is a pretty thing." After a moment he said, "Well, I've got some business up home myself. Tell you what, Adam. There's a little entertainment rigged up for tonight—I figure you fellows have earned some high jack. But when it's over, here's what we'll do. We'll ferry our Nigras across the river to Dundee's Landing. The boys can take them from there on down to the Yazoo Market. You and I will catch a steamer upriver—no goddamned

Barnyard this trip—and we'll be in Memphis town two days later. Head high and tail over the dashboard. How's that sound?"

"Sounds je-wholloper."

"All right, then. Now go and catch up on your shut-eye." He grinned again. "You'll want to be wide awake tonight."

Just suppose, Stewart thought to himself, as he undressed in the cubicle he shared with Albe Dean—just suppose it could somehow be arranged that the law was waiting at the Yazoo Market, or Dundee's Landing. Suppose he could set it up to have the law bushwhack Murrell—take him redhanded with this batch of stolen slaves. It would mean the finish of Murrell, the collapse of the Mystic Confederacy, and the end of this nightmare vigil. But how to get a message out of here to alert the authorities? Suppose . . . and he drifted off to sleep before he finished the thought.

·

The sound of two signal shots from across the lake, and subsequent movement in the outer room, barely penetrated his consciousness. He plummeted back into deep sleep and dreamed of Naomi. She was seated at the little harmonium in the Henning parlor, playing softly and singing in her dulcet voice. But she gradually began to play louder and louder, hammering on the keys and stamping her feet on the bellows. Her voice rose to a yowl and the song she was murdering became recognizable as a particularly bawdy barroom ditty. Stewart came awake to discover that the music was still going on.

Twilight had turned the room's little window to a pale patch of gray. From somewhere up the island came the sound of lilting music and women's voices lustily singing the ribald ballad of his dream, counterpointed by the kennel hounds' uproar. "What the hell now?" he muttered, and felt around for his trousers.

He stumbled out, rubbing sleep from his eyes, to find the rest of the Clan busy in the big room. Three or four were gathered at the wash-up bucket, scrubbing away with pieces of sacking and squabbling over the single lump of soap. Others were changing their socks or struggling into collars and neckties or stocks. Andy Boyd was fighting a currycomb through his whiskers. Dr. Cotton was picking the livestock off his tricorn hat. Murrell, the only one fully dressed—and, as usual, dressed to the nines—was humming as he put candles and lard lamps around the room.

"Ah, you finally stirred your stumps, Adam!" he called. "Go put on your best duds, if you've got any. Company coming!"

Stewart returned to the cubbyhole and fetched a clean woolen shirt out of his saddlebag. He ran a hand over his chin and nearly sandpapered the skin off his palm. He went back to the big room to find the toilette department still crowded, so he poured a gourdful of the coffee boiling on the stove and carried it back to his room to shave with.

Just as he finished, the mysterious traveling concert arrived in the clearing, and the dogs went out of their minds. Stewart stepped into the main room just as the biggest woman he had ever seen came through the front door. She had to turn sideways to accomplish it. The woman wore a nondescript traveling costume which appeared to have begun life as a tent. Her hair was the variegated color of an autumn sunset, and the stucco of make-up on her face must have constituted at least one of her three hundred or so pounds. She carried a concertina under one arm. Angus Donovan edged in behind the woman, smiling as proudly as if he had just that minute invented her; apparently she was the product of his errand across the river.

"Foursquare Fanny!" Murrell shouted joyously. "The old hell hole herself!"

"Black John!" she croaked. They rushed to embrace and pound each other's back. "And there's Hot-Pants Yance!" she roared. "And old Randy Andy! Jeez, it's good to see you ag'in, boys!"

"The rest of the bunch will be out to greet you in a shake, Fan. They're dressing up in your honor."

"Well, Saint Peter's peter!" she protested. "Don't let 'em see us till we've had a chance to doll up, too. Me and the gurruls didn't traipse all this way in our working clothes, Murrell."

"All right, sweetheart. You fetch them in and we'll all turn our backs. You can dress in the bedrooms yonder."

The big woman called out the door, "Git your asses in here, ladies!" The singing outside trailed off.

The clansmen were all back in the big room now, standing around grinning self-consciously. "Hide your eyes, boys," said Murrell. Everyone turned his face to the wall and listened to the sounds of giggling and skirts rustling as the girls tripped across the chamber and whisked into the cubicles.

The men scurried around, then, continuing the process of making the place as festive as possible. They stoked up the stove until it roared and threatened to come apart, prodigally lighted more candles, set out their best grade of whiskey, picked up their discarded filthy clothes and dusted the tables, benches and drinking mugs with them. They leered to one another at the occasional gusts of girlish laughter and whispering from the side rooms. Stewart was glad to see that they had not neglected to remove John Rogers' mortal remains.

"Old Foursquare Fanny O'Hoag," Murrell explained to Stewart, "runs the best house on the river. Not a skate in her whole stable"—he chuckled—"unless you except the great lady herself."

As if that had been her cue, Madam O'Hoag came sailing splendiferously out of one of the cubicles, wearing her "working costume." If this one, too, had originated as a tent, it had been a circus big top. Its flamboyance would have lighted the building adequately without the candles, and the egret plumes that sprouted from her shoulders and hairdress flicked soot from the rafters.

"Sister Fan," said Murrell, "I'd like to introduce you to our newest clansman, Brother Adam Hughes."

Stewart shook her soft, powdery hand and she gazed at him with a measure of amusement. "Adam," she repeated. "Well, now, if'n that ain't a coinkidinky. Show you what I mean, son, in a minute." She raised her voice. "All right, gurruls, y'all ready?"

A happy titter answered her. The big woman said confidentially to Stewart, "Ever'body here knows ever' body else. But I kinda like to stage a grand promenade, y'know?" She whipped open a huge, lacy fan and commenced to fan herself briskly. Her myriad feathers swirled in the breeze. "Jemima!" she called.

A tall, lissome, blonde-haired beauty came out of one of the rooms and dropped a graceful curtsy. All the men clapped hands, stamped feet and whistled appreciatively. Each of the girls made the same stagy entrance as her name was called—"Felicity!" "Timna!"—curtsied, smiled and was loudly applauded. Murrell had been right; there wasn't a homely girl in Madam O'Hoag's retinue.

"Deborah and Delilah! . . . They're twins," Fanny explained to Stewart, as two identically lovely and identically costumed brunettes appeared. "All my gurruls," she went on, "are named out of the Bible. Holier that way. *Haw haw!*" and Stewart gasped as she thumped his back. "Beatitude!" and out came a luscious, green-gowned redhead. "Integrity!" produced a diminutive and delicious doll of a girl. Fanny whispered another aside to Stewart. "That's my dotter—the image of me when I was her age. She's not for nobody but John Murrell; he made me guar'ntee it. Poor darling—it means she don't get laid but few and far between, and it's sp'iling her nerves. Takes Dr. Morse's Invigorating Elixir all the time now, like a spinster schoolmarm."

The applause for Integrity was discreet and gentlemanly. She came directly from her cubbyhole to curtsy only to the chief himself. Murrell raised her up with courtly dignity and kissed her hand.

"They do make a sweet-looking couple, don't they?" simpered the girl's mother, digging a meaty elbow into Stewart's ribs. Six more gurruls made their appearance—Abigail, Miriam, Modesty, Ruth, Joy and Vashti—until the room was swarming with scriptural heroines and personifications of various virtues, all in colorful ribbed taffeta.

"Now I want y'all to say howdy to somebody new!" announced Madam O'Hoag. "A little lady just j'ined our happy establishment." She turned to Stewart. "This is why I thought it was interesting, you being called Adam." He turned slightly pink, having an inkling of what he was in for. "Here, gentlemen—and you Adam—is our very own sweet *Eve!*"

What Stewart was in for did not look to be at all unbearable. She had long, curling hair the color of buttercups and, surprisingly, wide brown eyes. Unlike the other girls, she wore no paint or polish; her heavy dark eyewinkers and fresh pink lips were her own. The plain gray gown with its white collar made her look as prim and maidenly as a Pilgrim daughter in a "Harvest Home" print, but it did not discourage the intimation of unpuritanical curves and uninhibited warmth underneath. The total effect was a combination of artlessness and impudence.

The staring men applauded her in a subdued way, but the stares alone were appreciation enough. Stewart gaped as admiringly as the rest. And even while he was mentally counting the snares and pitfalls this newest temptation could lead him into, he was thinking that temptations would be a lot easier to resist if they weren't so blamed tempting.

"Come here, child," Fanny called, "and say hello to Adam."

That was a sort of signal. All the girls immediately shed their formal stage manners and scampered across the room to throw arms around their favorite men. Three of them jumped for old Andy Boyd and began to argue about who had got him first. Murrell mixed a hot whiskey toddy for Integrity and led her to a secluded corner. Modesty sat on Dean's lap and crooned over his bandaged hand. Beatitude went for Yancey, but he warded her off and came down the room to where Stewart was tentatively shaking Eve's tiny hand.

"I think it's just perfect," the madam was saying to them. "Adam and you both being new and not having a favorite yet."

"She's got one now," Yancey interrupted, taking the girl's arm.

"Wouldn't you know!" said Fanny. "Here's the sarpint already!"

"You just hold on!" said Stewart. It graveled him to have his temptation snatched away before he even had a chance to resist it.

"Mebbe you don't know the rules here, Hughes. Latecomers get last pick."

"Now you lay off these younguns, Yance!" rasped the woman. "Ever'body knows that Bea's allus been your woman."

Firmly putting away Yancey's hand, Eve spoke for the first time, "Excuse me, but I'm with this gentleman here."

"Well, ain't you the high and mighty!" Yancey snorted.

"Don't fret, honey child, you get paid no matter who you're with." And he chucked her roughly under the chin with his deer foot. At that, Stewart reached out and hauled Yancey around to face him. As long as it had been a matter of staking his claim to a female stranger, he was on uneasy ground. But when it came to defending one, he could act without troubling his conscience.

"I reckon you heard the lady."

Yancey's frown became menacing. "By the rules I've got first pickings, Hughes. But if you want to fight for her, I'll oblige. I just want to notify you: I ain't no clumsy young pup like that Albe you trounced. I don't go into a fight without I know I can win."

Stewart's attention was caught by a flash of light on metal, and his eyes dropped to the deer foot that the man dangled in his hand. A thin, bright blade slid slowly out of its brass ferrule, and Stewart suddenly recalled the odd, silent object that had killed the black-bearded man back in Providence.

He took a deep breath and started to cock a fist, but the girl gently touched Yancey's sleeve and said, "You wouldn't want to spile my first visit here, would you, suh?" Yancey looked at her in some surprise. "You come see me over to Greenville sometime, Mister Yancey, and welcome. But for tonight I'm already tooken."

"There'll come a time," Yancey said quietly to the girl, "you're gonna be mighty sorry for that." And then he spun on his heel and stalked furiously back to Beatitude. They heard her squeal suddenly, as he gave her a brutal pinch of greeting.

Eve possessively looped her arm through Stewart's and said to the madam, "You going to just play referee tonight, Fan?"

"No, by damn!" said the big woman. "Here's my darling now!" She seized Dr. Cotton, who had clattered up with two mugs. She explained to Adam and Eve, "He knows my style of loving—and I get free advice on my female ailments, to boot."

Eve smiled at them both, said very politely, "Excuse us, then," and steered Stewart off to an empty bench. He picked up two mugs of whiskey on the way, then sat down and looked at her. She propped an elbow on her knee, put her chin on her hand and stared just as owlishly back at him, until he had to grin.

"Reckon I ought to thank you," he said, "for cooling the fracas back yon."

"I ought to be thanking you. I think it's admire-able, for a gentleman to take up arms for the lady of his favor." Then they sat and sipped at their drinks, until the girl said, "You're uncomf'table with me, ain't you? I reckon you're not used to consorting with whores."

"Why—ain't that kind of a hard name to call yourself?"

She shrugged. "There's harder ones. Know something, Adam? There's as many names for me as there are words for love. A fact. I made a list oncet of all the words for whore and all the words for love, affection, passion and all—and they come out just about even."

"Now that's a funny observation," said Stewart. "What made you think of that?"

"I do a lot of thinking," she said, with shy conceit. "Some men—when you're with 'em—you just got to think of something else. I do a lot of reading, too. I gener'ly read Sir Walter Scott."

"Oh? Who wrote it?"

"*He* wrote it. I mean, Sir Walter Scott is the writer. I've just finished reading *Ivanhoe.*"

"Look, they're tuning up to dance," Stewart interrupted. "Would you do me the honor to dance with me, Miss Eve?"

"I'd admire to, Mister Hughes . . . Adam."

Boyd with his fiddle, Donovan with his jew's-harp and Bill Earle with the madam's concertina, all moved back against the wall and ripped into "Tom Bolynn," while the rest of the company faced off and romped through a Virginia reel. Then it was "Walk Jawbone" and, after that, "Old Dan Tucker." Then Murrell demanded that sophisticated novelty round dance, the waltz, and grabbed Andy's fiddle to play it himself. The girls put up a token show of shyness, then melted into the gentlemen's arms and made a very pretty show of dancing it. The men swapped partners several times. Eve didn't dance with one man for more than a few measures before another was cutting in; only Yancey pointedly and sullenly avoided her.

When the waltz ended, Eve made her way back to Stewart and said, "Whew, I'm all bedewed. Let's walk outside and cool off."

Stewart picked up two more whiskeys and followed her out

the door. Other couples were meandering off in different directions into the darkness: Vashti and Ruel Blake, Modesty and Albe Dean. Stewart led Eve across the clearing to a place where a grassy swale ran right down to the lake and a screen of bushes afforded privacy. They woke up an old razorback sleeping there and sent him grumbling away. Then they sat down side by side on the grass and for a while just watched the moon rise above the trees on the opposite shore.

"Warm night," said Eve, and suddenly stood up. "Can anybody see me here? I think I'll take a swim."

"You swim?" said Stewart, surprised.

"Oh, yes. I'm a reg'lar tomboy," she laughed, and began blithely to shed her clothing. "You come, too."

This was pushing things a little too fast, he thought, as he peeled out of his shirt. He discreetly averted his face while she undressed, but watched her out of the corner of his eye and, every time she took off another garment, so did he. When she dropped a starchy heap of petticoats, he took off his trousers. This left her in a chemise and pantalettes, and him in his union suit. He expected that she'd stop there. But, tra-la-ing a little tune, she pulled the shift over her head and stepped out of the drawers, birthday naked. Stewart doffed his long underwear and immediately plunged his nudity underwater. He looked back as he slid away from the bank, and saw the girl poised there on the grass for a moment, like a lovely piece of lawn statuary, before she slipped into the water after him.

Swimming was a sport not often indulged in, by women or men either, and seldom seriously practiced. So the best Stewart could do was a sort of dog-paddle that kept his head above water but didn't propel him anywhere very fast. The girl surprised him again by stretching out into a graceful breast stroke and shooting out across the lake.

"Don't go and drown yourself," he spluttered enviously.

"I won't. The Lady of the Lake, that's me," she laughed. She floated on her back and blew a spume of water into the air. Then she kicked her feet and became a stern-wheeler that churned over to bump its prow gently against Stewart's shoulder. They stood up in chest-high water and, acting provocative for the first time, she pressed herself against him.

"Ever do it in the water?" she asked.

"Er—no," he said, in some consternation.

"I didn't either. *Ow!*" She hopped up and down. "Let's don't. A crawfish or something just nipped me." She floundered back up the bank, dripping water and moonlight, and sat down to examine her pinched toe.

Stewart followed, to flop full length beside her and give himself up to wholehearted admiration. Eve was well named; she looked as pure and perfect as the Almighty's archetype for womankind. There was about her an air of innocence that was, even if put on, beguiling and beautiful. The time would come, of course, when she would lose it, or deliberately abandon it for more flagrant witcheries, but right now . . .

She was very young, not out of her 'teens, Stewart judged. Her ivory-skinned body was firm under its softness. Those delectable curves would not need corseting or cosseting for a long time. Her legs were long and slender, her waist two hands' span around, and her full, high breasts were the only forbidden fruit this Eve would ever need to tempt an Adam. Now she smiled a cherub smile, turned to him and her lips parted invitingly. In that moment, Stewart's heart went out to her, and his conscience went over the hill.

•

The tranquility of their afterglow was disturbed by a renewed sound of singing from the direction of the headquarters building. The dogs immediately pitched in and harmonized.

"Maybe you'd like to go back inside?" suggested Stewart. "You're missing out on all the fun."

"No," she said. "That kind of fun I get all the time. I don't have many chances just to be ca'm and peaceful like this."

They stayed where they were, and Stewart speculated to himself on what her kind of life must be like. At last, inevitably, he asked the question all young men ask all young Eves. How come?

She answered patiently, "My folks had a teensy farm and a big fambly; some of us had to budge. My sisters went north to Fort Dearborn to work, and I went to Vicksburg. I didn't like it there—awful bad men—and I heared that Miz O'Hoag had a more select setup. So, a month ago, I come there and she took me on."

Stewart said thoughtfully, "You've sure enough stepped into a nest of bad men here."

"I didn't know there *was* any good ones," she said with a smile. " 'Cept maybe the one I been reading about—Wilfred of Ivanhoe."

"Tell me about him," said Stewart indulgently.

She launched into the story on the instant. She told it with great gusto, only slightly garbled, and laid special emphasis on the poetical virtues and the trite noblenesses of the age of chivalry. "My, I wish things was like that nowadays," she concluded.

Stewart said he did, too.

"And me, I'd like to be like Rebecca. That other girl, Rowena, was sort of wishy-washy, but Rebecca had real sand. I think I druther be her. She stood up so spunky to everybody and everything."

Stewart remarked that standing up was a good way to get knocked down.

"If'n I had a shining knight and a shining ideal to live up to, I wouldn't be afeared to take chances."

A wild but winsome idea had planted itself in Stewart's head. "Sometimes, even these days, there's work for people like Ivanhoe." He added, elaborately offhand, "And Rebecca."

"How do you mean?"

"Well, call it a crusade," he said. He was determined to keep this on the sanctified level of her Ivanhoe's career. "Suppose your country, say, was in mortal danger, and you had a chance to save it. What would you do?"

"Why—if'n I had the chance—I'd do what I could to save it. Is that what I'm supposed to say?"

Stewart scratched his head. This was silly, both of them lying here as naked as their namesakes, in the languor of afterlove, and talking the salvation of the nation.

"Suppose there was a bunch of bad men scheming to throw over the whole country, and you were the only one who knew about it. What would you do?"

"Tell on 'em?" she essayed.

"Aha! But they'd try to keep you from telling, wouldn't they? It would mean danger. Going it alone. Giving up your home, your work, everything."

Eve pointed out with simple logic that her home and her work were wherever she was at. She sat up and stared at him. "Are you just spinning a conundrum? Or do you really mean something is . . . ?"

"I mean something *is,*" he said. "I mean there's a job for a Rebecca right here and now."

She rolled close against him again, her eyes shining into his. Stewart became suddenly aware that he had backed himself into a corner that would be hard to get out of. This notion of his was infantile, impractical and suicidally dangerous to both him and Eve. Maybe he had always known that sometime, somewhere, he would *have* to trust another person. But this glowing little darling of a trollop?

"I think maybe," he said after a moment, to the grass, "I better let it lay."

"Dogged if you will!" she said, and reached for her clothes. "If you won't tell me, I'll go and ask John Murrell. He will."

She might have kicked Stewart in the groin and got somewhat the same reaction. He blurted, "Good God, no!" and clamped a hand on her shoulder. She looked searchingly at him and then in the direction of the still audible music. When she turned back to him her brown eyes were no longer wide and ingenuous.

"What you talked about—it's got something to do with John Murrell. Now you *got* to tell me."

He dropped his head onto his arms with a groan. Ha-ha, Virgil Adam Stewart Hughes, what now?

"Well, to begin with," he said, his voice muffled. "My name's not Adam Hughes."

Eve was less than thunderstruck at this revelation. "My name ain't really Eve, neither." She went on to point out that just about every second man on the frontier was wearing a manufactured handle, which usually implied something about why he was lurking on the fringes of civilization in the first place.

"My right name is Virgil Stewart. I tacked on the other one

so this bandit Murrell and his hive of rascals wouldn't recognize me."

"Ain't you kind of calling the kettle black? Or else what're *you* doing here? You ain't no *lawman?*"

"Oh, hell," he said bleakly. "I might as well tell you the whole story. But look—Eve—right now I'm all alone in this. It's just me against Murrell's whole crew. Do you say one word and I'm a gone Josie. Maybe you, too."

He dredged up what he could remember of her Ivanhoe chronicle, and tried to arrange his story into that frame of reference. Some of his comparisons were rather farfetched. Andrew Jackson would have been surprised to find himself cast as Richard Coeur-de-Lion and Murrell as the traitorous usurper. Too, Stewart felt it expedient to paint Murrell a little blacker and himself a little whiter than he believed either of them really to be. But when he came to the end of his narrative, Eve said breathlessly:

"Why, you're almost like Wilfred of Ivanhoe yourself!" She leaned over and decorated him with a kiss. "Fancy taking all this on singlehanded. Like a quest!"

"None of it means anything, though, unless I can corral the whole Clan."

"Oh, yes, you got to! And I'll he'p you!" Her enthusiasm was so fervent that it was a little unsettling. On reflection, Stewart thought that maybe just keeping her mouth shut would be the one best thing she could do for him. He suggested this and was put firmly in his place. "No! I think it's the grandest adventure that ever was. This might be the only chance I'll ever have to be Rebecca. What do you want for me to do?"

"Well, there's a way to catch the whole bunch at one grab, if I can get a message out of here."

"You mean you want me to carry it." She hugged herself excitedly, her breasts lifting above her folded arms. "Oh, do let me, Virgil!"

"Call me Adam, if you don't mind. You pop out with 'Virgil' up yonder and you can add 'good-by.' Remember—just *remember*, for God's sake—this is a real life-and-death matter, not something out of a storybook!"

"Yes, Adam. Do let me he'p, Adam. You don't know how much it'd mean to me, to do something good for a change."

"You done *me* some good a while ago," he said, with a smile.

"I will again, whenever you want. But that's what I mean—that's all I've ever been good for. This other, if it all comes out right, we'll both be heroes, you and me! I'll be somebody new and better, not just a river tramp no more. Folks'll look up to me, and—and—why I might get offers to go on the stage. I might be another Fanny Kemble!"

"Hold on just a minute," he broke into her fantasies. "Let me tell you how I'd figured on using you. It might change your mind about there being any glory in this. The gang is taking a dozen stolen slaves across the river, come Sunday night . . ." She was quiet and listened with rapt attention. "That'll be my one best chance to catch 'em. To have a posse waiting there. And there's only one man I'd trust to see to that—my friend John Henning—but he's way to hell and gone up in Tennessee. I've got to get a message to him in time for him to gallop a posse down here by Sunday night."

All business now, Eve said, "Steamboat's the only way."

"Right. Somebody's got to steam from here to Memphis, ride like the very devil to Henning's place, and get him on the trail to Dundee's Landing with a company of lawmen."

"I can do it!"

"Can you? It'll be hard enough just getting you off this island."

"No, it won't. We come in a skiff from Mister Dundee's, ourselves, and walked overland from the river to this here lake. What we'll do, we'll wait until everybody's asleep up to the house. We'll sneak out on your hoss. You ferry me back acrost the lake, we ride to the skiff, you row me acrost the river, and I'll hail the first upriver steamboat that comes along."

"Won't no steamboat pull in for a lone girl."

"Shoot! They all know me," she said, without embarrassment. "I'll have less trouble flagging one than you would. With luck, I can be in Memphis by Thursday night."

"You do make it sound possible," said Stewart admiringly.

"If I'm gonna be Rebecca," she said, but now half mocking herself, "I'll do it up proper. Honest Injun!"

He smiled at her. "Blamed if I don't think you can. Well, we can only try. Here——" He rummaged in his discarded clothes and brought out the memorandum book. "You won't have to explain a thing—just hand this to Parson Henning. And he'll put you up at his place. Whatever you do, Eve, don't stir out of there until I come for you. I'll cover up your sneaking off from here, the best I can. But if anything goes wrong with this scheme, you'll be the first one Murrell looks for."

She shivered slightly, then said, "We better put in a showing up at the house, and act like we're just having a high old time."

"Good idea," said Stewart, reaching for his underwear. "I could use a drink."

"Wait just one little bit, Adam," she said, touching him shyly but significantly. "We—we won't have a chance—later. And I don't know when I might ever see you again . . ."

•

The party appeared to be in the last stage of bacchanale; the room smelled fiercely of whiskey, smoke, perfume, sweat, and the musk of animal rut. The girls had doffed all their pretentious manners and most of their clothes. Stewart stared in admiring amazement as they capered, staggered or simply lay around in chemises or pantalettes or less. In all this expanse of skin, the primly gowned Eve looked like a visiting missionary.

The public part of the orgy did not last much longer. Yancey and Beatitude reeled down the room, she whimpering at the iron clutch of his hand on her neck. They disappeared into one of the cubicles and, a moment later, her voice rose in a wail of pain. Bill Sanders vanished into another of the cubbyholes, taking with him both the twin sisters, Delilah and Deborah. "They like to work together," Eve confided to Stewart. Though no one was now playing any music, Dr. Cotton and the madam were giving an imitation of a willow sapling waltzing with a church—until Fanny collapsed and the doctor barely managed to angle her from falling into the stove. Conscientiously, the skinny old man tried to lug her toward his cubby; Eve said it looked like an ant dragging home a tumblebug. Eventually two stronger men did the job for him, though with difficulty.

The big room was quieting and darkening fast. The candles and lamps went out by twos and threes. The stove creaked and groaned as it cooled. The only other sound was of whispers and snickers from the curtained cubbyholes. Stewart sneaked a look into his own chamber and was gratified to discover that Albe Dean was still outside somewhere with his Modesty.

"Find your gear," he told Eve, "and let's start getting ready."

She vanished into the gloom, came back with a lumpy carpet-bag, and changed into her traveling clothes of woolen shirt and denim jeans.

"I can't leave these here," said Eve softly, indicating her gown and the bag, "but there's no sense toting 'em with me."

"We'll sink them in the lake," Stewart decided. He bundled them under one arm and bent down to hoist his saddle.

"No need to bring that," Eve whispered. "I can ride bareback now I got britches on. Let's hurry."

They tiptoed across the room and out into the now-moonless night, provoking only a sullen, sleepy growl from the chained-up dogs and a brief squawk from a chicken that Stewart trod on. At the corral, a few of the horses looked up without interest, but Israel came unbidden and eagerly to the gate. He stood docile while Eve and Stewart climbed on, and then strode as daintily up the clearing and past the house as if he understood the necessity of silence. Stewart poled the three of them across the lake on the ferry raft and, halfway over, dropped Eve's bag into the water. "Don't worry," he told her, noticing her expression as it sank. "Miz Henning and her daughter will fix you up with some clothes."

On the other bank they mounted again, and the horse picked his way carefully along the invisible trail. Half an hour later they came out onto the Mississippi shore, only a few yards away from the girls' boat. Eve had called it a skiff; it was more like a freight scow. "I didn't think to inquire how the whole lot of you came over in a skiff," Stewart grumbled. "I should've known it must have been something bigger. You'll have to help row."

He tethered Israel to a tree and set the big boat adrift. One on a side, he and the girl put out an oar apiece and awkwardly rowed the craft in a series of circles to nowhere. Then Stewart thought of striking up a cadence count and they did better. Even so, it seemed to take them the rest of the night to reach the eastern bank.

"We're about half a mile downstream from Dundee's Landing," Eve said. "I'd best hurry up there." They both still talked in subdued voices, though the nearest possible ear would have been Dundee's.

Stewart glanced uneasily at the sky, beginning to silver with the light of the false dawn. "I'd admire to see you there," he said, "but it's going to take me hell's own time to get back to the island. Can you walk it alone?"

"Oh, yes," the girl assured him. "It's only my arms is tired. Don't fret about me."

He did, though. It seemed like heartless abandonment, marooning her here in the bleakest hour of night in an all but empty land.

"Are you sure?" he said uncertainly. "We can still go back."

"You hesh!" said Eve. "We've done begun, now, and there ain't going to be no back-wheeling. Gimme that li'l book of your'n and I'll be off."

He handed over the memorandum book, plus a come-in-a-hurry note he had scribbled before they left the island. He also gave her all the real, or un-Murrell, money that he possessed. "Take it," he insisted, when she tried to refuse. "I don't have need of it. You will. To pay your passage, hire a horse and all."

"All right," she said. "Now let me be away and doing. Gimme a kiss for luck."

He gathered her into his arms; her lips were trembling. "I'm proud of you, Eve," he said into her long hair. "You be careful, now, and do just like I told you—because I want to see you again. You hear?"

"I won't forget. I want to see you, too." She turned to the track that led upstream.

"Good-by, Rebecca," he called after her, "and good luck." By then she had disappeared into the night. She was, he reflected, carrying his life in her hands, and God only knew how much else besides. Good luck to me, too, he thought ruefully.

•

When he got the scow back into the river, he could propel it only by the mosquito power of sculling over the stern, and the big thing slewed ponderously and swung in every direction except due west. Dawn had long since arrived when he finally touched again on the Arkansas shore, soaking wet, shivering with cold, and so tired he could hardly lift his arms. He estimated that he was a good five miles downstream from his horse, but otherwise the deflection wasn't a misfortune, because the craft had to disappear anyway.

Stewart did the five miles at a staggering lope. Most of his way was along a sand and gravel beach, so it took him not much more than an hour to get back to Israel. It was broad day by now; he could only hope he was right in the assumption that the clansmen would still be unconscious. At the ferry landing, anyway, there was no one waiting for him, and, as far as he could see, no breakfast smoke arising anywhere down the length of the island.

According to his plan, the raft had to remain on this side of the lake. He kneed Israel into the water and swam him across, getting thoroughly wet and chilled all over again. Then, as the horse splashed up the island bank, Stewart got a nasty shock. An illogical thought went briefly and horribly through his head: *"They caught her!"*—before he realized that what he saw was not Eve's drowned body. Her gray pilgrim-daughter gown had floated into the shallows and lay at full length, undulating eerily. Stewart swallowed his fright, fished out the garment, and wrapped it securely around a heavy rock before he threw it far out into the water again.

There was still no evidence of activity when he reached the headquarters clearing. The dogs, confused and grumpy at all the night's queer comings and goings, did not even bother to signal his arrival. Stewart turned Israel into the corral and then stumbled wearily back up to the building. He couldn't make his first move until his clothes were dry, but he mustn't chance falling asleep while he waited. So he sat down on a chopping block at the corner of the house, in the full warmth of the sun, and began quietly to steam. Occasionally he dozed in spite of himself, but each time he would topple off the block and wake up again.

It was nearly noon when the Clan showed the first sign of life. Murrell himself came out of the door, half dressed and carrying a wooden bucket, and tottered uncertainly in the direction of the spring. Possibly his eyes weren't open yet; he took no notice of Stewart.

"Mine iniquities are gone over my head," Murrell was intoning to himself. "My wounds are loathsome and corrupt, because of my foolishness. I am pained and bow down greatly. I go mourning all the day long."

He splashed around down at the spring for a while and then came back, toting the bucket gingerly but managing to slop water all over his trousers. He trudged on into the building, still without noticing Stewart's presence, and could be heard bumping around in there and bawling, "Everybody up! New day a-dawning! Everybody up!" The sound of the other people beginning to stir was Stewart's cue for action. He slipped in unseen through the front door and headed direct for Yancey's cubbyhole.

"Goddamn you, Yancey!" he shouted for everybody to hear, and lunged at the pile of blankets. "What've you done with her, you bastard? Oh, excuse me, ma'am." It was Beatitude he had hauled out by the hair.

Yancey floundered out from the other side of the pallet, blinking. "What in tarn——?" he began, but Stewart seized the slack of his underwear and yanked him to his feet.

"What'd you do with her?" Stewart roared at the astounded man. There was a hubbub in the outer room, as the half-awake company stumbled out to see what was going on. Beatitude stared up at Stewart, clasping the blankets around her bare chest.

"What in Christ's name is eating you?" asked Yancey in bewilderment.

"Goddamn it!" Stewart shouted again. "Don't make out like you don't know what I mean!" He gave Yancey a shove that sent him out through the curtain flap into the main room.

"Now lookahere," said Yancey, bringing up against a table. "Nobody han'les me like that!" He glanced around the circle of wondering faces, as if for verification of Stewart's sudden seizure of lunacy. The whole gang was there now, men and women in their underwear or wrapped in bedcovers, all staring sleepily and befuddledly.

"Afore I kick in your aitch-bone," said Yancey, "mebbe you'll tell me why I got to do it."

"My gal's gone!" Stewart shouted, trying wearily to simulate frenzied rage. "Eve's done disappeared, and I know you had something to do with it! You said you were going to get her! Miz O'Hoag, you heard him say it!"

The madam, her frowsled head topping a mountain of blanket, nodded hesitantly. "Why, yes, he did say . . ."

"Well, I didn't!" Yancey protested. "I call Bea there to witness that I was right beside her all the livelong——"

Stewart bellowed wrathfully and went for him. It was Stewart's idea that, by being the first to sound the alarm, and by making this hair-trigger accusation, he would absolve himself of suspicion when the Clan realized that the girl had truly gone. Furthermore, he went into the fight purposely intending to lose. Taking a beating ought to be further evidence of his sincere bereavement.

It was admittedly a little presumptuous of him that he had *decided* to lose the fight. That part of the plan, he soon discovered, was not at all hard to arrange. Yancey might have been sapped by hangover or sexual excesses, but he was in a sight better shape than his assailant. Stewart had had no sleep or food, had spent the night wrestling a heavy boat back and forth across the wide Mississippi, and the morning running an overland endurance course. Besides, he had other things on his mind—which is no way to go into a knockdown drag-out fight.

He got in that first punch, all right, and it shook Yancey. But from then on Stewart had the impression that he was uselessly pounding away at an unfeeling bag of feathers—and that the bag of feathers was pounding back at him with cudgels of pig iron. Stars swam before his eyes, and comets swooshed out from between the stars to clout him in the face. He swung wildly back at Yancey and felt some of his blows land, but did the feathers care? All the women's eyes were wide and their mouths puckered in a silent "Ooooh!" The men, including Murrell, were poker-faced. They didn't yet understand what this ruckus was all about, and so seemed unsure whether they ought to be rooting for one man or the other.

Stewart stayed on his feet somewhat longer than he really wanted to. At the end he was fighting blind, weaving and staggering too helplessly to get any force behind his fists even if he could have seen to aim them. He was just a standing punching bag for Yancey, who could have kept up his quick, hurtful blows all day. But there was a murmur from the audience; somebody would soon step in and declare it a technical knock-out if Yancey didn't finish it. So, while Stewart stood shakily pawing the air, Yancey wound up his arm like a siege cata-pult, and unleashed a blow that would have careened a healthy horse.

•

Stewart became slowly aware that he was no longer being hammered to death, but drowned. It took painful effort to will his eyes open, and at that only one of them obliged. It stared up into Fanny O'Hoag's big face, and the sight was such that it closed again involuntarily. Her make-up had been so rav-aged during the night that she looked like an old barn wall covered with several years' accumulation of tattered poster ad-vertisements.

Wincing, Stewart urged his eye open once more, just in time for it to receive another bucketful of water. Spluttering, chok-ing and cursing, he reared up to a sitting position. Taking stock, he discovered that he was on the floor near the wall, that his face was painfully bruised and swollen, one eye shut and both of them doubtless colorful, a back tooth missing, and his head and trunk competing to see which could ache most unbearably.

Fanny, in between sloshing water over him, was saying to someone, " 'Couldn't imagine what he was jawing about. But dogged if'n she *ain't* gone off somewheres."

Stewart hastened to verify this, but his voice came out in a feeble quack: ". . . Gone . . ." Dr. Cotton knelt down beside him and said, "Let me do a little patchwork, Adam, before you go to jump off Lover's Leap." He set to work with hot water, salves and wads of cotton wool.

"He must have fallen hard for the wench," said Murrell's voice. "I wonder where she's gone."

" 'Twas Yancey got her!" croaked Stewart. In his addled state of mind, he was half beginning to believe this.

"I didn't! I'm sorry I had to beat up on you," said Yancey, sounding not at all sorry. "But you wouldn't listen. I ain't had nothing to do with the damned little hellcat. I dunno where she's at."

"Well," said the madam, "ain't nobody going to be satisfied till she's found. Y'all getcher clothes on and scout the island."

The searchers returned, singly and in groups, with baffled expressions and nothing to report. She was nowhere. There were no horses missing from the corral. The dogs hadn't got her, or, if they had, they'd made a clean job of it. It was not until Donovan came back from the head of the island that the first light was shed on the mystery.

"The raft's lodged over on t'other side of the lake," he said. "Looks like she's gone sure enough."

"Now why would she do a thing like that?" murmured Miriam, with a sidelong glance at Stewart.

"Ask Yancey, I tell you!"

Yancey sighed patiently and virtuously, and pointed out that if he *had* ferried the girl off the island, he would have ferried himself back again and the raft would be on this side of the lake.

"Her carpetbag is gone," reported Integrity, upon investigation. "It ain't with the rest of our'n."

"Funny," grunted Foursquare Fanny. "She *must* of gone back over to Greenville."

"Are you *sure,*" Timna queried Stewart, "you didn't—uh —hurt her? Unintentional, I mean?"

"Naw," grunted Stewart. He heard one of the girls whisper to another, and all of them looked at him with undisguised interest.

"Sometimes Eve was took bad with the flowers," Fanny muttered. She produced a little pocket calendar from her reticule, studied it, and shook her head. "Wa'n't near time for her'n."

Stewart was coming in for some curious looks from the whole gathering. He was relieved when Murrell said, "Well, let's all have some breakfast, hey, Andy? And then we'll go over and sniff at her trail. Maybe we'll learn something."

Stewart insisted on accompanying them when they set out, ignoring the doctor's advice to rest his battered body. Not that he didn't already know what kind of trail they'd find, but he wanted to hear what was said about it. The women all carried their baggage with them, and rode pillion on the men's horses.

Big Tip swam over and retrieved the raft, then ferried the men, women and horses across the lake. They followed the trail to the riverbank and exclaimed over the absence of the boat.

"Could she of han'led that big barge?" Donovan wondered. "With me paddling and all the gals he'ping, we had a helluva time getting it over here."

"Glory!" said Vashti. "Might be she's a-drifting off down the river right now!"

"No more than she deserves," said Murrell drily, "if she was fool enough to put out in the thing. Fan, was this girl maybe a little bit—scatterbrained?"

"We-ell," said the madam uncertainly, "I've only knowed the wench about a month, John. But I never seen no sign of mooniness."

"She read a lot," Jemima contributed, as if this might have been a sign.

Murrell stifled a grin and said, "Well, she's sure to be waiting for you when you get home. Enjoying a laugh at your expense —and Adam's. Tell the little chit that she earned her man a beating. Maybe that'll chastise her."

The group waited there on the strip of beach until two flatboats hove into view around the upstream bend. Then they all shouted, waved and fired shots in the air, and one of the boats pulled inshore to see what the to-do was about. It was loaded with pigs, but the O'Hoag raised no objection, so Murrell peeled off some paper money and paid the four crewmen to transport the girls across to their home territory.

The parting was accomplished only after all the women had kissed all the men. Then all the girls had to kiss Stewart "especially," and tell him how sorry they were that he'd been so shabbily treated. More than one of them also managed to convey to him, in a whisper, that *she'd* be happy to substitute for the faithless Eve next time there was a party. Stewart's impression was that he had somehow become something of a curiosity and a challenge.

During the rest of that week he managed to maintain the pose of inconsolable bereavement. He sat around and moped and sulked convincingly, and the other men tactfully left him alone. Stewart's mien of preoccupation was not entirely put on. For the first couple of days he lived in expectation that Fanny

O'Hoag would reappear with the news that Eve was still lost, and resume the search all over again. When she did not, he began to worry that maybe the girl had thrown over her notion of adventure and really had gone meekly home to the madam.

Whichever, the days crept on without event or excitement of any sort. He finally made himself believe that *of course* Eve had carried through according to plan, and that right now Henning and a band of stout-hearted men were galloping southward. This thought merely served to inspire him with new trepidations. What would happen at Dundee's Landing when the bushwhackers jumped the Clan? Would the trap succeed? Would he himself be shot in the melee? By the time they began ferrying the slaves off the island, at sundown on Sunday, Stewart was twitching visibly. Fortunately, the other men still did not discern anything sinister in this. They humorously appraised his condition as being the worst case of heartbreak they'd ever seen, and let it go at that.

•

The landing of the steamboat *Ben Sherrod* at Memphis seemed to be accomplished by a combination of lung power and bell power. As it backed and filled to maneuver to the dock, the continuous jangling of the bells and the shouted commands and curses of the deck hands and dock hands completely obliterated the sound of the unobtrusively laboring engines and paddle wheels. Stewart stood at the rail looking out over the river front, sick with despair, confusion and high agitation—a condition not unnoticed by his companions, Murrell, Ruel Blake and Lee Smith.

"I'm glad I brought you home again, Adam," said Murrell solicitously. "I don't know which affected you worse, losing that girl or losing that fistfight, but you sure haven't been yourself lately. Maybe a little vacation on your farm will perk you up again."

Stewart smiled wanly and said he figured it would. But when the *Ben Sherrod* had finally been cussed and gonged into its moorings, he walked down the gangplank like a man going to meet the firing squad—and, for all he knew, he was.

Something had gone terribly wrong back there down the Mississippi. During the Sunday night, Stewart had held tight rein on his excitement and apprehensions while he worked alongside the other clansmen. When they unloaded the first bargeful of Negroes on the Mississippi shore—without incident or intervention—Stewart told himself that Henning's posse was merely lying in wait until the whole gang and the complete cargo were gathered there. The barge went back and forth across the river. By daybreak the population of Mississippi had been increased by a dozen Negro slaves, the thirteen surviving clansmen (including Stewart) and a milling herd of horses—and still there was no sign of an ambush. Murrell issued his instructions, and the greater part of the Clan rode off southward, shepherding the coffle of blacks toward the Yazoo Market. Murrell, Blake, Smith and Stewart remained behind. They turned over their horses to Mr. Dundee, to be forwarded to Memphis by some trustworthy boatmen, and sat down to wait for an upriver steamer.

The voyage on the *Ben Sherrod* should have been great fun and adventure. Murrell engaged the most luxurious saloon-deck accommodations and spread himself lavishly in the matter of prime liquors and choice viands. He and the other two spent most of the trip in the gambling saloon, alternately losing their own counterfeit and winning other people's real money. Stewart spent much of the trip fighting an urge to fall overboard and end his misery.

All he knew for certain was that Henning had not kept the rendezvous. All he could imagine was that Eve had failed to get the message to him. Or that she had simply got bored with the intrigue and abandoned it somewhere along the way —which he somehow could not believe. Or that she had fallen into the hands of one of Murrell's multitudinous henchmen or "respectable" hirelings. In that event his whole undercover plan would have been busted wide open, and he could look forward to immediate exposure when the boat landed and Murrell got the word. Eve could be either dead by now or held to witness against him.

His fellow travelers, still thinking that his gloom was the aftermath of the island debacle, did their rough and hearty best to cheer him up. They plied him with whiskey, taught him to play roulette, and introduced him to the various unattached women they came across on board. Stewart did make a valiant effort to respond; if he wasn't already in jeopardy, his gallows-stair demeanor could be enough to arouse suspicion. But his attempts at bonhomie rang hollow. At his drunkest and jolliest, he still looked like a man wrestling with demons. The nights were bad, too. Once, inexplicably, he dreamed of Hester in the arms of Murrell, while her husband looked on and beamed approvingly. Of all girls, why should he dream of Hester? he asked himself on awakening, when it was Eve he was worried sick about, and Naomi whom he might not live to see again.

Except for the feeling that he had made the trip stretched on tenterhooks, Stewart remembered only one specific facet of it. That was the evening when Murrell, fairly in his cups, remarked on the "business" that was bringing him back to Tennessee.

"One o' my neighbors—blamed old fool—been hintin' that I stole two of his Nigras," he said, and belched. "Pease-porridge parson name o' Henning. I gotta go pacify him."

"How?" asked Stewart.

"Dunno. Maybe I'll tell him his lousy Nigras were more trouble'n they were worth."

"I 'member them two," Blake put in. "Tried to tell ever'body they was stole."

"Did they?" asked Stewart.

"They *tried*." Blake drew a hand like a blade across his belly and laughed. Stewart gulped.

That was all that was said about it; the conversation drifted on to other subjects. Stewart automatically made a mental note of the revelation, as just one more item in the catalogue of crime he had compiled. Then it occurred to him, with a shock, that this wee fragment of information was what he had sought from the beginning. Here at last was the confession he had risked so much to get, and now it would probably never be of any use.

There was, as always, a considerable crowd on the Memphis wharf to watch the arrival of the steamer, and numerous men greeted Murrell by name as he stepped ashore. Stewart waited nervously for one of them to beckon Murrell aside, whisper in his ear, and point. When no one did, Stewart decided that of course it wouldn't be done out in public and in broad daylight. Most probably it would take place somewhere like——

"The Bell Tavern!" Murrell exclaimed. "Come on, boys. I need a hair of the dog."

Stewart plodded along with the other three, through the riverside streets of the Pinchgut and down Smoky Row to the sign of the brass bell. Paddy Meagher's squalid saloon had changed not at all since his last visit. It was crammed to the doors with a mob of roisterers and tawdry fancy ladies. Murrell was given the same whoop of welcome as last time. They took the same table as before—it seemed to be reserved for the Clan—and the same orange-haired girl brought them whiskey, got intimately fondled in the process, and twitted Stewart about his previous mix-up with the funny money. He managed to grin at that, but sat from then on in uneasy silence. He poured glass after glass of whiskey into himself, feeling no effect from it, and died a little more each time one of Murrell's acquaintances stopped by the table for a chat.

They stayed in Memphis for two days, putting up again at the Pedraza Hotel, but spending most of their time at Meagher's tavern. Murrell held court there, receiving deputations from what Stewart assumed to be far-flung regiments of the Clan. They gossiped, bundles of money changed hands, and Murrell dispensed instructions, congratulations, advice or censure, as the interviews required. Stewart paid scant attention; he had ceased even trying to take notes. He sat dully through these audiences, speaking only when spoken to, and otherwise ignoring the comings and goings. That none of these ruffian strangers brought a report of Eve's capture and confession should have lightened Stewart's mood, but he was unable to imagine any amnesty, just a painful stretching out of the suspense.

Then, late on their second night there, he was galvanized to attention when a man he had never seen before came to the table and said, "Mister Murrell, I got news for you."

"What's that, Squint?" Murrell asked idly. Stewart slid his chair a cautious few inches back from the table.

"Keelboat unloading down the foot of Story Street," said the stranger. "Sent me to say they got four hosses consigned in your name."

Murrell thanked the messenger, gave him a silver dollar, and smiled around at Blake, Smith and the limp Stewart.

"Well, we're mounted again. And I don't think I've got any more business to keep me here. What say we push on first thing in the morning?" The others said that was jake by them, Stewart adding his acquiescence with the first eagerness he had shown in a long time. Murrell grinned slyly at him. "Ah, I thought that would fetch a rise. Real anxious to get home to that wife of yours, hey? Going to show her some of the tricks you learned, gandermooning with Eve? Well, before you light, Adam, I want you to come along with me and the boys and see *my* place. Have supper, spend the night there, get yourself spruced up really pretty to surprise your Marybeth."

Stewart almost asked, before he thought, who Marybeth was. Then he accepted the invitation, and without any real reluctance. Though all he wanted now was to get out of the Pinchgut, get shed of Murrell, get back to Naomi, this would at least save him the necessity of inventing a locale for his fictitious farm; Murrell might have wanted to escort him right to the door of it.

The hotel hostler had their horses saddled and waiting for them at dawn. After his long spell of inaction, Israel was inclined to stretch his legs, and Stewart let him, setting a pace that only Murrell's Tempest could match, and quickly outdistancing Blake and Smith. Not until the last straggling houses of Memphis' "liberties" were behind them did Murrell and Stewart hold up and wait for the other two.

After that first headlong flight, they rode leisurely. The Tennessee countryside was considerably more sightly and enjoyable than when Stewart and Murrell had come through it in January. The chocolate-cake soil was now richly frosted with buttercups, butter-and-eggs flowers and jonquils. The very flowers seemed to hum, so numerous and busy were the bees among them. The hum was counterpointed by a melodious, low-toned song, warbled by the golden orioles hidden among the dogwood trees that bloomed everywhere.

The dogwoods' cross-shaped bracts were as big across as saucers and almost blindingly white in the sunlight, except at the crosses' tips—rust-stained, some superstitious people said, by the nails of the Crucifixion. Fittingly enough, the dogwoods were interspersed by even more flamboyant redbud trees. Their flowers, some superstitious people said, had once been as white as the dogwoods', but had worn a permanent blush of shame ever since Iscariot hanged himself from a branch of one. Such people called the redbud the Judas tree.

The four men were now pleased to camp outdoors along the way instead of enduring the local doggeries. Once, at dusk, they spotted two wild turkeys courting. The female was acting as coy and coquettish as any country maiden, swishing her wings like a dappled dance skirt in the grass. The male was puffed up, fan erect, strutting like any country swain. Ruel Blake shot the female for their supper that night. They dined to the orchestral accompaniment of a multitude of frogs: squeaking, croaking, grunting, peeping, ga-lunking. For liqueur with their meal, they had the smell, almost literally intoxicating, of the wild plum trees' blossoms, which breathed their tart and fruity aroma only after nightfall.

In some measure relieved of immediate anxiety, Stewart's spirits rebounded. He took lively pleasure in this unhurried journey and bucolic surroundings, enjoyed the company of even these questionable fellow travelers, and was good company himself for a change. Almost too bad it had to end, he thought, on the afternoon they circled north of Jackson toward Murrell's estate.

The end, when it came, came with startling suddenness, but so quietly as to be almost anticlimactic.

There was a mounted man idling at the far end of the Estanaula toll bridge, where Stewart had first set eyes on John Murrell. Before they got across the bridge, the rider had spurred his horse and vanished. "My, do we look that ugly?" Murrell murmured lazily, but Stewart was struck with a premonition. Sure enough, there were a dozen men on horseback waiting for them when they ambled up the road toward Murrell's gate. Murrell pulled Tempest to a standstill, studying the group with narrowed eyes. Blake and Smith each dropped a hand to the pistol at his side and glanced at the chief for instructions. He laughed suddenly, deprecatingly, and said, "It's only that old banty hen Henning, boys. No cause for alarm."

Stewart said nothing, but his heart was racing—he had recognized another of the men as the sheriff of Madison County. He eased back on Israel's reins until he was riding at the tail end of the little procession. He, Blake and Smith stopped a few yards short of the waiting crowd, but Murrell rode right up face to face with Parson Henning and Sheriff Cullen and wished them a good afternoon. "You gentlemen are blocking my carriage-way," he added affably. "If you'll allow me, I'd like to rest and clean up before receiving visitors."

"No social visit, Squire Murrell," said the sheriff, brusque and ill at ease. "I'm afeared I've got a warrant for your arrest."

Murrell raised the white-ticked eyebrow. "May I inquire the charge?"

"Slave stealing. Parson Henning here is the complainant and I have a warrant signed by——"

Murrell interrupted sharply, "Isn't this a trifle high-handed, Parson? You intimated suspicions, but——"

Sheriff Cullen interrupted in his turn. "A warrant for arrest ain't issued on *suspicion*, Squire Murrell."

"On what then?" Murrell's voice and color were rising. "You've not a tittle of evidence."

"We have all we need." Henning spoke for the first time, as if impatient with this rigmarole. "Virgil, are you ready to testify for the prosecution against this man?"

Murrell frowned, then turned in his saddle and looked around to see whom Henning might be addressing. His face was a study in bewilderment, but it froze and turned pale when Adam Hughes cleared his throat and said, rather too loudly, "Ready, Parson."

The other two clansmen also swiveled and stared at Stewart. For an instant everything was very still. Then, in a quick scramble of movement, the two went for their pistols and Murrell slammed his heels into his horse. But the sheriff's deputies were ready for this; their guns were already out, aimed and cocked; Smith and Blake appeared to take second thought and didn't bother to draw. At the same time, Murrell found that the posse's horses had quietly ringed him in during the conversation; Tempest could only rear and plunge helplessly.

"That's enough of that!" snapped Henning. "Drop your pistol belts and rifle guns!"

The sheriff gave the parson a look of annoyance. One after

another, Blake's and Smith's well-worn weapons and Murrell's proud Jonathan and David dropped ignominiously into the dust of the road.

Henning said, "Sheriff, do your duty." The lawman gave him another peevish look.

"Squire Murrell, I have to inform you that you're under formal arrest for a crime of felony. Any sudden move on your part'll be taken as an attempt to excape, and'll be dealt with accordently."

"Damnation, Sheriff. Can't I even go as far as my own house up yonder and speak to my wife?"

"Miz Murrell's already been notified of this action," droned Sheriff Cullen. "One of my men'll fetch her down to the jailhouse after you been booked."

"For Christ's sweet sake! You know I'm not going to light out like a chicken thief!"

"No more sass, Squire Murrell!" commanded Cullen. "Turn around, all three of you, and commence traveling. You got to come along, too, Stewart. We'll need a deposition."

Murrell glumly pivoted his horse and moved past Stewart at a funeral pace. The man hadn't spoken to him during this colloquy, nor even looked at him after that one startled glance. But now, as Murrell passed, his head turned slowly, pale eyes fixed on him with an expression hard to classify, compounded of disbelief, disgust, disillusionment and—something like compassion. Stewart felt suddenly very small and drab. There should have been fireworks and brass bands, he found himself thinking, when a man as big as Murrell was run to ground. There should have been thunder and lightning.

•

Devoid of fanfare, the procession meandered listlessly toward Jackson. The deputies rode in a hollow oblong formation that boxed in the three prisoners. Cullen, Henning and Stewart were side by side at the rear of the formation.

"You've done a good job of work, Virgil," said the parson, the first personal remark he had yet made.

"Well, thanks," said Stewart in a dull voice. "Most of the credit's yours, though, for springing the trap."

Henning glowed and looked modestly heroic, while the sheriff looked sour at being left out of the congratulations.

"I take it the girl got through to you," said Stewart. Murrell, riding slumped in his saddle just ahead of them, seemed to stiffen upright for an instant.

Henning laid a cautionary hand on Stewart's arm. "We'll talk about it after all the formalities are over."

There was the usual sprinkling of loafers around the Jackson jailhouse. They nudged each other, whispered and gawked as the crowd of men dismounted and trooped inside. Murrell was given a cell to himself, and Lee Smith and Ruel Blake lodged together in the one next to it. But first the sheriff had them empty all their pockets; he ticketed their weapons and personal possessions with little tags, and gave them written receipts for their cash money, which, as well as Stewart could tell, was all real legal tender for a change.

"All this here may be evidence," said Sheriff Cullen. "I'll have to 'propriate your guns, too, Stewart."

"I don't have any."

The sheriff's eyes bugged a little. "Ain't—got—a gun?" He gulped. "Not atall? And here you been riding with a gang that's supposed to be . . . !"

"I'm a peaceable man," said Stewart drily.

While Murrell and his boys were being locked away, Stewart dictated a brief, barebones account of his association with the Clan. After he had signed the clerk's transcript of it, he asked if he could have a few minutes' talk with John Murrell.

"Come, come," said the parson chidingly. "Let's not consort with the enemy."

The sheriff didn't much like the idea either, but, perhaps to spite Henning, told Stewart to go ahead. A deputy let him into the cellblock and then stood guard against the door to the office. Stewart spoke to Murrell through his cell bars. "I just wanted to say that I'll leave off Israel at your place on my way back to the Hennings's."

Murrell gave him a long, flinty look and then said crisply, "Keep him. You're going to need a fast horse."

"Going to need a helluva lot more'n that," growled Smith from the next cell, "when I get out of here."

"No, I mean it," said Murrell, less inimically. "I gave you

the animal without reservation. And you ought to get some reward for this. Keep him. I have a feeling you won't be getting much else."

"Well . . ."

"Just do me one favor in return," suggested the dark man, stepping close to the bars. "Tell me about it. How you came to —well, do all this." Stewart obliged, haltingly. He told how Henning had proposed their "accidental" encounter, how he had reluctantly let himself be conscripted, how he had kept a record the whole time, and, finally, how he and Eve had conspired to alert the authorities.

"By damn!" said Murrell, almost jovially. "I knew I was picking a good man when I brought you in. Never did a man so neatly pull the wool over my eyes. You have my heartiest admiration, Virgil Stewart." He shook his head. "A shame, that name—I kind of liked Adam Hughes. The name *and* the man."

"Thanks," grunted Stewart.

"But tell me. With all your high-minded intentions, why didn't you simply shoot me, lad? Hell knows you had the chance often enough. Why stoop to all this pussyfooting?"

"A bullet don't settle anything. It just ends it."

"Well, that I fear was your one mistake. But since you spared my life, Virgil, I'll spare yours. I could have you gunned down before tomorrow's breakfast, but I won't. I'm going to let you live."

"Am I supposed to thank you humbly?"

"No." Murrell's voice was steel again. "You won't thank me for it if you live to top Methuselah."

There didn't seem any point in continuing the conversation. Stewart motioned to the guard and was let back into the office room.

"All done, Stewart?" said the sheriff. "Don't reckon you sneaked him a hacksaw. Haw haw." Stewart didn't laugh. "Harrumph. Well, I thank you for your cooperation. We won't need you for a while, but you'll be hearing from us. I reckon the citizens owe you a lot. You ought to feel purty good, son. Purty proud."

"I don't feel anything," said Stewart, climbing wearily into his saddle. Then he added six words that he was later to recall, often and bitterly. "I'm just glad it's all over."

Book Three

THE HEMP

As they rode out of Jackson, headed for Henning's place, the parson explained why his posse had not been waiting at Dundee's Landing as Stewart had requested.

"I wanted to hit the trail as soon as I got your message," he said, "but it was impossible. For one thing, there was the time factor. I was afraid we wouldn't get there by Sunday night, and, if we'd missed Murrell there, we might not have been able to swing back in time to find him here. Besides, I ran into problems of legal jurisdiction. I could only swear out a complaint charging him with theft right here in Madison County, and it appears I'd have been bending the law to ride after him into another state . . ."

The explanation went on at great length and into great complications. It seemed to Stewart that the parson's every sentence began thunderously with "I" and ended windily with "impossible." But it didn't matter; he was barely listening to the man. Stewart felt like an antique clock that had finally been allowed to run down.

When they turned in through the gate, and the girl came pell-mell down the hill from the house, Stewart smiled through his haze of tiredness at the memory it evoked—from a long, long time ago, it seemed. He was off his horse and holding out eager arms before he noticed that the girl was a bit taller and a lot blonder than the Naomi he remembered. He stood puzzled for a moment, frozen in the act of reaching for her, and then Eve rushed into his arms and flung her own about him with a happy cry of welcome.

"We done it, Virgil! Just like Ivanhoe 'n' Rebecca, that's us!"

Stewart heard the parson behind him sniff disapprovingly. And over the girl's shoulder, now, he caught sight of Naomi standing waiting in the dogtrot. That was some distance away, but he could tell that she was standing very stiff with her arms tightly folded across her breast. A slight fluttering of her skirt suggested that she might be tapping her foot. Gently and quickly, Stewart disentangled himself from Eve's exuberant hug and stammered some noncommittal words of greeting.

Parson Henning said, "I'll lead your horse around to the stable, Virgil." There was a touch of coolness in his voice. "I imagine you're in a hurry to see Naomi. Too."

Stewart strode up the hill toward Naomi's ramrod figure, feeling rather as if advancing under fire. He tried to act as if he was only coincidentally walking in the same direction as the golden-haired sprite who skipped along at his side, still prattling.

". . . Didn't get but two hours' sleep the whole way! . . . What happened back on the island? . . . Hired a buckboard in Memphis town and changed hosses twicet afore I got here! . . . What'd Miz O'Hoag say when she missed me? . . . Never such excitement in my whole life! . . . Oh, Virgil, we done good together, didn't we? . . ."

They were close enough to the house now to see Naomi's eyes snapping, her toe tapping. Stewart gave Eve a clenched-teeth smile and said, "Yes, we certainly ought to compare notes, *Miss Eve*. We'll have to have a long talk about it all. Later." Eve comprehended and clapped a hand over her sudden impish grin. She flashed a merry glance between Stewart and Naomi and said brightly, "Well, 'scuse me, folks. Work to do." In a twinkling she had dodged around the unmoving Naomi and whisked into the kitchen building.

Stewart moved to the edge of the flower border that separated him from Naomi, and looked up to where she stood on the porch of the areaway. She looked back at him, aloofly. There ensued a silence, while he felt the local temperature drop by several degrees. Stewart was awaiting the recriminations: for his long absence, for his excursion into outlawry, for whatever she might have surmised about Eve, for his neglect of his Tuscahoma enterprises. Naomi appeared to be simply waiting. Finally, Stewart sheepishly mumbled something.

"I beg your pardon, *Mister* Stewart?"

"I said, could you tell me what today's date is?"

The girl had probably been expecting him to say almost anything else in the English language; she could only exclaim, "What in the world has *that* got to do with anything?"

"I just wondered if I was late for our wedding."

Her eyes misted and a kaleidoscope of expressions flickered across her face. She half laughed, half wailed, "Oh, you ever-lasting ninny!" and threw herself from the porch into his arms.

•

Half an hour later, Stewart had paid his respects to Mrs. Henning and the house servants, had parried all questions, begged out of attendance at supper, stumbled to his room, sloshed around in a washtub of hot water, and fallen into bed. He slept like a dead man until after noon the next day. He descended from his room, clean-shaven, freshly garbed and feeling civilized for the first time in recent memory, to find only Naomi waiting for him in the parlor.

"Won't you sit down, Virgil?"

"Er—thank you." He perched tentatively on the edge of a straight chair across the room from her. There was a leather-bound book on the table beside him. He raised an eyebrow at the gilt title: *Ivanhoe.*

"Oh, not way over there, Virgil." She patted the settee cushion beside her, and he moved to it. "Would you care for a glass of sherry?"

"Thank you," said Stewart again, and she poured from the crystal decanter.

"I'm so very glad you're back, Virgil."

"So am I. There were times I wasn't sure I ever would be."

"You wouldn't have got into that mess if you'd heeded me. You promised me you wouldn't take any chances. Or do anything to hurt or embarrass the family."

"I got back safe, so whatever chances I took don't count. And I sure haven't hurt anybody, except maybe Murrell."

"How about me? How do you think I feel, being the one and only person you didn't take into your confidence. That girl Eve, oh yes. But not me."

"I had to have her help, Naomi," Stewart protested. "I'd still be in Murrell's clutches, wasn't for her."

Naomi sniffed and said, "Do you know she hasn't yet explained just how she happened to be so handy when you needed help? We know her name, and that's about all we do know about her. Not that we've pried, exactly, but she manages to fend off every question about her connection with Murrell—and with you."

Stewart was inexpressibly glad to hear this; it inspired him to a mild invention. "Didn't she tell you? She was a prisoner on Murrell's island. I helped her to escape and in return she agreed to help me. Us."

Naomi appeared a little less than convinced, but she put her hand over his and said, "It's all right, Virgil. You did go into this against my wishes and advice. And I don't suppose I'll ever really know——" She stopped, sighed and said, "But it's all over now, praise heaven, and we needn't talk about it any more."

"Thank you," Stewart said humbly, addressing God.

"Do you remember what you said to me before you went away? That once this was over, *I'd* have the keeping of you from then on. Do you still want it that way?"

"You know I do, Naomi. I've got to see this business out to the end—whatever that involves—going to court and all. But from there on out, it's just you and me."

She smiled slowly, triumphantly. "Then nothing else matters." She leaned toward him; the thick dark lashes lowered over her violet eyes; Stewart bent toward her seductively parted lips.

"Oh, par'n me!" said a shy voice, and Stewart and Naomi leaped apart. Eve, in the doorway, said, "I was just coming in for that there book."

Eve picked up the *Ivanhoe,* showed it to Stewart and explained, "I'm reading it out loud to Lena in the kitchen."

Stewart glanced uneasily at Naomi, and cautioned Eve, "Don't you think maybe you better let Lena get on with her cooking or whatever?"

"Oh, it don't distract her." She added complacently. "Lena's like me—she's rooting for Rebecca over that spunkless other gal."

Naomi said ever so sweetly, "Then she's in for a disappointment, dear. In the end, you know, Ivanhoe weds the *Lady Rowena*."

"I wouldn't want to spile it for Lena," said Eve thoughtfully, as she moved to the door. "Maybe I'll tack on a diff'rent ending." She left a small laugh in the air behind her.

"Really, Virgil!" Naomi burst out. "Why did you have to get mixed up with that common little baggage? Now she's out there consorting with our Nigras like she was brought up in slave quarters! And all this fa-la-la about you being Ivanhoe and her being——"

The stem of Stewart's wine glass snapped abruptly in his fingers. He drew himself to his full height, towering over her. "Naomi Andrea Jackson Henning," he said quietly, menacingly. "Not five minutes ago you said we wouldn't thrash over this mess any more. Now—one more by-Jesus word out of you about it and I swear I'll go into town, bust Murrell out of jail, and ride off with him and his cutthroats to where *I can have some PEACE!*"

Naomi had bristled, but as his voice rose she shrank back in her chair, and said meekly, "Yes, Virgil."

•

At the supper table Stewart told the (only slightly expurgated) story of his adventures. Though he skipped lightly over the bloodier events and more hazardous moments of his bandit career, Naomi gasped at some of his disclosures, and Mrs. Henning breathed "My!" and the parson shook his head somberly. When Stewart came to the portion that included Eve, he fixed her deliberately with his eye and repeated the "prisoner" fable he had already fed Naomi. A dimple in Eve's cheek deepened just for an instant.

"Why, you poor dear!" cried Mrs. Henning, turning to the girl. "You never said a word."

"No'm," Eve sighed tragically. "I didn't want y'all to think I was trading on your symp'thies." She blinked back a realistic tear and stared down at her plate, either not seeing or ignoring the skeptical look from both the parson and his daughter.

"You tell the rest, Miss Eve," urged Stewart. "The next part of the story is yours, anyway."

"Well . . . It was near a month agone, this band of riders come to the house. Our *farm*house, I mean. Dead of night it was. They—they wanted fresh hosses. My Paw was away and —and my Maw said she couldn't sell or trade without him there. The men, they laughed and said 'sell, *hell!*'"

Mrs. Henning jumped slightly.

"They drug our prime hosses out of the barn, and when Maw tried to stop 'em, one of the men clubbed her with his whipstock. That's when I run out. Maw was stretched on the ground, but when I run to her, one of the men swiped me up to his saddle and next minute we was off into the night . . ."

The parson was lounging back in his chair, tapping a finger-nail against his teeth. Naomi leaned her chin on her hands and regarded the storyteller with eyes the color of glacier shadows.

"Going to hold me for a king's ransom!" Eve went on, warm-ing to her fiction. "Said I'd stay on the island, and work and slave for 'em the rest of my life, if'n my Paw didn't send 'em gold. Well . . ." Stewart was wishing the girl had never learned to read; she obviously caught the pained expression on his face, reined in her imagination and came back to credibility by fetching Murrell and Stewart onto the island. From there on she told the story straight, or almost: how Stewart had engineered her escape, how she'd made her wild courier ride to the Henning plantation. "And you know the rest."

"So after she left the island," Stewart pitched in, to avert any cross-examination, "we all just lazed around until Sunday, when we started ferrying the darkies . . ."

They were interrupted by the entrance of the houseman, Lance.

"Your par'n, Mas Henning. Dey's a gennulman at de doah wishin' a wud wid you'n Mas Stewart. Say he name Majuh Mahtin."

"Ah, from the County Attorney's office, Virgil!" chirped the parson. "Come to discuss court strategy, no doubt. Show him into the parlor, Lance, and fetch cigars and brandy. You'll excuse us, ladies?"

Major Gayne Martin was a tall, stoop-shouldered man with salt-and-pepper hair and mustache, who wore his rank and a slightly crippled leg as mementoes of the British sack of Washington City. He gave Henning only a curt nod as they shook hands, but studied Stewart gravely and at length through his steel-rimmed spectacles. Then he sat down and got right to business.

"Mister Stewart, Parson Henning, it may look like I've come in unseemly haste. But this case has got to go to court in a hurry." He took an object from his coat pocket and dropped it on his chairside table. It was the beat-up little memorandum book which Stewart had filled with his jottings. "Mister Stewart, you are the sole witness against John Murrell. If the prosecution has a case at all, you are it. To be quite blunt, we want to get you before a jury before Murrell gets you before a gun sight. That's why I've come in such a hell of a hurry, to find out what kind of case we've got."

"Air tight," said the parson around his cigar. "Iron bound."

The lawyer threw him a look and said drily, "There appear to be a couple of holes in it already. Big enough to let his henchmen slip through. Smith and Blake were released this morning."

Stewart choked on a swallow of brandy.

"Murrell's working fast, too," Martin told them. "He's already lined up one of the slickest attorneys in the West—Milton Brown. He showed up with a writ and fifteen minutes later Murrell's sidekicks were just a cloud of dust on the horizon."

"But—how——?" coughed Stewart.

Martin shrugged. "Plaintiff's complaint named only John Murrell. There was no mention of Blake or Smith or anybody else. Milt Brown merely had to say 'show cause' and—hey presto!, *habeas corpus!*—Judge Webb practically saddled their mounts for them."

Henning stormed to his feet. "By heaven, that Webb must be in Murrell's pocket! This is an outrage! Obstructing justice and——"

"Since you've brought up the subject of obstructions, Parson," the major overrode him, "I might mention that I've talked to Judge Webb and Sheriff Cullen, and I was appalled at what they told me."

The parson opened and shut his mouth and sat down again.

"I gather that when you showed Judge Webb this memorandum book, he was all for calling in a U.S. Marshal. Making this a federal case against Murrell. Charging him with treason at worst, conspiracy at least—and hunting down the man and his whole Mystic Confederacy. But you withheld the book and the information it contained, pleaded a private grievance, insisted on entering a comparatively measly complaint of grand theft, and demanded deputation to join the posse. You not only blindfolded Justice, Parson. You hamstrung her, deflowered her, and spayed her as well!"

The major's words were hammers driving the little man, like a tenpenny nail, deeper and deeper into the recesses of his chair.

"I only——" he said weakly.

"You only wanted to be known as the man who caught Murrell," said the lawyer cruelly. "Well, you've got him, sir—like a buffalo by the tail!"

Stewart stared at the parson, aghast. Henning's eyes were flickering everywhere in the room except in his direction. So that was why there'd been no ambush at Dundee's Landing. The man who had launched him on this fool's crusade had made it all but worthless at the last.

Henning tried an ingratiating smile. "After all, Major," he said, "what difference does it make what charge is written on Murrell's death warrant? Slave stealing is a hanging offense."

"A snake doesn't stop wiggling when its head is cut off," said Martin. "If Murrell hangs for this, possibly half a hundred other men equally guilty will remain free to rob and kill some more. Were he to hang for conspiracy, they'd swing with him. Now do you see the difference?"

For a change, silence from the parson.

"His counsel, Milton Brown," the major went on, "is a man with high political aspirations. Not a man to sully his record defending a hopeless cause—or even an unpopular cause. No amount of money could have hired him if he suspected any taint of treason or sedition to figure in this case. So it's obvious that he expects to fight a simple charge of larceny—and that he expects to win."

"How can he?" Stewart asked wonderingly.

"How can you prove Murrell stole Henning's hands?"

"Damn it, he told me so."

"Hearsay, Mister Stewart, inadmissible as evidence."

"Well, how about the other slaves I saw him ferry off for the Yazoo Market?"

"Is there anything but your say-so to prove that he did? Or if he did, can you prove that they weren't his own?"

"Then what about the killings I saw with my own eyes? What about this stuff?"—and he hauled a handful of Murrell's paper money from his pocket.

Martin yawned. "Squire Murrell is not being tried for murder, counterfeiting, witchcraft, cannibalism, or anything but the specific theft of two colored bondsmen. You can expose him as the Antichrist and it won't help the case we've got to work with."

"Major Martin," Henning put in, obviously trying to work up to self-important bluster again. "Aren't you admitting defeat a little prematurely? Virgil is not quite alone in this. I intend to stand by him every inch of the way. After all, I am the aggrieved party. I, too, shall speak out in court, loud and clear."

"You." Martin leveled a forefinger at him. "You'll testify that you lost two slaves. Period. Pontificating may be your sole talent, but the court won't allow any suspicions or baseless accusations. You pulled the trigger on this business, Parson. All you can do now is hope you don't get a backfire. Any more of your know-it-all bombast——"

"Major, I must respectfully protest your attitude! This outright discourtesy in my own parlor——"

"Better I say it to you here than for you to read it on a court warrant charging slander, libel, defamation, false arrest, and all the other things your swaggering has left you wide open for."

The parson turned a little pale. Stewart took pity and came to his rescue.

"I don't know beans about the law. But this all seems a

little ass-backward to me. Here we go to all this trouble to put Murrell behind bars, and now it's us that's on the defensive."

The lawyer smiled, slightly contemptuously. "Henning here was out for glory, but he hadn't the mustard, so you were his simple-minded dupe." Henning glared at him. "It was just dumb luck, in my opinion, that you succeeded in jugging Murrell. But you didn't look any further ahead than that. Happily or otherwise, the Constitution protects Murrell just like any other citizen, and he's innocent until *you* prove him guilty. Your story and your notes are not enough. You need corroboration, concrete evidence."

"Wait," said Henning. "What about the girl who brought Virgil's message? There's your corroboration."

Stewart frowned uncertainly. "Not much she can add to my story, Mister Henning. All she really knows is what I told her."

"She may be better than nothing," said Major Martin, getting to his feet. "I'll talk to her some other time. Right now, I'll thank you for the brandy, Parson, and be on my way. Mister Stewart, my offices are in Third Street. Will you drop by there about noon tomorrow? I want to write down your deposition in every detail."

When the major had gone, Henning and Stewart stood in the hall, suddenly embarrassed in each other's presence. The parson ran a hand distractedly through his profusion of excess hair. At last he said, in a low voice, "I told you once, Virgil, this was my only chance to face up to evil and destroy it." He hesitated, and Stewart waited for him to frame some sort of apology for having botched the opportunity so thoroughly. Instead, surprisingly, the man's eyes flashed and he pounded a tiny fist in his palm. "And by the saints," he gritted, "they're not going to cut me out of the show! Murrell is *mine* now, and it's *my* hands will swing him to the top of the hanging tree!" With that, he whirled and pelted up the stairs as if the Fool Killer were at his heels.

•

When Stewart had talked himself hoarse and the secretary had covered six foolscap sheets with his spidery script, Major Martin leaned back and nodded judiciously.

"Yes, if you tell it just that way in court, it certainly ought to make an impression on the jury. However ... " He sat forward again and his expression was not hopeful. "Brown's main objective will be to discredit your testimony. As it's just a matter of your word against Murrell's, he'll do this by discrediting *you*. And he and Murrell won't hesitate to pry or pay for gossip to hurt your reputation." The major waved a hand at his secretary. "Elkins here just got in from Memphis. Tell Virgil what you heard out there, Elkins."

The secretary glanced at Stewart and said, "Fellow name of Ableworthy is telling how you bilked him out of his land, down in Mississippi."

"Come again?"

"Says the Yalo Busha County Assessor has valuated your property at three times what you settled to pay him for it."

"Well, goddammit, I ain't surprised!" Stewart exploded. "I worked my ass off, dredging that farm out from under the river!"

"See what I mean?" said Martin. "You're celebrated now, Virgil, and a prime target for malicious and meddlesome people to take potshots at, whether they're being bribed by Murrell and Brown or not. And you're in for some other nuisances, too. There's already a newspaper reporter from the *Western American Argus* nosing around the courthouse. There'll be more of them from every paper except maybe *The Female Advocate and Factory Girl's Friend,* and they'll be pestering you to death."

"Damnation," said Stewart. "Wish I could get away somewhere."

"You're going to," the major told him. He began to riffle among the papers on his desk. "I'm sending a transcript of your story to the Attorney General at Nashville. Maybe it's not too late to interest the federal government in Mister Murrell. Meantime, I've already applied for the necessary warrants, extradition papers and whatnot, for you and me and Sheriff Cullen to take a little trip down to Murrell's island in Arkansas."

"What do you expect this to accomplish?"

"I don't rightly know. But if we can track that coffle of

slaves to the Yazoo Market, well, it'll be something. Or if there's any possibility of finding some of the clansmen and persuading them to talk . . ."

"I know two that might," Stewart said thoughtfully. "There's an old-timer named Andy Boyd who didn't go for Murrell's empire idea. And a steam doctor named Cotton who despises the whole Clan."

The major made notes of this and murmured, "If we could offer them a measure of clemency, in exchange for exposing Murrell . . ."

"I reckon I never will understand the law," said Stewart, shaking his head. "Here you despair of catching Murrell up on a simple stealing charge, because you figure it's easier to hang him for treason."

•

The company made the long trek to Murrell's secret island only to find it occupied by nothing more suspicious than a family of derelict Chickasaws. Since an Indian of the squatter type could litter his home plot with what looked like a generation of rubbish and filth in a matter of days, it would have been impossible to prove that the Chickasaws hadn't lived there since before Columbus. Naturally, fearing eviction from their happy squalor, the Indians swore that they *had* been there forever, and denied any knowledge of Murrell, the Clan, or any other claimants.

Another disappointment waited on the Mississippi side of the river. Dundee's Landing was now Tupper's Landing. Mr. Tupper informed the visitors that he had purchased the establishment just a week before, and had not yet seen anything that looked like a desperate outlaw or a captive slave. In fact, he added disgustedly, he hadn't seen anything that looked like traffic or trade either, and he devoutly hoped the posse was looking for the sharp-trading Mr. Dundee to hang him.

Sheriff Cullen and two of his men went on to continue the search, riding south for the Yazoo Market, but without any real hope of being able to trace a dozen unidentifiable blacks through the busy auction marts. Major Martin and the rest of the company turned back for Tennessee, emptyhanded and disgruntled. Stewart decided, as long as he was this far south, to swing over east to Tuscahoma to see how his properties were doing and to make his apologies to partner Clanton for the long absence from duty.

It was still early morning when he rode into the settlement, and only a few people were yet on the street. They paid him no attention beyond a quick, wary glance—a disturbing sign; that wasn't their usual way. He hitched Israel in front of the General Store, stepped up on the boardwalk, squared his shoulders and marched in. Clanton was leaning on his elbows across the counter, grinning and chinning with two rawboned farmers. The fat man looked up when Stewart entered, and the grin melted off his face like grease sliding. His two customers turned and looked impassively at the newcomer, flicked an inquiring eye at Clanton, and appeared to receive some silent dismissal.

"Well, see you 'nother time, Ed."

"Lemme know, Ed, when that turps cooker gets here."

The storekeeper's spectacles were like two disks of ice fixed on his erstwhile partner. "You got a nerve," he said quietly.

Stewart tried gallantly for some show of the prodigal returneth. "Reckon you thought I never was coming back," he said.

"Reckon I hoped not," said Clanton.

"Hey? How come?"

The fat man gave a snort of laughter. "Yes, sir, you really got gall. I see you're not even wearing a gun. First suicide I ever saw *advertise*."

"Now look here," said Stewart, his irritation beginning to mount. "If you're put out on account of my staying away so long, I had a good reason."

"You sure as hell did. Don't you suppose we've all heard about it down here?"

"Well?"

"Well, ain't nobody invited you back, that's all. You ain't welcome in Yalo Busha County, you ain't welcome in Tuscahoma township and, most particular, you ain't welcome in this store."

"Damn all, Mister Clanton, you might tell me why."

"Heh! I told you, boy, that first afternoon you set foot in here. I told you John Murrell has friends. Just put it that I'm in business here, and I want to go on being. You're so much walking dirt now, Stewart, and dirt ain't good for my merchandise."

Stewart flushed in anger, but couldn't think of a retort.

"And you can sure 'nough figger," Clanton went on, "there's others take an even dimmer view of what you done. I'd soonest you rode elsewhere in a hurry, 'cause blood ain't good for the merchandise neither."

"I reckon I should have expected something like this," Stewart said to himself. He was already out the door when Clanton called:

"One more thing, If you're bunking down at the old Ableworthy place, don't count on staying too long." Stewart turned and looked at him in perplexity. "I got an attachment on it," the fat man explained.

"An attachment? How come?"

Clanton took off his glasses and polished them on the hem of his apron. "Well, my lawyer'll give you the details, when you're summonsed," he said offhandedly. "But it's a little matter of unfulfilled money obligations."

"What are you getting at?"

"There's them would call it—embezzlement," murmured Clanton, fixing the spectacles back on his nose with slightly unsteady fingers. Stewart started impulsively back across the store. "Hold on, now!" Clanton shrilled, reaching for a cleaver. "One beller from me and the whole town'll be on your neck, no questions asked!" Stewart stopped himself, quivering.

"Don't forget, we had an agreement," Clanton said hurriedly. "You got paid out of store funds here, on the promise you was to add stock from your wares up at Memphis. I never seen that merchandise and you know it. You took money under false pretenses."

"Why you greedy, slimy——"

"Now don't take on so." Clanton's voice was oilily soothing. "It'll all be straightened out in court. Chances are you won't go to jail or nothing. All you'll have to do is make good. But in the meantime, Stewart—in the meantime, think how it's gonna look, up yonder in Tennessee, when you get on the stand to crucify Murrell. And they say, 'Why, who can believe this feller? He's already an accused embezzler.'" Stewart was keeping his hands at his sides with an effort. "That won't be

all, neither," Clanton added. "There's others got gripes against
you. Now me, I'm a reas'nable man. Wouldn't take much to
make me squelch that charge of mine. Like if you was to deed
over that farm to me without no court fuss. Out of the goodness of my heart, I'd accept it in full payment and restitution."

Stewart stamped out the door, fuming. As he walked Israel
up the street, his mind was in a tumult. He had expected a
certain coolness and standoffishness from the Tuscahomans—
even open hostility from Vess, whom he knew to be a Murrell
partisan. But, considering this instant, spiteful, vindictive mal-
ice from a man he had thought his friend, well, he could
probably expect to duck potshots from mere casual acquaintances. Let's get the worst over with, then, he thought, and
turned his horse for the Vess house.

There was a long wait after he knocked at the door, though
he thought he heard scurrying movements just inside. Then
the door opened and Vess's big square body filled the frame.
He cuddled a cocked rifle in his arms.

"All I come for is my gear," said Stewart evenly.

"You're liable to get more'n you come for, turncoat," Vess
snarled. "But not here and now. I don't want you dying on
my doorstep."

"I don't want anybody dying on it," snapped Stewart. "Just
let me get my belongings and I'll clear out."

Vess stepped back into the hall and jabbed his rifle muzzle
at a small pile of gear already stacked against the wall. "Here
'tis. Take it and git."

Stewart kept tight hold on his temper. He carried the bags
and bundles out and tied them untidily around his saddle
skirts. Vess lumbered off the doorstep and followed him down
to the road, still carrying his weapon. "I just want you to
know one thing," he said, while Stewart worked. "I could of
shot you right up yonder when you knocked on the door, and
not a man would of spoke against it. There's what they call
the unwritten law about these things."

He seemed to be trying to talk himself into a state of aggrieved anger. Stewart couldn't make it out; it didn't seem to
have anything to do with anything. He shrugged, checked the
horse's packs for balance and prepared to mount.

"You hear me?" Vess's voice rose. "You try to muck me in on

that Murrell business, all right; I'll fight you square, man to man. But you come trying anything else, I'll shoot you down on sight, so help me! Hear that? Now *git!"*

•

With an involuntary surge of pleasure and pride, Stewart noted that his lands were no swamp this year. His hand-built levee had definitely held back the river's spring floods. That twinge of pleasure was quickly gone, though, when he reminded himself that this might not be his property much longer. He looked rather gloomily, therefore, at the gaunt skeleton that was the framework of his might-have-been house. Since he last had seen it, the uprights, stringers and rafters had weathered away their bright-cut look. The house had grown old before it had ever been lived in.

Of course, the original cabin had already been senile when he took it. The door fell off its rotted leather hinges into his arms; the one window pane had been cracked by frost or an errant bird; the fireplace had collapsed into a heap of stones; otherwise, the Ableworthy manse was just about as he had left it. Stewart unloaded and unsaddled Israel and turned him loose in the field beside the cabin. He threw out the moldered remains of the two shuck pallets and swept desultorily with a leafy branch.

He brought his packs indoors, but didn't bother to open them. He laid out his saddle and a blanket on the earthen floor, for a bed, and then just sat in the doorway gazing mournfully out over his fallow acres and wondering why he had come at all. Obviously, the whole settlement was against him. No point in hanging around here, as he had planned, until time for the Jackson trial; might as well leave as soon as he'd got a night's sleep. On the other hand, if he rode right away, would they claim he was fleeing the embezzlement charge—and those shadowy, unrevealed other charges that Clanton had hinted were waiting for him? Stewart cussed to himself at the injustice of being made a pariah and a fugitive because he had done what he thought was a public service. Then he cussed *at* himself, for having got mixed up in it in the first place.

He stood up with a grunt that damned the whole ungrateful world. He'd go down and admire his levee handiwork, and at least have the gratification of preening himself on *one* job well done and worthwhile. Stewart stayed down by the water until about noontime. He meandered the length of his wattle-and-daub construction, straightening a leaning pole here and there, plugging a few eroded holes with stones, and, afterward, just meditatively skipping flakes of shale across the surface of his river. At last he began to feel hungry, and started back to get the cornbread and jerky out of his saddlebag.

He came into sight of the cabin with a sudden impression that time had somehow flipped back, and that he had never left this place at all. Once again there were two horses cropping grass around the cabin, and Hester was pacing up and down before the door. She was dressed as she had been that other time, in mannish shirt and breeches, and her flame-bright hair was fluffed out loose. Stewart did not halloo this time; he came up the field unnoticed. She paced to the end of the cabin, wearing a frown of concentration, and he was standing silent before her when she turned to march back again.

"Virgil!" she said, and she smiled happily.

"I reckon *you've* come," he said, trying to keep his voice firm, "to tell me I'm being sued for back rent."

"Don't be silly," she said, a little uncertainly, but maintaining the smile. "Is that—is that the kind of welcome you expected from me?"

"It's the kind I've been getting. All right, then, what do you want?"

"Just to see you. I wanted a chance to . . . Oh, Virgil, did you think you didn't have a friend left?"

"If you're a friend of mine, Hester, I'll give you a piece of friendly advice. Clear out, so nobody'll know it."

A trace of hurt came into her brown eyes. "You've decided William is on Murrell's side, so I must be, too."

"I learned about Bill Vess from Murrell himself," said Stewart, surprised at how calm his voice sounded. "It's no mere opinion. And I know damn well it wasn't any secret from you."

"All right, Virgil, it wasn't. But what could I do? I never knew you'd get mixed up in it."

"I'm not despising your loyalty to your husband," Stewart said. "But now that him and me are on different sides of the fence, you've got to stay on his side of it."

"No, I don't!" she said suddenly and heatedly. "Listen, Virgil. 'Twas long before your time that he threw in with Murrell. I grant you I put up no argument. Because it truly wasn't anything but hero worship. Even his crookedness has been only a piddling little thing. He's supplied Murrell's men with mounts, hid their goods for them sometimes—that's all."

"I believe you," said Stewart gently. "But I had to give his name to the law people, and what they do about it I can't——"

"Oh, for heaven's sake! Did you think I came here to plead for him? He'll get whatever's coming to him, and so will I."

Stewart went inside the cabin and began rummaging in a saddlebag for his victuals. Hester stood in the doorway.

"I kept quiet because, well, who did I care about on any other side? William at least had his fancy of being a bold, bad bandit. Me, I just plugged along, feeding his puny little vainglory. And then I got to know you . . ."

Stewart bit into his hunk of stale cornbread.

"That was when I begun to care where I was going, what I was mixed up with, what I was doing with my life. That was when all the things that hadn't mattered before begun to mean something."

Stewart continued to eat, his back to her.

"I took a good look at myself and I thought, why I'm not just Missus Vess, not just another one of his stable nags to follow him around. I'm *me*, I'm the Hester-Clarke-that-was, and I can be what I want to."

Without looking around, Stewart said, "Hester, I already told you I'm not holding any of this against you."

"You really think I'm telling you this just to get myself out of trouble, don't you? No, Virgil, all this came to me before you ever left here. Do you remember what I told you back then? Not to let anything change you. Well, you haven't changed— you're still the man I admired—but I've changed. Ever since I first met you, I've been looking at things different. And I don't like much of what I see—especially in the looking glass."

"Oh, hush," said Stewart. "What you see there is the handsomest thing in Mississippi."

She made an impatient gesture of fending off the compliment. "Then *why* won't you *look* at me?"

He turned, came close and looked down into her tilted-up face. There were tears in her eyes, and she was trying hard to resurrect the smile with which she had first greeted him. But that attempt failed. She suddenly closed her eyes, opened her lips and forced them passionately upward onto his. Stewart was surprised, but found it the most natural thing in the world, to take her in his arms and return the kiss. She was the first to pull away, shaking her head.

"I reckon," Stewart said understandingly, "it's *not* exactly the time or place."

"It wouldn't really matter," Hester said wretchedly. "William has already sworn out a paper, accusing us of—being lovers—last winter, when you stayed at our house. I suppose he's got some kind of witnesses paid to lie for him."

"Why?"

"Oh, Virgil, he's doing it for John Murrell! He's willing to brand me an adulteress and himself a laughingstock, just to help the chief."

Stewart clenched his teeth and said, "You're going to let him go through with it—paint you black along with me?"

"No. If he does take it to court, I'll start my own suit against him. But you know it's a long drawn-out business, especially when it's the wife asking for divorce. It can't possibly be settled before Murrell's trial. And that's where people will point at you and say, 'Can't believe a man like *that.*'"

Stewart leaned limply against the log wall. She put a hand on his arm. "Don't let them hurt you. Don't get mixed up in it atall."

"Don't get m———! Just how in tarnation do you think I could get any *more* mixed into it?"

"Nothing's really happened to you yet. Nothing like what *can* happen. Just ride away and disappear. Murrell will be let loose, but who cares? You'll be forgotten and that's all there is to it. Nobody slinging mud at you in court, nobody tainting you with a stain that you'll never rub off."

"Maybe I care more about what I think of myself than what anybody else thinks."

"All right," she said desperately. "So you do go back and you do stand up against the man. If he doesn't hang, there won't be a safe place for you on this earth. And if he does, you know what's going to happen? It won't be Virgil Stewart the hero. It'll be Virgil Stewart the outcast, the dirty dog who split on the romantic rogue Murrell. They'll turn *him* into a martyr, a legend—there'll be a Murrell statue in every wax museum in the country—and *you'll* go down in history as the sneaking villain that stabbed him in the back. Oh, ride away, Virgil!" She paused, then said in a whisper, "Ride away and I'll ride with you."

Stewart didn't trust himself to speak. The proposition was too tempting.

"We'd make a good life together," she said, still whispering.

Stewart could only shake his head. There was a long silence before Hester spoke again, in a dispirited voice.

"It's your Naomi, isn't it? I reckon she's sticking by you through all this?" She turned away, winking back the tears. "She'll stick by you to the bitter end—and beyond."

"I trust so."

"You do realize the end will be bitter?" Stewart said nothing. "I'll go now. I don't know whether to admire you or weep for you, but I pray with all my heart that you come through it clean and safe. And Virgil——?" She turned again, and her eyes shone a plea that he understood.

"If there was no Naomi . . ." he said softly.

"If ever there's no more Naomi . . ." she said, just as softly.

•

It was the middle of the night when the bright light woke Stewart. He struggled out of the rolled-up blanket and lurched to the cabin doorway. Across the road, the unfinished frame of his house was a furiously crackling tracery of bright orange flame. Even as he watched, the fragile skeleton crumbled in on itself and fell crashing into the foundation excavation. An astronomy of sparks swirled gaily upward into the night sky and the house was no more.

•

William Vess was among the dozen or so unsmiling men who pointedly neglected to greet him when Stewart stalked into the General Store next morning. He swept them with a look calculated to provoke a free-for-all, but no one took up the challenge, so he spoke to Clanton, who was in his favorite leaning pose behind the counter.

"Somebody burned down my house last night."

Clanton clucked and said was that so. "Depreciates the value of the property. Now it might not cover the compensation I'm asking. Too bad."

Stewart roundly damned his compensation and snarled, "I want to know who did it!"

"Oh, I can easy tell you that," Clanton said. "They was a bunch of likkered-up Choctaws raising a ruckus around town all last night. Didn't know they'd got out to your place, but they sure made town purty hot for a while. The women and chillun all run and hid."

"You're a goddamned liar."

"You're not the only one suffered, Stewart," the fat man went on, as if he hadn't heard. "They broke into Bill's livery stable, too, didn't they, Bill?"

"Sure did," said Vess indifferently.

"Might of burned that down, too, if he hadn't rousted 'em out with a shotgun full of rock salt. As it was, all the damage they done was run off with that pack mule you stabled there."

"I might have known," said Stewart, not giving much of a damn any longer.

"Yep," said Vess ruminatively. "There's times this neighborhood can be downright unsafe."

"There's times this neighborhood stinks to high heaven," Stewart retorted, turning to the door. "Wish I had time to clean it up, this trip. Reckon it'll have to wait till I come back from hanging John Murrell."

•

Yearning for the caress of a cool, soft hand on his brow, Stewart rode straight to see Naomi, not even pausing in Jackson to report to Major Martin. But the only hand extended to him at the Henning estate was, in effect, a fist. Parson Henning emerged from the big front door and was waiting at the top of the verandah stairs when Stewart rode up, dismounted, and handed his reins to the little black stableboy. The parson gestured and halted the boy in the act of leading Israel away.

"Morning, sir," said Stewart. "You look a trifle perturbed."

The man's lips were set in a thin, sharp line. They opened and shut like slicing blades, almost clicking, as he said, "Mister Virgil Stewart, I have the sad duty of informing you that you are no longer welcome in this place."

Stewart stopped in his ascent of the broad stairs and gaped up at the grim little man. Henning clenched and unclenched his hands nervously, and shifted his eyes.

"My daughter's compliments," he continued, "and she is pleased to consider your betrothal at an end. Naomi begs you will respect her desire never to see or speak to you again." Stewart stood rock still. "Or if you came here," the parson went on remorselessly, "to disport yourself with that harlot Eve, she is no longer in residence."

Stewart made a strangled noise combining interrogation, disbelief and outrage. He caught the flutter of a curtain at one of the porch windows, and glimpsed Mrs. Henning's motherly face peeping out, pale and apprehensive.

"I bid you good-by," said Henning. "Now you'll oblige me by clearing my boundary line immediately." He stretched an arm behind him and unlatched the front door. It swung open to reveal Lance standing there with a couple of black field huskies. The three of them were equipped with antique rifles which they held gingerly at arm's length. The impromptu home guard appeared to be as flabbergasted at all this as Stewart was. They goggled back and forth from one white man to the other, their eyes like boiled onions. Stewart made an effort to restore sanity to the situation, saying, in as reasonable a tone as he could muster:

"You can call off the vigilance committee, Mister Henning. I don't aim to bust in. But I do think I deserve some explanation. This ain't like you."

Henning retorted stiffly, "A gentleman would not ask the reason for a rebuff. And a blackguard needs none."

Stewart restrained an impulse to grab the wee bravado and break him over his knee. He went on quietly, "Parson Henning, if I knew what's riled you, maybe I could explain or apologize. Did something happen whilst I was down South?"

The parson unbent enough to say, "Your sudden notoriety, Mister Stewart, has turned up all sorts of people who knew you in other days. It seems you were not always the man I thought you to be. I can only regret that I ever allowed you to besmirch my household with your presence and my daughter with your attentions. Certainly *that* should be plain enough, sir."

"You seem almighty willing to believe whatever you've heard," Stewart said, in a quiet but awful voice. "I can't even defend myself without the slightest idea what it was. But it's a poor imitation of a man that condemns without a hearing."

"That will do!" the parson said hotly. He beckoned to the three Negroes cowering in the doorway. "You'll leave at once, sir, peaceably or otherwise." The three intended enforcers of this shrill threat crept out onto the verandah.

Stewart laughed at them indulgently, then said to Henning, "If Naomi's throwing me over, she could at least have the courage and courtesy to tell me to my face. Or has she lost her wits and manners same as you have?"

The parson's face was mottled and his shock of white hair bristled like dandelion down. "My daughter sends this token as evidence." He reached out and dropped something into Stewart's palm. It was the tiny, gold, heart-shaped locket Stewart had once given her. He sorrowfully regarded it, then flicked the catch to open it. Inside, where the face-to-face silhouettes had been, were only two small dots of dried glue on the velvet lining. "Now, if you'll excuse me, sir," the parson continued, "I have work awaiting me indoors—when I've seen you depart the premises."

"Oh, get off your high horse, Parson!" Stewart said. "I'll go when I'm ready. And I won't be ready till you've answered one more question."

The Negroes moved uneasily, looked to the parson for a command, then looked at their weapons as if wondering which end to point.

"You said Eve had gone," Stewart persisted. "Why? Where?"

"Presumably back to the gutter that spawned her," said Henning self-righteously. "It became increasingly apparent from her language and behavior that she was not what she pretended to be, but a common woman of the streets."

"Did you throw her out? After what that girl did for you and me?"

"I did not. Her sins were not for me to judge, though frankly I have my opinions of your interest in her welfare. She left when her cousin called for her. I must say in all honesty that I was relieved to have my home clean of her contamination."

"Cousin? What cousin?"

"The sort of kin you'd expect her to have," said Henning. "A rough-looking, rudely dressed man with a built-in scowl and all the refinement of a ground hog. He was accompanied by his man servant, a species of giant ape."

"Yancey!" Stewart groaned in dismay. "And Big Tip. She went willingly?"

"I couldn't say. When he came to the door and identified himself as her kinsman, I was only too happy to bundle her out to him, with all the clothes and trappings we had given her. The last I saw, she was riding pillion behind his saddle and they were headed west. I say good riddance."

"Real Christian of you!" Stewart exploded. "You've likely sent that girl to her grave, and you stand there and congratulate yourself on your confounded pygmy virtue!"

Henning suddenly seized a rifle from one of the Negroes, cocked it, threw it to his shoulder and spat, "That's enough from you, sir! I'll tolerate no more abuse! Begone this instant or I'll shoot you for a trespasser!"

Stewart stepped forward through a red haze.

"He'll do it, Virgil!" Mrs. Henning suddenly screeched from her window. "Please go—for all our sakes!"

Stewart hesitated, nodded in the woman's direction and said shakily, "Your servant, ma'am." He turned on his heel, vaulted to his saddle and rode away without looking back.

•

To Major Martin, he bitterly recounted the series of kicks in the teeth he had enjoyed since their recent parting. There was precious little sympathy forthcoming.

"You went into this crusade with your eyes open," the lawyer reminded him, "or should have. Did you really think Murrell would neglect any opportunity to make you regret it? Frankly, I'm surprised you're still walking around vertical."

"Oh, the hell with what he's doing to me," muttered Stewart.

"Maybe I ought to be grateful for finding out how many fair-weather friends I've wasted my affection on. But that girl, Eve . . ."

"Yes, too bad he got her," Martin agreed. "I wanted to talk to her. She likely wouldn't have been much help, but she was all we had in the way of a corroborating——"

"Is that all you care? That it hurts your case?" Stewart asked angrily. "Yancey's almost sure to murder the girl. He already had a personal grudge to settle with her. Eve should have had protection. She'd earned it."

"Simmer down," said the major. "Of course I'm concerned. And, believe me, anything that tries to hurt our case right now is flogging a dead horse." Stewart lapsed into a morose silence, while Martin studied him speculatively. "That girl," he said after a while, in a kindly voice. "She meant more to you than just a handy conspirator, didn't she?"

Stewart loudly said nothing.

The lawyer coughed, and got back to business. "I haven't exactly been leaning on the hoe while you've been away. I've circulated reports to the various law agencies in Missouri, Louisiana, Mississippi and the Arkansas Territory. That is, the ones I was sure weren't in league with Murrell. They're enthusiastically prepared to grab any perambulating clansmen that might pass through. I've got warrants for the dozen or so men you knew personally, including Smith and Blake—a pity I couldn't have managed that before Counselor Brown got them loose. And I've subpoenaed almost everybody else you listed in your little book, but you can guess how few I expect to serve—and how *fewer* I expect to respond. I'll alert the cooperating law agencies to be on the lookout for your lady friend, too. What's her name?"

"Eve," Stewart said dully.

Martin waited, pen poised. "Well? Eve who?"

"Oh, dog it," said Stewart. "I don't know her last name."

Martin drummed his fingers on the desk top. "How," he asked, with gentle sarcasm, "am I supposed to identify this particular Eve? Does she wear a fig leaf, perhaps?"

Stewart groped for his scattered wits and proceeded to describe the girl as best he could. He contributed what little he knew of her history, which was very little, as he omitted any mention of her profession or her mentor, Foursquare Fanny O'Hoag.

"Well, don't get your hopes up," said Martin, as he wrote. "But then, on the other hand, there can't be *too* many brown-eyed blondes on the frontier."

"Not much use looking for her anyway," Stewart said darkly. "She won't be found till her body floats up at some woodyard on some river somewhere."

Major Martin changed the subject. "I checked on those two clansmen you thought might turn state's evidence," he said, producing a sheaf of documents. "Naturally, they've both emigrated to the Sandwich Islands or someplace, for their health, but I did get some fragments of information. Andrew Lofton Boyd, for instance, seems to be the nation's oldest active blight. He has spent some twenty of his sixty-six years behind bars, and the rest of them running. Then there's Joshua Hiram Cotton, M.D. His dossier comes from New Orleans, and I swear I can't make head or tail of it. He's wanted for malpractice, misprision, malversation, manslaughter and I don't know what all. Neither one strikes me as the world's most persuasive witness for our side."

"Even so, Cotton and Boyd are the only two of the whole bunch that deserve to go on living."

"Well," Martin said, closing the folder with a slap, "that's the sum total of our progress to date. In other words, nothing. Unless some backwoods constable stumbles over one of your rascal friends, and can fetch him in without getting himself plugged in the process, we're right where we started. I wish to Christ you had shot Murrell in the head when you had the chance. I'd a whole lot rather be defending you on a murder charge than——"

"Than defending me as a public nuisance?" Stewart finished for him.

"Now wait a minute," Martin protested. "If you convince yourself that you're on the defensive, the jury's going to know it and respond accordingly. About the only weight on our side of the case is your genuine indignation and belief in what you're doing."

"Belief in what I'm doing?" Stewart repeated wonderingly to himself, and Martin looked sincerely worried. "Whatever Murrell may be, I know he'd never have backed out on me in a tight spot, the way all the good, honest, churchgoing, law-abiding folk are doing. No, by God, I'm beginning to sympathize with his point of view." He paused, then added viciously, "Right this minute, I can nominate a good many worthier candidates for the gallows than——"

Martin rocked his head in his hands.

"Oh, don't fret," Stewart told him, with a harsh laugh. "I ain't going to walk out on you or the sovereign state of Tennessee. But I tell you one thing. I don't intend to settle for doing Murrell in. I want Yancey, too. And if he's harmed that girl . . ."

•

Stewart had some difficulty in finding a place to stay in town; the Murrell case was attracting visitors from all over that western country. Jackson's two hotels, the boardinghouses, and spare rooms were rapidly filling with correspondents from big-city newspapers, out-of-town law officers and jurists interested in the legalistic aspects of the case, and a growing horde of just plain sensation seekers. But he finally managed to obtain a mean room under the eaves of a Widow Finlay's private house, where he was passably comfortable—and thoroughly miserable.

The trial was ten days off, and he spent some of the time desperately trying to track Eve and her abductors. A strikingly lovely young girl, in the company of two such brute thugs, one of them black, was not too hard to trace. Numerous people living along the Memphis pike recalled having seen them go by, riding westward, and an itinerant peddler had passed them not many miles this side of Memphis. But there the trail petered out, and Major Martin forbade Stewart to range any farther afield.

The major had been right about one thing. The Murrell affair was being avidly followed by newspaper readers as far away as New Orleans and New York. Stewart's original statement concerning his sojourn among the clansmen was supposed to have remained confidential, but a copy leaked out to the press, and Murrell was thereafter variously described as "The Would-Be Emperor" and "White Ruler of a Black Empire." Milton Brown protested vociferously that his client's interests were being prejudiced, issued repeated statements that Murrell was merely (and mistakenly) being charged with simple theft, and even petitioned the court for a change of venue (denied). Actually, the newspapers were impartial. They took snide licks at Stewart, too, usually identifying him as "the whilom gang member" who had betrayed his chief.

In an attempt to keep their readers' interest whetted until the trial did get underway and provide genuine news, the reporters besieged Stewart whenever and wherever they could find him. Stewart grudgingly answered their questions about his past, present and future. Inevitably, his life story appeared in print as an amalgam of what he had told his pesterers and what they had been fed by Murrell's paid rumor retailers. Stewart learned—first with angry surprise, then with disgust, finally with weary resignation—that his father had been hanged as a horse thief back in Georgia, that he himself had been caned off a riverboat for cheating at cards, that he was wanted in Alabama as a counterfeiter, that he had fled from Kentucky just a jump ahead of an irate, shotgun-toting father. In vain he protested that he had never in his life set foot in either Alabama or Kentucky.

The newshawks so persistently haunted Mrs. Finlay's house (she gloried in the attention) that Stewart stayed away from there as much as possible. When he wasn't roaming the roads in futile search of the lost Eve, he spent his evenings in taverns, sitting usually alone, always late into the night, and drinking rather too much. But the Murrell business was naturally the prime topic of conversation in all these places. So, in saloons where Stewart was known, the general confabulation always came to an abrupt stop when he entered, and for the rest of the night the patrons would alternate between conversing aloud on innocuous subjects and whispering to each other about what really interested them. When he sought out a grogshop where he was still a stranger, Stewart was likely to overhear personal and painful remarks.

Once, for example, he fell to talking with a leathery old mule skinner who was drinking beside him. The old man had just that day brought a team into town and was, like everyone else, full of opinions, philosophies and judgments on the Murrell question.

"Way I feel about thisyer Jawn Murrell," he confided to his mug of whiskey and to Stewart, "there ain't none of us as good as what we oughta be. And might be any man'd turn to a friend or a teammate to air his troubled soul—like Murrell did to this whatchamacallim Sturd. And a friend that'd turn right around and spill what he heard, well, I'd deem him the worser of the two . . ."

Stewart finished his drink with unwonted haste, made his excuses and left the tavern, feeling very much as if he could exit through the crack under the door. He slunk, or stumbled, back to his rooming house to find the landlady waiting up for him, heedless of the hour. She came flying to meet him at the door, untidily clad in wrapper and slippers.

"Oh, Mister Stewart!" she gushed. "There's a young *lady* waiting to see you. In the parlor." Mrs. Finlay dropped her voice to a whisper. "She's been waiting for *hours*."

Stewart weaved unsteadily and a little apprehensively to the parlor. Unbelievably, it was Naomi who rose from a chair as he entered. They approached each other slowly, then in a rush. The embrace was impulsive and mutual, and the kiss was sweet. It lasted for a long time before they stopped to breathe and Stewart opened his eyes. The first thing he saw was Mrs. Finlay at the parlor door, practically palpitating in vicarious bliss. Stewart shut the door in her face.

"Papa would disinherit me if he knew I was here," Naomi said. "I'm supposed to be staying the night with Sarah Hobbs, over on the other side of town. But I had to see you. I was worried sick, wondering what you must be thinking of me."

"Couldn't you imagine?" He grinned, and kissed her again.

When she could speak, she said, "Did you think I'd really jilted you? Oh, Virgil, you'd never believe what things are like at home now. Papa's just gone half crazy, that's all. He thinks he's Andrew Jackson for real, I swear he does!"

"I did get that impression."

"Remember how he used to be so meek and henpecked around Mama? Well, he's lording it over her so *she's* the meek one now. And he bosses the hands around and interferes

with their work. Every Nigra on the plantation has got the
leaping fantods. He even burst into the kitchen one day and
tried to tongue-lash Lena about something, but she threatened
to brain him with a skillet, and now she's the only one he
doesn't try to browbeat."

Stewart almost smiled. Lena seemed to have absorbed something of Rebecca's grit from Eve's readings aloud.

"He talks wild, too. Claims he's going to march on the jail
with *his own militia* if Murrell doesn't get what's coming to
him. The militia is poor old Lance and two of the field hands.
Papa parades them around on the lawn doing what he calls
drills, until they're ready to fall over dead. And the sermon
he preached last Sunday! 'If I be a man of God, let fire come
down from heaven and consume thee.' The congregation just
sat there looking at each other, it was so savage and incoherent.
It gave me the grue to listen to him. What's got him riled,
Virgil, is that the state is depending on you to hang Murrell,
and he's being ignored. He buttonholes every newspaperman
he can find, but he can't even get his name in the papers. Papa
envies you and hates you for that."

"He envies me." Stewart's laugh was like a razor scraping on
glass.

"He doesn't really believe all those lies that are being told
about you," she went on. "He just turns purple because you're
getting all the attention—so he used the stories as an excuse to
tear the pictures out of my locket, and call you all kinds of
awful things, and forbid me ever to see you again."

Stewart said earnestly, "Well, I'm sure glad to find out you're
still——"

"Oh, still!' she cried, throwing her arms around him. "Still
and always! I don't care what anybody says, I don't care what
Papa does. We can only hope that he'll come to his senses,
after this is all over."

"There's just one thing I don't know if I can ever forgive
him for," Stewart said, troubled. "That's the way he treated
Eve. The *cousin* who came for her is one of the Clan's meanest
killers. She may be dead by now. At the very least, she won't
be testifying for us in court." Naomi said nothing. Feeling a
twinge of uneasiness, Stewart asked, "Couldn't you have stopped
him sending her away?"

"Why, I wasn't even home at the time," she said guilelessly.

This was so patently a lie that Stewart, in a sort of horror, tried to justify it to himself. Why, after all, should Naomi have interfered on behalf of a girl she considered a rival? Then he winced, knowing that *she* must have known Eve was being thrown into mortal danger. "Well, it doesn't matter now," he said, dreading to delve any deeper into the jungle world of female morality.

"I have to run, Virgil," Naomi said, as if equally anxious to get off the subject. "Sarah's waiting up to sneak me back into the house so her folks won't know I went out."

"Will I see you again soon?"

"I don't know. It'd be hard. But I'll be in court with Papa."

"Good. I could use a friend there."

"More than friend," she said, and kissed him passionately.

When she had gone, Stewart plodded slowly upstairs to his cramped and lonely room, wondering dully why that farewell kiss had seemed less sweet than the one of greeting. Why, he asked himself, after the things he had learned about people in the last few weeks, should he be bent on hanging just one particular specimen of them? Murrell wasn't by any means entirely wicked; he knew that from experience. What was it Andy Boyd had once said? "There's some white wool even on a black sheep." And Stewart was more and more coming to realize, to his sorrow, that there was no such thing as an entirely white sheep, either.

•

Though fairly capacious, the courtroom could not begin to accommodate the crush of expectant spectators. The word was that people were selling their places in the waiting line for two-figure prices, and no paper money accepted. The railed-off front end of the room was all business: the heavy furniture was positioned foursquare; the crisscrossing traffic of clerks, bailiffs and other officials was constant but orderly. In the spectator rows back of the railing, however, the people wriggled, elbowed, spat, cussed with abandon, crawled over the seats.

The newspapermen had a table to themselves at the front of the room, where they were already busily scribbling. Two other tables, facing each other across the width of the court, were for Stewart and Major Martin, and Murrell and Milton Brown, and their separate staff underlings. Parson Henning had stiffly declined to sit at the prosecution table; he was in the audience, Naomi beside him. Stewart could espy no recognizable clansmen present, and even Murrell's wife was not in attendance—or so Stewart was told; he wouldn't have known her if she had been.

The judge's high bench towered against the front wall of the room. Above it hung a slightly frayed and sooty American flag and a stern-visaged portrait of President Jackson. Both the bench and the jury box were empty when Stewart took a seat at his table. The unwashed, grime-thick windows let in only a pale intimation of daylight. The room was illuminated by whale-oil lamps bracketed around the walls and pedestal lamps on the tables—a sufficiency of them to permeate the air with the odor of fish. The uncovered floor planks were stained with generations of tobacco juice and littered with cigar butts, nutshells, and scraps of paper.

All in all, Stewart thought, it was a most inappropriate setting for the high drama of John Murrell's being brought to justice. He felt remotely sorry for the man, who so loved dash and color, being bayed in a squalid arena like this. Stewart glanced over at the object of his sympathy. As might have been expected, Murrell was the best-dressed man in court, and he looked as hale, happy and uninvolved as if he had just strolled in for a look around. Stewart searched the crowd for other familiar faces; except for Parson and Naomi Henning and a few townsmen whom he hardly knew, there was none. Nobody from Tuscahoma was there, either.

Then Martin was nudging Stewart to his feet, as a bailiff shouted something and the presiding magistrate, Judge Tibbetts, came in through a door in back of his bench, black robes swirling dust up from the floor. The judge had a bourbon-colored face, corduroyed by lines and wrinkles, and fringed by white tufts of side whiskers. With a show of gravity and majesty, he sat down in the rocking chair that was his personal idiosyncrasy and trademark. It was said that more juries had been influenced by the tenor and tempo of its squeaks and groans than had ever been swayed by evidence.

The complicated maneuvers of court protocol that ensued were inclined to blur bewilderingly, as far as Stewart was concerned. He stood up obediently when he was told to, answered to his name when it was spoken, sat down again when commanded. Once, when the judge ordered, "The prisoner will stand to hear the indictment," Stewart started unthinkingly to his feet, drawing a startled look from the bench, a scolding hiss from Martin and a sardonic smile from Murrell.

The dark man stood erect, head high, as though critically auditioning the clerk's chant:

". . . In that the defendant, John Alexander Murrell, not having the fear of God before his eyes, but being moved and seduced by the false and malignant counsel and instigation of the devil, is hereby charged with the felonious crime of stealing and diverting to his own aggrandizement, or otherwise depriving the said complainant, Michael John Henning, of the persons and services of said Negro bondsmen, by name Henning's Caesar and Henning's Rustum . . ."

"The prisoner has heard the arraignment," said Judge Tibbetts. "The plea is now in order. Guilty or not guilty?"

Milton Brown stood up beside his client but, before he could open his mouth, Murrell sang out, in his best pulpit voice, "Not guilty!" so calmly and assuredly that it sounded like the verdict. The judge favored him with a cool glance and did not respond, obviously waiting for the attorney Brown, who, looking annoyed, seconded: "Not guilty, Your Honor."

After that there was another mechanical rigadoon of people standing and sitting down, questioning and answering, picking up documents and putting them somewhere else. At one point Stewart dimly heard himself explained to the judge as ". . . appearing in the role of *amicus curiae,* may it please the court. Mister Stewart will testify in corroboration of the plaintiff's charge and in support of the state's case against the accused, but he is equally available for call by the defense or for questioning from the bench."

Then a parade of ordinary-looking, country-type men filed into the veniremen's roped-off section of seats and were called, one at a time, to the front of the room. They looked frightened, pleased, eager, or awed, as they submitted in turn to the scrutiny and rapid-fire questioning of the lawyers.

"Are you a freeholder of this county, Mister Stone?"

"Yes, sir."

"Have you expressed any opinion as to the guilt of the defendant?"

"Well, only to my old lady, mister."

"Move this talesman be excused, Your Honor."

". . . A freeholder of this county, Mister Runnels?"

"Yes, sir. Got a farm three mile west o' Denmark."

"Have you any scruples of conscience to prevent finding the accused guilty, on account of the severity of the penalty to which he could be sentenced?"

Wide eyes and grin. "That mean he go' be *hung?*"

"Move this talesman be excused, Your Honor."

There were challenges for cause, peremptory challenges, arbitrary challenges. This went on all through the first afternoon of the trial. To Stewart it seemed an ungodly amount of argle-bargle, just to get twelve men seated in that box. Apparently the veniremen thought so, too. The later ones summoned began to answer the questions so laconically as to seem ignorant not only of the case at hand, but of their own occupations and religious leanings. From this group of ostensibly unbiased and impartial clams, Martin and Brown finally culled a dozen that were satisfactory to them both.

The preliminary formalities and jury selection had taken one whole day. It was not until the next morning that Major Martin stood up to make the opening statement for the prosecution.

". . . And the state will prove, from eyewitness testimony, that the prisoner is not only guilty of slave stealing as charged, but has engaged in such a career of other criminal victimization of his fellow man that there can be no doubt of the necessity for conviction and for putting him where he cannot strike again.

". . . Will present a witness who can describe, from his own experiences in the company of this man, what sort of brute monster John Murrell is. Mister Virgil Stewart risked his life to venture into the very strongholds of this consummate criminal, to amass the startling and damning testimony that he will put before you.

". . . And so the state of Tennessee has brought this man to trial on just one count, but one which carries the ultimate penalty on conviction. He has been called to account for stealing another man's Negroes, and the state will demonstrate his capability of that crime by citing his culpability in a multitude of sins against the American people and the American nation. When you have learned the extent of his vile and nefarious activities, the state believes you will agree that he must be found guilty as charged, and made to pay the extreme penalty."

It was necessary for Martin to call Parson Henning as the first prosecution witness, to establish the complaint against Murrell. The old man stood up there like Jackson at his inaugural: erect, fierce, dignified, taut as a coiled spring, and obviously ready to launch a diatribe. Martin, who had said he was afraid of just that, effectually held the parson on a tight rein.

". . . So you suspected your slaves were stolen?"

"I *know* they were stolen. I *suspected* they were stolen by——"

"And you asked Mister Stewart to investigate?"

"I asked him to scrape up an acquaintance with John Murrell, to engage him in conver——"

"You did not, of course, encourage Mister Stewart to bedevil the man or coerce him into confessing the theft?"

"Of course not," Henning said huffily. "I had no wish to make anyone a scapegoat. I merely wanted——"

"But you are satisfied with the evidence which Mister Stewart brought back? Satisfied that it was the man Murrell who was responsible for the disappearance of your slaves?"

"Oh, absolutely. For one thing, the man admitted it to him. Now I should like to make a state——"

"Thank you, Parson. That will be all." He turned to Milton Brown. "Your witness, sir."

Parson Henning turned red, and opened and shut his mouth, obviously as hurt and angry as if he had suddenly been amputated at the knees. Then the defense attorney stepped up to cross-examine.

"You said, Parson Henning, that you were satisfied with Stewart's accusation of my client?"

"I was and am. He exposed Murrell in his true——"

"You consider Stewart a reliable investigator? Trustworthy? Truthful?"

"I believed every word of his story. He——"

"If Stewart is such a paragon of probity, why did you turn him off your land and forbid him to see your daughter again?"

Silence. The parson lowered his eyes in confusion. Half the people in the court turned to stare at Naomi, where she sat pale-faced in one of the front rows. Half of them turned to scrutinize Stewart.

"That has nothing to do with the case against Murrell," the parson said, considerably deflated.

"Will you tell the court just *why* you broke off your friendship?"

"Well . . ." Henning gulped, audibly and visibly. "When the news of this business got out, a lot of people turned up who had—who had known Virgil before. They told me things about him, things I hadn't known . . ."

"Things that convinced you he was not a fit candidate for a son-in-law?"

"Well, I didn't make any snap judgment. I just wanted to suspend any understanding between him and my daughter until I could find out the facts about——"

"And yet," Brown persisted mercilessly, "even though you were revolted by what you'd heard about him, you still considered him fit to malign and accuse Squire Murrell?"

The parson's forehead was shining with perspiration. "My personal feelings about Mister Stewart have nothing to do with——"

"Now, you're a reasonable man," the lawyer said, leaning confidentially toward him. "You've suggested that you had good cause to doubt Virgil Stewart's rectitude, his personal worth. As a reasonable man, Parson, and in the face of all this, how can you pretend that you would trust him with another man's life and reputation?"

"I——" the parson began, then choked on whatever he had been about to say.

"Come, come," said the defense attorney chidingly. "Do you really credit Stewart's talebearing against my client? Are you that gullible? Otherwise, why are you still defending Mister

Stewart's honesty, even when you know he is sadly deficient in it?"

By now Henning had slumped until he was almost invisible in the witness chair. Judge Tibbetts had to lean far over his bench to stare down at him. The parson wiped his forehead, licked his lips and managed to stutter, "I—well—perhaps I did lean upon a rather slender reed."

"Thank you, Parson," said Milton Brown. "That will be all for now."

"I should like to make a statement of my——"

"You may stand down," Brown said firmly.

•

And then it was Stewart's turn. Major Martin made the preliminary questioning as brief as possible. ". . . And you trusted none of these revelations to your memory?"

"No, sir. I didn't want to chance forgetting the names and dates he reeled off at me. Every night when he was through talking, I'd write them down in my memorandum book."

"Is this the book?" asked Martin, picking it up from the table.

"It is. Yes, sir."

Martin waved it at Judge Tibbetts. "The state enters this book as Exhibit A for the prosecution."

"So entered," rumbled the judge. "The jury will examine it at the first recess."

"Now, Virgil, I'd like you to tell the whole story of your meeting and association with John Murrell. I'll try not to interrupt. I want the court to hear it all in your own words."

Stewart began slowly, in a mutter, and had to be told by the judge to speak up. Then he caught Murrell's mocking gaze, faltered, recovered himself with an effort, and avoided looking in his direction from then on. He sought out Naomi's face, shining with pride and encouragement, and spoke the story directly to her.

The judge folded his hands over his belly, closed his eyes, and would have seemed dead asleep except for the gentle eek-eek of his rocker. Milton Brown hopped up at regular intervals, to protest again and again that his client was in jeopardy for a specific charge of theft, and that Stewart's rambling testimony amounted to a series of supererogatory accusations, immaterial to the issue. Each time, Major Martin countered that Stewart's narrative confirmed Murrell's motive, opportunity and means of acquiring and disposing of stolen property. And each time, Judge Tibbetts overruled Brown's objections—though with less enthusiasm and a deepening frown as Stewart's monologue grew longer and more complicated and dragged in the names of more and more people. Gradually, too, the chirruping punctuation of the rocking chair slowed to an infrequent long-drawn rumble.

Otherwise, the court was hushed, fascinated. Martin stood quietly before the witness stand, his hands clasped behind his back. Naomi sat tall and bright-eyed. Her father slumped beside her, still crushed. The reporters' pens waggled furiously. The jury tried to look solemn, wise and magisterial, and succeeded in looking like a box of assorted owls. Milton Brown drummed his fingers on the table and set his face in a derisive half smile. The prisoner fixed Stewart with an unflinching stare.

In this umptieth retelling of the story, Stewart again slid evasively over Eve's role in it. "So this girl that had come to the island, I persuaded her to carry a message for me . . ." He had been talking for nearly two hours before he came to the posse's capture of Murrell and company, rubbed his aching jaw and trailed off with, "Well, I reckon that's all of it . . ."

Martin started to say something, but stopped at a forbidding grunt from Judge Tibbetts' rocker.

"Is the prosecution aware," the judge asked the major, "that these disclosures, implicating a number of persons who are *not* on trial, leave the witness uncomfortably open to charges of slander?"

Martin blinked in surprise and pointed out rather stiffly, "Not only slander, Your Honor. Perjury as well, if these disclosures were not true. But I remind the court that my witness is under oath."

The judge cleared his throat and said directly to Stewart, "I should just like to make clear to the witness that such accusations are not to be tossed around irresponsibly. For instance, Mister Stewart, you mentioned the name of Judge Awdward. My own personal feelings must not color this proceeding, but I might inform you that Justice Awdward and myself have been fraternity brothers and friends ever since college. I find it difficult to believe anything ill of him." The judge seemed suddenly to realize that he had overstepped the bounds of impartiality, and hastened to add, with a wink at the courtroom, "Except, of course, that he is a lawyer."

There was a rustle of dutiful laughter from the spectators, but Stewart winced painfully, Martin was flushed with angry outrage, and Brown's smile widened. The judge said, "Proceed," and leaned back again with a melancholy moan of his chair.

Martin went on to take Stewart back over a few details of his story, questioning him closely on the counterfeit money switch at the camp meeting, the rescue of Barney and Tucker, the killings of the Providence jailers, the slave shipment to the Yazoo Market. Brown continued to play the jumping jack, interrupting to object that his client was not on trial for accepting a gift offering from a grateful congregation, nor for maintaining law and order in defiance of a lynch mob—and that a specially deputized posse, *including the witness,* had failed to turn up any evidence whatever of any slave shipment.

Judge Tibbetts sat and rocked in short, peevish arcs and finally demanded, "Do you really find it necessary, Mister Prosecutor, to slather on the mud so thickly? The defendant is on trial for the theft of two slaves from an estate not eight miles from here. So far, you've wandered as far afield as Louisiana and . . ."

"If it please the court," Martin said through his teeth. "As I maintained earlier, the state is attempting to establish motives and means——"

"Major Martin, unless continued questioning of this witness can elicit new facts for the record, please desist from plowing the same furrow over and over again."

Martin shrugged wearily and turned the witness over to Brown for cross-examination. The defense attorney came up close to the witness chair and peered narrowly at Stewart for some moments. Then he turned half aside and said loudly, "Mister Hughes . . ."

He paused and of course Stewart corrected him: "My name is Virgil Stewart."

"You prefer that one for this occasion, eh?" said Brown, as if respecting a confidence. "Very well. Mister *Stewart,* then. I have only a couple of questions to ask you." He picked up Exhibit A. "This little booklet." He flicked it against his palm. "Mister Stewart, where did all these notations come from— the names and dates and so forth, in this little book?"

"Why, I put 'em down at the time they——"

"*You* wrote them in here, Mister Stewart? They were not inscribed by any other authority than yourself?"

"That's right. Every night I'd——"

"Then, if we choose not to believe the words you speak, there's no reason why we should credit the words you've written, right?"

Martin was immediately on his feet. "I object, Your Honor! Counsel has in no wise disproved either my witness's written or oral testimony. This is not refutation—it's defamation!"

Before the judge could rule, Milton Brown said coolly, "Your pardon, Mister Prosecutor. I'll withdraw that question if you wish. And I don't think I have any others at this time."

On returning to the table, Stewart grumbled to Martin, "I wouldn't say we're exactly setting the world on fire. What now?"

"Oh, that was the easy part," Martin muttered unhelpfully. "Now we really start to suffer."

He rose and addressed the bench. "I would like to repeat, for the record, that the state's case has been severely hampered by the disappearance of every possible corroborating witness for the prosecution. I remind the court that subpoenas were issued for practically every person Mister Stewart listed in his notes. None of them has responded." Martin read the names, from Smith and Blake to Boyd, Cotton, "and the girl known only as Eve," then continued resignedly, "It is unlikely that any of these witnesses will ever be procurable while this trial lasts. However, should a miracle occur and one of them show up, the state begs leave to reopen its brief. For now, and with that proviso, the state rests its case."

Judge Tibbetts consulted the clock on the back wall, decided to postpone the opening of the defense until the next morning, adjourned the court for the day, remanded the prisoner to jail, and had the bailiffs escort the jury to their secluded quarters in the Jackson Hotel. Stewart waited while the courtroom cleared. So did Naomi. She hung back until her father was swept out in the crowd and then came to Stewart, crowing, "You were just wonderful!" as he gathered her into his arms. "Standing up there so proud and unafraid and alone. I felt like saying to everybody, 'that's *my* Virgil!' "

"You'd best not own up to it yet. We haven't won, not by a long shot."

She sobered, to match his mood, and said, "That's what Sarah Hobbs keeps telling me. But she and all my other friends admire me for staying on your side and paying no mind to the gossip and all."

"I admire you, too," Stewart said, kissing her lightly on the tip of her nose.

"I have to go now," she said, kissing him back. "Papa'll be looking for me." As he walked her up the aisle to the double doors, she added solicitously, "Wasn't that a shame, the way poor Papa got all balled up when he was on the stand? He wanted *so* to make a good show." Stewart manfully refrained from saying anything about poor Papa's showing. "Well, tomorrow'll be Mister Brown's turn," Naomi chattered on blithely. "Just one more day, darling, and that should finish everything."

•

Excerpts from the third day's trial
transcript by Mr. Earnest Hobkins,
court clerk (altered only slightly from
the original spelling and punctuation):

> COUNSEL MILTON BROWN opening for the Defense in this wise:
> "Your Honor, gentlemen of the jury, it is guaranteed by our sage and sacred Constitution that a man is innocent until proven otherwise. Unfortunately, not even the Constitution can defend a man from the danger of being maliciously or mistakenly charged of crime by a self-

seeking, ill-intended, or simply misguided fellow mortal. In that event the accused has no recourse but to spend his time and money, and expose himself to slander and vilification, to refute the charges.

". . . Not one of you in this jury-box who is impervious to such an attack by some enemy that seeks to bring you into disrepute or jeopardy. Not one of you who could not tomorrow find yourself labeled Defendant, and suffering the humiliation and discomfort of being held up to public amaze. And that simply because someone had his own personal reasons for putting you in peril.

". . . The State has admitted that its brief contains nothing but the charges of the plaintiff and the testimony of one volunteer 'friend of the court.' The case before us boils down to one thing: that one volunteer's unsupported word against the word of the Defendant. It will be up to you, gentlemen, to decide whose word is worth belief. Defense will present testimony which will shed grave doubt on the plausibility of the charges against Squire Murrell, and on the questionable intentions and veracity of the man pretending to validate these charges. When you have compared the two men's stories, and the two men themselves, I have no doubt that you will bring in the only conceivable verdict. Not guilty."

. . .

COUNSEL MILTON BROWN calls his first witness, viz: Mr. Abner Lloyd.
(The Oath is administered.)

. . .

COUNSEL BROWN: "Mr. Lloyd, you have represented yourself as a citizen of Nashville. But I believe you have lived elsewhere?"
WITNESS LLOYD: "Come from Georgia, a place they didn't have a name for, back then. Now it's Peachgrove City."
COUNSEL BROWN: "You knew the witness Stewart in Peachgrove City?"
WITNESS LLOYD: "Didn't know him personal—just a squirt. Knowed his paw. Seen old man Stewart run out of town, when people started missing horses here and there roundabouts."
(Brief disturbance at Prosecution table. Quelled without comprehensible remarks for this record.)

PROSECUTOR MARTIN: "Your Honor, I object. I fail to see what bearing this testimony, true or false, has on——"

COUNSEL BROWN: "Please the Court, I feel Defense is as much entitled to explore the antecedents and background of witness Stewart as he was to impugn those of my client."

JUDGE TIBBETTS: "Objection overruled. Proceed, Mr. Brown, but try not to go back more than three or four generations."

(Laughter.)

. . .

COUNSEL BROWN calls his second witness, viz: Mr. Jos. Piper.

(The Oath is administered.)

. . .

WITNESS PIPER: ". . . didn't know he was in these parts until news of this-here trial got about. And I'm no longer an Alabama law officer. But I've sent word down home that if they're still looking for Stewart on that counterfeiting charge, here he is."

. . .

COUNSEL BROWN calls his third witness, viz: Mr. Thos. Dark.

. . .

COUNSEL BROWN: ". . . And you were aboard, Mr. Dark, the night Virgil Stewart was disembarked from the riverboat at Memphis?"

WITNESS DARK: "Disembarked, h——l. He were caned off."

COUNSEL BROWN: "By whom, Mr. Dark?"

WITNESS DARK: "By they fellas what caught him a-cheating at the cards. Caned him proper, they did."

. . .

COUNSEL BROWN calls his fourth witness, viz: Mr. Hayes B. Jakobssen.

. . .

WITNESS JAKOBSSEN: ". . . Yes, sir, I'm a process-server by trade. What you'll hear a lot of ignorant people that think they're funny call a vulture."

(Laughter.)

COUNSEL BROWN: "And you have come from Mississippi, I believe, to serve a summons upon Mr. Virgil Stewart?"

WITNESS JAKOBSSEN: "That's correct. Only by law I can't lay it on him till these-here proceedings is over. Then I bet he'll go on the dodge. Most people do when they see me coming."

(Laughter. Judge Tibbetts admonishes
the witness to confine his remarks to
the charge alleged in the subpoena.)

WITNESS JAKOBSSEN: "D——d if it's alleged, Your Honor. I say it's a fact, and anybody'll tell you that old Hayes B's word is good. I happen to be a senior deacon in——"

COUNSEL BROWN: "Please, sir. Just inform us why Mr. Stewart is being summoned."

WITNESS JAKOBSSEN: "Mr. William Vess of Tuscahoma, Mississippi, is seeking a divorce from his wife and re-dress from that-there Stewart, on the grounds that her and Stewart committed adultery right under the poor man's own roof, when the poor man's wife was Stewart's landlady. And you won't catch old Hayes B serving no summons that he don't know in his own heart is the gospel——"

(Brief disturbance at Prosecution table.)

COUNSEL BROWN: "If the Court will instruct Mr. Stewart to cease these unseemly commotions, Defense promises to call him to the stand after a while and give him the opportunity to present his own version of his history."

. . .

COUNSEL BROWN calls his fifth witness, viz: Mr. Daniel Black Gum Tree.

. . .

(Justice Tibbetts interrogates the witness.
It having been ascertained that witness is not
of the Christian persuasion, he tenders an
Affirmation of Faith in order to be sworn.)

. . .

COUNSEL BROWN: "Mr. Black Gum Tree, you are a member of the Cherokee Nation?"

WITNESS BLACK GUM TREE: "I am Cherokee."

COUNSEL BROWN: "You now reside on a reservation in North Carolina?"

Witness Black Gum Tree: "I do. Many do."

Counsel Brown: "And where did you live before that?"

Witness Black Gum Tree: "My farm. In Georgia country. Near place now they call Peachgrove City."

Counsel Brown: "Why did you leave there?"

Witness Black Gum Tree: "White man say want gold under farm. My farm, others. Come. Run us away. Beat. Burn. Kill children. One children mine."

Counsel Brown: "You mean more than one white man, of course. And I believe, Mr. Black Gum Tree, you know the name of one of those men."

Witness Black Gum Tree: "One, he name Stewart. Father of him there Stewart. I know. I see him young boy, watch while father, others burn, kill, steal."

(Sensation. Justice Tibbetts demands order.)

. . .

Counsel Brown calls his sixth witness, viz: Mr. Virgil Stewart.

. . .

Counsel Brown: "This will be brief, sir. You have attended carefully to all the foregoing testimony of the Defense witnesses?"

Witness Stewart: "Yes."

Counsel Brown: I presume you will deny the testimony that your father was expelled from Peachgrove City for horse-theft?"

Witness Stewart: "I d——d sure will."

Counsel Brown: "A simple yes or no will suffice. I presume you will deny the testimony that you were caned off a Mississippi riverboat for cheating at cards?"

Witness Stewart: "I do deny it."

Counsel Brown: "I presume you will deny the testimony that you are wanted in Alabama for counterfeiting legal tender?"

Witness Stewart: "I don't only deny it. I dare anybody to show I've ever set foot in Alabama."

Counsel Brown: "And, to judge from your conniptions during Mr. Jakobssen's testimony, you will also deny that you are required to appear before a circuit court of Yalo Busha County, Mississippi, to answer charges of adultery preferred by your former landlord?"

Witness Stewart: "There may be charges. There was no

adultery. That William Vess and his righteous Hayes B
are both God d——d liars."

COUNSEL BROWN: "Just answer my questions, please. *You*
are not being tried. Yet. Now, you say you deny the alle-
gation of adultery?"

WITNESS STEWART: "I sure do. And not just on my account.
Those two b——ds are conniving to smear a good and
upstanding woman."

JUDGE TIBBETTS: "Mr. Stewart, your chivalrous attitude
may be laudable, but your language is not. One more
profanity out of you and I will charge you with contempt of this court."

COUNSEL BROWN: "So far, Mr. Stewart, you have impugned
every one of the Defense witnesses I have quoted to
you. Accused them of perjury, no less, which is tant-
amount to accusing me and my colleagues of suborna-
tion. I'll ask you only one more question. Do you deny
that you stood by, some years ago, and watched, without intervening, while your own father participated in a
mass rout of innocent, peaceable, land-owning, law-
abiding Cherokee Indians? Do you deny that?"

(No reply from the witness.
He shakes his head.)

COUNSEL BROWN: "Come. No commotion? No sulphurous
denunciations? Not even a simple yes or no? Did that
happen or didn't it?"

WITNESS STEWART: "Yes. It happened."

COUNSEL BROWN: "No further questions."

•

Excerpt from a news story in
the *Western American Argus,*
datelined July 17, 1834:

. . . at which the State prosecutor hung his head and
looked almost as sick and ashamed as the witness Stewart
on the stand. Defense Attorney Brown turned away with a
triumphant air. Plainly, he had made his point; i.e., that
if Mr. Stewart could not refute *one* of the damaging revelations anent his past, he could not refute *all* of them.
Q.E.D., he could not refute *any* of them. Specious logic,
perhaps, but the men in the jury-box are hardly logicians.

Counselor Brown next created a mild stir by calling

the Defendant, Mr. John A. Murrell, to the stand to testify in his own Defense. This was a daring but skillful tactic, shewing strong confidence in his client's innocence, inasmuch as it implied that Mr. Murrell did not fear the gantlet of cross-examination.

No more did he. Mr. Murrell took the stand as it had been a pulpit, and both the jury and the spectators appeared awed by his mien of dignity and martyred innocence. Mr. Brown posed only one blunt query: "Are you guilty as charged?" and his client, well-rehearsed, did not reply. Instead, he said in resonant, deep-belled tones: "Mr. Brown, gentlemen of the jury (turning to the box), Your Honor (turning to the bench), to save the time that would be consumed by a repetition of all the questions that have been fired during this trial, I beg leave to make a statement that should cover everything. Have I Your Honor's permission to address the Court?"

The venerable Justice Tibbetts considered for a moment this, as it were, unorthodox request, but at length acquiesced with a curt inclination of his head. Thenceforward His Honor's sometimes irksomely creaking rocker was as silent as everything else in that Courtroom, the while Mr. Murrell made his quiet, dispassionate, solemn address to his captors. Truth to tell, your Correspondent was as spellbound as the rest of the audience by this redoubtable man's simple, classic story and the mesmerism of his strong, rich voice. So enthralled were we that we failed to attempt to record verbatim notes of his statement. This, though, was the pith and gist of same:

Squire Murrell commenced by averring that he bore no ill will against those who had brought him to this sorry pass, not even the misguided fortune-hunter who had attempted to make *his name* in this wise. These were fierce times, he said, and it were but natural that the victims and bemoaners of the sad state of Society today should seek a scapegoat. "Mine enemies speak evil against me," quoth the Defendant, "saying, when will he die and his name perish?" He went on to add that he would not dignify the charges against him by replying to them *item* by *item,* nor would he conduct his Defense by aspersing his prime opponent. Instead, he said, he would simply demonstrate the absurdity of the accusations.

Mr. Murrell's advocate, Mr. Brown, smiled beatifically,

the while his Webster-tongued client encapsulated a history of his own life. The Defendant told of his harsh childhood, spent in grinding poverty with a tosspot father and a harlot mother; and of how he escaped at a tender age, to make his own way, friendless, penniless, and alone. It was to be observed that several females among the spectators, and not a few grown men, surreptitiously dabbed at their eyes.

"Be strong and of good courage; fear not," was the motto Mr. Murrell claims he adopted early in life. (Indeed, Mr. Murrell impressed his auditors as a pious and a godly man, with his ready grasp and apt employment of Scriptural allusions.) He told how, through unstinting labor and upright living, he overcame the adversities of his youth-time and eventually became a man of modest means. Then he limned the manner in which he had improved his holdings, by judicious investments and by seizing opportunities which lesser men had overlooked, &c. He dwelt at greater length on his religious conversion; how he had come to realize that his material attainments were owed not to Luck or Sagacity, but to a Power greater than he.

Mr. Murrell concluded with the frank and practical admission that, "The value of my holdings right now is in excess of one hundred thousand dollars. I only wish to inquire, in all modesty, is it conceivable that a man of comfortable means, of not inconsiderable reputation, and in expectation of a glorious Hereafter, would imperil it all by consorting with outlaws? More ludicrous still: why in the name of common sense would such a man stoop to abducting two black men, and them the property of his next-most neighbor?"

When he had done, there were few dry eyes in the Courtroom, and scattered hurroars were to be heard here and there. Admittedly, the man had replied not at all to a single charge against him; but the power of his oratory had done much to cast doubt on the credibility of the indictments. Mr. Brown, at least, seemed satisfied with the performance, professed that he had no further questions, and handed over his client for an expected merciless cross-examination. But Major Martin confronted the Defendant to make only this demand, weighty with sarcasm: "Please extend your left thumb, *Reverend,* that the jury may see."

Mr. Murrell smiled rather wearily, as if he had been expecting this, and complied. Even from the news-reporters' bench, where we sat, the white scar was visible against the dark complexion of the ball of his thumb. "The scar consists of two letters," the Prosecutor explained, for those who could not see. "H and T. Mr. Murrell, is it not true that you served a year in Nashville Penitentiary as a convicted horse thief?" "Sir, it is true," said the Defendant, in tones of painful emotion and remorse. Major Martin retired.

Mr. Brown was quick to leap up for re-direct examination. "This crime you have so honestly and unhesitatingly admitted," he said. "How old were you at the time?" "I was one-and-twenty, a mere callow stripling," came the reply. Mr. Brown continued, "Do you feel that you have atoned for that long-ago indiscretion?" Mr. Murrell nodded positively. "I was young and foolish; I had no guidance; I had no God. But I obtest and objure you, dear friends, to reflect on the meaning of the word *penitentiary*. A place of penitence. And believe me, a year in prison is time enough to repent for the most heinous crime. When I came out, I was neither young nor foolish. I have already mentioned the adversities I had to best to make a man of myself; the stigma of that prison sentence was the hardest to surmount. I can only hope that my life since then is adequate testimony that I spent it trying to live down that shameful episode."

With that, Mr. Brown concluded his examination, and the Defendant stood down. The atmosphere of the Courtroom was such that, had the trial ended at this juncture, Mr. Murrell would almost certainly have been handily acquitted, and, no doubt, carried from the dock on the shoulders of a myriad weeping, cheering admirers. He may yet be. The trial was but adjourned until the summations on the morrow, when will begin the fourth and likely the last day of this extraordinary tournament of hard words and turbulent passions.

•

From the *Western American Argus,*
datelined July 17, 1934:

UNEXPECTED DEVELOPMENTS
IN THE MURRELL TRIAL

———

His Acquittal Appears Certain,
Our Correspondent Reports

———

The trial at Jackson, Tennessee, of a rich planter named
John Murrell, who is accused of slave-stealing and numerous other reprehensible activities, completed its
fourth day on this Thursday. And, although it will take up
again on Monday, the 21st inst., Mr. Murrell's friends and
supporters are already parading torchlights through the
streets, celebrating his imminent acquittal by inviting pass-
ersby and absolute strangers to partake gratis of the spiri-
tuous conviviality of the town's overflowing taverns, singing bibulous victory songs, &c.

In yesterday's dispatch, your Correspondent implied
that Mr. Milton Brown's brilliant and adroit handling of
the case for the Defense bade likely to assure Mr. Murrell's acquittal, on the strength of verbal theatrics alone.
But today came a startling new development which, to
almost everyone's thinking, is a certainty to set Mr. Murrell free. The development came in the person of a drab
young female person named Susan Slocum. The first anyone knew of her was when Defense Attorney Brown
announced to Judge Tibbetts, at court's opening, that the
woman had voluntarily presented herself at his offices
early this morning, and he begged leave to put her immediately on the witness stand. This was not accomplished
without considerable and vehement protest from the
Prosecution, Major Gayne Martin being understandably
aggrieved, not to say dismayed, at being caught unprepared for this surprise witness. But after some spirited de-
bate, Judge Tibbetts ruled that the woman was eligible
to testify, and, almost from the moment she took the Oath,
Miss Slocum had the Court in an uproar.

•

"The defense calls Susan Slocum."

Martin frowned blackly as he returned to the prosecution table. "All right. Who the hell is she?"

Stewart looked genuinely blank. "I never heard of her."

For a minute he really did not recognize the woman who walked to the front of the court. From the halting slowness and stiffness of her movements, he would have reckoned her to be in late middle age. Her hair was dull and lifeless, severely swept back into a schoolmarm bun, and her lips and complexion seemed drained to a uniform colorlessness. She slumped dispiritedly in the witness chair, her arms folded across her breast, clutching the fringes of a shabby brown shawl. But then Stewart caught his breath and half arose.

"State your full name, please," said Milton Brown, after the oath had been administered.

"Susan Taliaferro Slocum," she said without expression.

"I believe you work under a sobriquet? A professional name?"

"Eve. Just Eve."

Major Martin flicked a glance at Stewart, whose eyes—bewildered, horrified, pitying—were fixed on this enfeebled slattern.

"Were you subpoenaed to testify at this trial, Miss Slocum?"

"Not as I know of," she said faintly. "I come of my own free will."

"To testify for the defense. Why?"

"Because it's partly on account of me that there *is* a trial. I was the one what carried the message to Parson Henning."

"And what was the content of the message, Miss Slocum?"

"Well, I don't rightly know." Sitting hunched over, she seemed to suffer pain in forcing the words up through her concave chest. "I had a li'l pocket mem'randum book full of writing to give him, but I never took no notion to read what all it said."

Stewart whispered agonizedly to Martin, "She's telling the story all right, but what's she doing on *their* side?"

"You tell me," said the major.

"Miss Slocum," said Milton Brown, holding up Exhibit A, "where did you get this book full of writing?"

Slowly one of her hands let go the shawl, lifted and pointed straight to Stewart. She closed her eyes—the lids were unnaturally dark; for a moment her face was skull-like—and said, "He guv it to me after I laid with him. We was——"

"One moment. Do you mean that you and the prosecution

witness engaged in carnal congress?"

A low murmur from the spectators. A loud "Objection!" from Martin. "Must my witness be subjected to still another dastardly attack on his——"

"Major Martin—Your Honor——" interrupted Brown. "May I point out that this witness came on the scene uncalled and unexpected? She has not been coached—I hardly even took time to go over the outlines of her story—so her testimony and her ways of expressing it are almost as much a surprise to me as to anyone here. I'm sorry if Mister Stewart is embarrassed by the truth. But this testimony is directly concerned with the reason for Miss Slocum's possession of the book and her subsequent disposition of it."

Judge Tibbetts swept both Brown and the woman with a look of distaste. "Solely on that basis, Counselor, I will overrule the objection. But I caution you most strictly to avoid sensationalism for effect." Then he rapped his gavel and announced, "Any spectators who feel they are liable to be sensibly offended by this witness's testimony may take this opportunity to leave the courtroom."

No one stirred.

"Miss Slocum," Brown continued. "Where and when did you and this man indulge in this intimate relationship?"

Her dead-woman's voice resumed. " 'Twas two-three months agone, on an island in the Arkansas Territory. Me and some other girls from—from where we worked—was invited there to a party. In a big log house. Like it might of been a hunting lodge for Mister Murrell and his friends."

"It has been asserted, Miss Slocum," said the lawyer, "that this hunting lodge was actually the den of a desperate band of outlaws. Did you see any evidence at all of the island's criminal utility? Were there, for instance, stolen goods hidden there?"

"Not that I could tell," droned the crone who had been Eve.

"Most particularly, Miss Slocum, did you see any Negro persons on that island?"

"Nary a one."

"Very well. To get back to Mister Stewart. You have testified that you submitted to his embraces. Did——?"

"Objection, Your Honor," from Martin. "There has been no

testimony as to *who* submitted to *whose* embraces."

A pandemonium of whoops and catcalls from the spectator benches. Naomi looked ready to die, and Stewart looked as if he already had. The woman on the stand never changed her corpselike expression. Milton Brown stood smiling, examining his fingernails. Finally the judge's pounding gavel, his rasping rockers and the bailiffs' frantic shushing subdued the crowd.

"One more outburst like that," warned the judge, "and this court will be permanently cleared. You hear me now, Mister Brown. This line of inquiry may have its value in these proceedings. But, unless you care to risk having the witness's entire testimony stricken from the record, you will proceed with the utmost delicacy."

Brown coughed apologetically and said, "Miss Slocum, for the sake of sensibilities, let's make the rest of this as brief as possible. Tell the court how Mister Stewart came to entrust you with his little book."

"Well, it was after—afterward . . ."

Hurriedly, "Yes-yes."

"I told him how much I despised this—well, the work I do. And he told me he could he'p me quit it, he could he'p me make something decent of myself. He said he'd marry me."

This insouciant bombshell again blew the courtroom into conniption. The spectators jabbered, the jurymen put their heads together, the bailiffs jumped around and waved their truncheons, the judge rocking-horsed around his platform and nearly made kindling wood of his bench top. Martin did not leap up this time; he was exerting all his strength to hold Stewart down.

"But she can't do this to me!"

"She's doing it, dammit!" snarled Martin. "Whatever made you think she was on your side?"

". . . And unless this testimony gets down to rock-ribbed relevancy in about the next fifteen seconds," Judge Tibbetts was demanding, "the remainder of the questioning will be done by me, in chambers."

Brown said quickly, "I intend to show that the girl was duped into acting as an agent for the man Stewart. Miss Slocum, *was* it because of this promise of marriage that you obeyed Mister Stewart's subsequent instructions?"

Weakly, "Yes. For that, I'd of done anything."

"And he asked you to sneak away from the island and carry this book to his friend. Did he tell you why he was doing this?"

"He said . . ." She took a deep, shuddering breath and seemed to recite from a drummed-in memory. "He said he was mixed up with crim'nals and the only way he could get shut of 'em and keep a whole skin was to rig a trap for John Murrell and make him the goat."

Martin started to rise, but Stewart beat him to it. "You *know* that's not true, Eve!" he bellowed across the room. "What've they done to make you lie?" For the first time, she let her eyes meet his. There was so much anguish in hers that his own pain was instantly extinguished. Stunned, he sat down without being told.

Tibbetts threw him a look of irritation, and spoke to Major Martin. "I would request you, Mister Prosecutor, to remind your star witness that Miss Slocum is under oath, and that her testimony is no less deserving of consideration than his own has been. *Remind Mister Stewart.*" He nodded another go-ahead to Brown.

Eve resumed, and, as she talked, she drew the shawl closer and tighter around her shrunken body. "Well, I took Adam— I mean Virgil Stewart—at his word. I wanted to believe him. I had to get him out o' his fix so's he could get me out o' mine. But he went back on his word. After I'd come all this way to deliver that li'l book, I found out he was already bespoken —to marry the parson's daughter."

Milton Brown meditated for a moment, then said, "I think, Your Honor, I'll pass to my esteemed friend, the Prosecutor. If necessary, I'll ask an opportunity later for redirect examination."

"In that case, Your Honor," said Major Martin, "may I request an adjournment for a day or so before I proceed with cross-examination? Miss Slocum was originally sought as a prosecution witness. Her sudden appearance for the defense—well, I'd like a little time to restudy the state's brief."

The judge scowled. "Any objection to an adjournment, Mister Brown? Very well. This is Thursday. Court will reconvene at ten o'clock Monday morning." He rapped his gavel and whirled into his chambers, his robes billowing and his rocker banging angrily behind him.

As Martin gathered up his books and papers, he said frigidly to Stewart, "I've got to consult with Judge Tibbetts for a while. But, by damn, you and I've got some consulting to do, too. You come around to my office right after supper. Hear?"

Stewart nodded absently. All his attention was on Naomi. The room was emptying rapidly; her father had already gone; but she delayed, fiddling with her hat and gloves. Stewart waited for the few remaining stragglers to clear out, although half wishing they would linger and postpone this painful interview. What could he possibly say to Naomi? How beg forgiveness for the hurt he had done?

Finally the chamber was empty. She made her way along the row of seats to the center aisle; he rounded the railing to meet her there. To his surprise, her eyes were not pools of melancholy; they were as shiny and piercing as Crucifixion nails. And what she had to say was not at all what he might have expected.

"Virgil! How could you *humiliate* me so?" Her voice was not hurt, but bitter. "To have such a thing dragged out in front of all these people? I'll never be able to hold up my head in Jackson again!"

"Is that all that troubles you about it?" he asked wonderingly. "Not that I did a sinful thing—not even that I did a bad thing to *you*—but that it came out in the open?"

"I never mistook you for a saint," she said sharply. "But here everybody was congratulating me, praising and admiring me, telling me how spunky I was for standing beside you in all this mess. Now—now they'll laugh at me for a fool!"

"I came to you, just now, wondering how to say I'm sorry for my misdoings. Well, all right, now I know. I'm sorry for my misdoings being aired in public."

"Oh, you needn't be so cockahoop about it. This is the finishing touch. Everything's gone sour now. From here on, Virgil, you're on your own. After what that—that creature said, your crusade is finished. I reckon you see that."

"I reckon I see that your heroics were misplaced," said Stewart. "That's what you mean. You don't give a damn about that girl and me. She's just the excuse for you to get off the sinking ship."

"Do you blame me?" Her voice was strident with indignation. "I told you long ago this business was going to make a laughing-stock of you, and it has! The court's going to turn John Murrell loose and you're going to be hooted right out of the country. There won't be anywhere you can show your face without being pointed at and laughed to scorn. All you've got for your Ivanhoe play acting is contempt and ridicule. Are you offering me a piece of *that* for a wedding present? Do you think I'll throw away my friends, my standing, my reputation—for that? No, thank you!"

"Did it ever occur to you, Naomi," Stewart said shakily, "that I wouldn't be in this fix if everybody else involved hadn't deserted me? What I did, I thought I was doing for the good of this whole country. And now every single soul in it is damning me for a meddler and a liar and a rascal. Your father, that windbag poltroon, started me on this whole thing —and then turned his Christian tail. Everybody else I trusted turns out to have his own reasons for wanting Murrell left alone and me stomped into the ground. You were the very last one I had on my side. If you walk out, Naomi . . ."

"If you cared for me the least little bit," she said stonily, "You certainly wouldn't want to drag me down with you. No, I just won't let you. You made your bed and you can lie in it, but I won't lie beside you."

Stewart collapsed slowly onto a bench and put his head in his hands. Naomi never even said good-by. When he raised his head again, a considerable time afterward, he was alone in the big, empty, darkening room. Only a few of the lamps were still feebly guttering. A crippled old Negro clattered in from somewhere with a mop and pail, and whined, "I gotta mop an' lock up." Stewart looked dully at him. "You ain' got no bizniss being hyar, Mas Boss." Very slowly, Stewart got to his feet, flinching when his eyes met the soul-piercing stare of President Jackson's portrait, and shuffled miserably up the aisle and out the door.

•

On his way home, Stewart stopped at a tavern and drank three large tumblers of whiskey in quick succession. The barroom was crowded with spectators just come from the court, and he knew several of them, but no one ventured to speak. Stewart had intended to stay and guzzle until he fell over, but he felt responsible for the sudden clammy silence in the place, and went on his way. He was still stupefied by the rapid turn of events, and by the rapid ingestion of whiskey, but he was alert enough to sense an alien presence the moment he entered his dark, shuttered room.

"Don't be afeared," said a tiny voice. "It's only me." Stewart grunted and lighted the lamp on the chest of drawers. Eve said meekly, "I didn't dast show a light. I paid the black boy to let me come up. Your landlady don't know."

There was a silence, during which Stewart—staring down at her—tried unsuccessfully to muster up some resentment against this wan and shrunken woman. At last he said only, "What you want?"

"Virgil," she said huskily, "I know you don't want me here, but I just had to——" She broke off as Stewart turned to the bed and threw himself on it face down. "Virgil," she pleaded, "I wanted you to know why I *done* what I done."

"I reckon they made you," he said into the pillow.

"Let me show you," she said, in a taut voice.

"It's all right, Eve. Just go on away and don't think any more about it."

"It ain't all right," she insisted, but her voice had no spirit in it. "You know, don't you, how Yancey come and drug me away from the parson's place?"

"I know you went with him."

"I was afeared if I didn't, he'd come after you." Stewart heard the rustle of cloth, and wondered woozily if she was undressing to try and tempt him into some new complication. "The two of 'em, Yancey and that Big Tip, they took me to some place over in Arkansas. A big log house like the one down on the island. And look—*look* what they done!" Stewart didn't move. Eve's shout was a sob: "LOOK!"

Stewart turned reluctantly, and then froze, staring. He was stone cold sober in that instant. The girl had thrown aside the shawl and peeled off her bodice. Under it, her whole upper body was swathed in rough bandages of ragged cloth that she was now unwinding. Two small, slow tears crept down her cheeks as she bared her breasts. Stewart remembered the beautiful body he had adored in the moonlight, and his whole insides seemed to writhe with nausea.

"What——?" he choked, getting to his feet. "How——?"

"I *wasn't* going to lie about you," she said, beginning to cry in earnest. "I wouldn't of, no matter what Yancey said. I thought I could stand anything they could do to me. But *look*."

Stewart's face was sick, and his mouth curled in revulsion, but he couldn't take his eyes away.

In the same dull, dead voice with which she had spoken in court, the girl explained. "They took me in the house. They ripped off all my clothes. I thought it was going to be—you know. I could of stood that." She swiped futilely at the tears that continued to spill. "But they tied me to a ch-chair, so then I thought they was fixing to whup me. And I could of stood that, too. I *wasn't* going to lie ag'in you, Virgil!"

"No . . . no . . ." he said brokenly.

"Big Tip went out and brung in these dogs. You know, them same awful brutes they kept on the island. He tied 'em to the wall acrost the room from me. They was snarling and barking, meaner'n any dogs I ever seen. Yancey come and said to me, real soft, 'We ain't let 'em have a bite to eat for three days—just a-waiting for you to come and feed 'em.' That was when I begun to get scared." A note of hysteria had come into the flat voice. "Then Yancey turned to Big Tip and said, 'Go fetch me their vittles.' The nigger come back with a big flitch of side meat and handed it to Yancey. The dogs, they smelled it and they just went wild. Th-then Yancey turned to me . . ."

Stewart was seeing the man's face in his mind, knowing the kind of grinning, sadistic frown it had worn. The girl drew a long, sobbing breath.

"He tooken the flitch of meat and he rubbed it—rubbed its grease all over my breasts. All over, back and forth and up and down, and them dogs watching with their red eyes. Yancey kept saying, 'My, them hounds is awful hungry, awful mad, awful anxious.' And then he sent Tip to hide the meat away.

He went over where the d-dogs was tied, and—and th-then . . .
Oh, God! He cut the dogs loose!"

Stewart leaped to catch her; Eve had slumped against the
wall, sobbing uncontrollably. He grabbed her, taking care not
to touch the awfulness, and helped her to the bed. Her hands
were over her face, and tears and little whimpers trickled out
between her fingers.

In a moment, her voice muffled, she went on. "It couldn't of
tooken the dogs more'n a minute or two, but I don't know. It
felt like forever. Then Big Tip fought 'em off of me and
hauled 'em away. I was just a-bleeding all over my front.
But Yancey'd already had this here shovel a-heating in the
fireplace. He brung it over, fiery red—so hot he had to hold
the blade of it way away from him—and he—he laid the flat
of it acrost where my breasts had been. There was a sizzling
and smoking, but by then I couldn't even hardly feel it. And
I had screamed so much I just couldn't scream no more. But
I reckon that shovel cooking me was the only thing that kept
me from bleeding to death." She suddenly reared up on the
bed. "Virgil, you know I wouldn't of told lies! But that Yancey,
he said—if I didn't—the next time it'd be my *face* that was
tore off!"

"Eve . . . Eve . . ." Stewart said helplessly. "I know you
didn't want to say what you did. I wouldn't have held it against
you. I knew there had to be a reason."

"I shouldn't of lied, though," she whispered. "He'd already
done this. And he'd of done it anyway. And I'll prob'ly die
from this. My lies didn't save me nothing."

"Eve . . ." He cuddled her close to him. "Hush now. You're
not going to die—and you don't have anything else to fear from
Yancey. I'll see to that. Where is he now, do you know?"

She shook her head against his chest. "Him and Tip brung
me back as far as Memphis. Sent that feller Blake the rest of
the way with me—clear to the door of the courthouse. And
then he hid, but he said he'd be waiting with a gun p'inted
at the winder in case I didn't talk like I'd been told. I ain't
seen him sincet."

There was silence in the room for a while. Stewart was
thinking—how unfair it was that the one bravest, most de-

serving person in this whole unholy mess should have been the cruelest hurt. He recalled, with a pang, how he had failed to recognize her in the courtroom; how she had moved and walked like an old, old woman. And here *he* had gone out drinking to drown his measly miseries.

"You listen to me, Eve. You're going to have the best doctor in Tennessee fix you up." He forced conviction into his voice. "Be surprised what a doctor can do for you. You'll be healed and healthy again in no time—and prettier than ever."

She looked up at him, not daring to believe. "But you. What about you?"

"I'm going after Yancey."

"You can't just run out on the trial," she protested. "You're in enough trouble as it is. On account of me."

"Forget that. I've forgot it already. All I want to remember is that you went through more for me than anybody's ever done."

"Can I—can I go back on what I've told?" She seemed slowly to be drawing strength from his assurances. "Can I go and tell the judge the truth?"

"Not yet. If I'm not here when court takes up again, you tell 'em anything they want to hear, and be-damn to 'em. It won't matter then. But when I've settled with Yancey and you don't have him to fright you, then you can spill the truth. Right now, let's get you out of here."

Gingerly, wincing occasionally, she rewound the bandages. Then he led her, unobserved, down the back stairs and around through the alley to the street.

"You do something for me while I'm gone," he said, at parting. "You loose your hair down the way it was, and let me see some color in your cheeks when I get back. Do that?"

Eve smiled tremulously and nodded. She went away from him reluctantly, stopping once to call softly, "Please be careful, Virgil." When she was out of sight, Stewart set off at a run for Major Martin's office.

He flung open the door without knocking and strode in without waiting for an invitation. The lawyer looked up in surprised annoyance, but said only, "You're early, Virgil. I'm glad. We've got a lot to——"

"Have you got a gun?"

"Huh?" said Martin, nonplussed. "Why—just my old Army pistol yonder." He indicated an unwieldy, brass-framed weapon hanging from a wall hook by a thong through its rusty trigger guard. Stewart took it down, checked its load and jammed it into his waistband. "Now hold on!" warned Martin, getting up from behind his tableful of papers. "What numbskull notion have you got this time?"

"I want to shoot somebody," Stewart said quite simply.

"You quit this foolishness and sit down. I'm saving that one shot to do myself in, unless we can think up some sensational shenanigans before court reconvenes. Sit down, dammit!"

"I got no time to palaver, Major. I've got a long way to ride."

"You've what? You can't leave now!" Martin shouted. "You're the state's only witness. If you're not in court on Monday morning——"

"If I'm not, I won't be giving a damn what happens here. But if I am, I'll have another witness along. This time, by Christ, I'll be believed." He opened the door.

"Stewart, this is gross contempt of court!"

"You bet it is. Oh, I almost forgot." Stewart lifted his shirt and stripped off a canvas money belt. "If I don't get back by court time, would you do one last good deed and hand this over to that girl Susan Slocum? It ain't much, but . . ."

"What?" said Martin, astonished. "After what she's done?"

"Someday maybe I'll tell you truly what she did," said Stewart, and closed the door behind him.

•

Stewart was nearly as lathered and breathless as the good horse Israel, when he drew up outside the Bell Tavern late Friday night and tossed his reins to the omnipresent urchins. He paused there for a minute, to ease up on his panting and to loosen the big pistol in his belt. Then he pushed through the swinging doors and stood spread-legged and ready.

The grim purposefulness in his stance was a dangerous sign of temperament to haul into a saloon full of Pinchgut ruffians and rowdies. Perhaps the only reason he wasn't immediately challenged was that many of the habitués recognized him from his previous visits in the company of Murrell. At any rate, a silence fell on those nearest the door. They eyed him furtively as he swept his gaze up and across the big room. The puddle of apprehensive silence widened and deepened, and more and more of the people at the bar and tables turned to see what had cast the pall. For perhaps the first time ever, the piano player's tinny music could be heard; when he realized this, he stopped playing and turned like the others to watch. The bartenders looked at Stewart as impassively as everyone else; only the orange-haired barmaid Sally Meagher made an overt move. She brought a double-barreled shotgun up from somewhere and laid it on the bar. Stewart paid her no attention. Three men at the very back of the room were the last to halt their conversation, lower their mugs and swivel to meet Stewart's eyes. And there they were, just as he had first seen them: Dr. Cotton, Yancey, and Big Tip.

As if a signal spark had flashed at the instant of confrontation, all the people seated or standing between the two parties lunged to the bar side of the room, out of the line of fire. In a moment the room was a desert of unoccupied tables, two of them overturned, and the only sound was the forlorn clinking of an abandoned whiskey bottle rolling back and forth on the floor planks. For a frozen fraction of time, Stewart and the three clansmen held their tableau—and then in one quick burst of movement it was broken.

Dr. Cotton dropped to his knees behind the table and scuttled toward the shelter of the bar. Big Tip shoved forward from his place against the wall and started ponderously but rapidly down the room, like a tree attacking. Yancey, leaping up from the table, and Stewart, dropping to one knee, drew their pistols and fired simultaneously. Both of them missed their targets; Stewart heard glass shatter somewhere behind him, and saw his own ball smack splinters from the wall to Yancey's left. Neither had a second gun, neither made any attempt to reload.

Stewart launched himself up the length of the room at a dead run. He sidestepped nimbly around the onrushing Negro and flung a chair into his path to trip him up. At the same time, Yancey whipped the ever-ready deer hoof from his belt and flicked it to expose the gleaming blade. Without slowing his run, Stewart snatched up a bottle and smashed it against the tavern's big central stove as he passed. Wielding the jagged fragment that remained, he hurled himself on Yancey. Each man seized the other's weapon hand and for a static instant they wrestled, standing, their grimacing faces inches apart.

Then a heavy hand struck Stewart's shoulder and slid away—it was Tip's gorilla paw reaching to clutch him. He managed somehow to wrest Yancey around between him and the Negro, but the buffer could only be temporary. If he was to fight at all, he would have to contrive to fight them one at a time. Roaring, Big Tip flung tables and chairs out of his way and circled to grab for him again. At that moment Yancey took advantage of Stewart's divided attention and made a quick stab with his knife. Instead of tightening his grip on Yancey's wrist or attempting to dodge the thrust, Stewart fell back before it. He gave way so suddenly that Yancey fell forward, off balance, and in his surprise let go of Stewart's weapon hand. But Stewart didn't use his broken bottle; he dropped it, seized a chair by its back and swung it up from the floor. It crashed into Yancey's chest before he could recover his footing, and knocked him backward.

Several things happened then all at once. Yancey fell on his back under a table just as the black giant overturned it out of his way. The table—a long, rectangular and very heavy puncheon affair—tipped over on Yancey so that its edge axed into the pit of his stomach. The breath was knocked out of him; for a couple of minutes he was trapped helpless with his head and arms on one side of the tabletop and his legs and lower body on the other. And in those minutes the other half of the fight was finished.

It seemed to Stewart that he had no sooner hit Yancey with the chair than a black fist barreled out of nowhere and caught him on the side of the head. It was a glancing blow, but such was the Negro's strength that it careened Stewart sideways. He caromed off a table, hit the floor and slid against the stove. The door of its firebox banged open and salted him with sparks. As he jerked away from it, smelling singed hair and cloth, Big Tip stooped and picked up Yancey's fallen knife. A horrible grin distorted his features and his tiny eyes glittered, as he began ominously to stalk toward the downed Stewart.

There was one means of deliverance offered, and Stewart

took it. He grabbed the little hand shovel that lay by the stove and plunged it into the embers of the firebox. Just as the Negro raised the knife and hurled himself forward, Stewart flung the loaded shovel at his face. It hit Tip in a splash of flames, coals, ashes and smoke, and he reeled backward with a yell. There was a brief sound of frying and a sudden stench. Stewart rolled away and floundered to his feet, but he was no longer in danger. The Negro howled and danced in agony, slapping at the embers that clung to his skin. His black face was now mottled with blue-gray and, hideously, it smoked. He groped about him, trumpeting like a wounded animal, and Stewart could see that his eyes were cinders.

But blindness, and the fact that portions of himself were still cooking, did not deter Tip's purpose. He held onto the knife and lashed about, seeking the elusive enemy. He found one, when he stumbled over the legs of the hapless Yancey, still pinned by the table. Out of his mind with pain and rage, Tip did not pause to question the evidence. He fell roaring onto Yancey, grappled his kicking legs and began wildly to hack at the man's groin, the only part of him in reach.

Yancey had got his breath back sufficiently to cry out in pain and terror. He hammered on the table but could not move it. Tip paid no attention to his yells, but ripped the blade again and again through the man's lower body. Stewart stood limp and panting, staring transfixed like everyone else at the macabre scene. On one side of the toppled table, Yancey's head screamed and pleaded for mercy and his arms thrashed; on the other, the raving-mad Negro, his face still smoking, mechanically raised and lowered the bloody knife.

The girl Sally was the only one to snap free from the mass paralysis. She lifted her shotgun and, when Tip's head showed for an instant above the table barrier, let him have both barrels. The recoil slammed her back into the stacked kegs and bottles, and from there she fell out of sight behind the bar. The other end of the blast lifted Tip's body stiffly, almost reluctantly to its feet—though most of his head disappeared toward the other side of the room—and then it collapsed and lay still.

The booming shot unfroze the crowd of people cowering

against the bar. Several of the women dissolved into hysterics. One man vomited onto the floor. Three or four others leaped to lift the heavy table off the still-crying Yancey and help him to his feet. His trousers were drenched bright crimson, and he was already flaccid from loss of blood, but the men managed to stand him up in the pool that widened around him. He feebly clutched at himself, as something slipped down the inside of his trouser leg and fell onto the floor. Yancey looked down dazedly and, when he recognized what it was, shrieked long and piercingly and fainted like a woman.

Stewart had not even bothered to glance at him again. He shoved his way through the horror-struck crowd and leaned over the bar. On the floor behind it sat Sally Meagher, pale-faced, rubbing her bruised shoulder. Dr. Cotton lay at full length beside her, whimpering and hiding his head in his arms. Stewart reached down, seized the slack of his coat collar, and hauled him to his knees. The old man rolled his eyes up with the look of a hamstrung horse waiting for the finishing bullet.

"Once upon a time," Stewart reminded him, in an unsteady voice, "you said your calling was to help suffering people, Doctor Cotton."

The old man nodded, trembling, and croaked, "Y-Yancey?"

"No," Stewart said gruffly. "Me. Get up. We've got a hard ride ahead of us."

•

It was high noon on Monday, and the town had been astir for hours, but Stewart was too sound asleep to hear the pounding on his room door. Finally, in desperation, his caller bribed the houseboy to unlock the door. And then Major Martin had to shake the slumbering man for nearly five minutes to get him to open his eyes.

Stewart muttered a peevish oath. "Lemme 'lone. First snooze in four-five days. Don't tell me they *still* want me in court?"

"No, all that business is coming along handsomely," said Martin in great good humor. "Court's in recess right now. I'm sorry to have to wake you, Virgil, but there are some details . . ." Stewart suggested a vulgar disposition of the details, and rolled over on his pillow. "No, no," said the lawyer, rolling him back again. "Man, you've busted the whole thing wide open. Don't you want to hear about it?"

"Wanna sleep."

"Did I act like this when *you* woke *me* at that Christly hour this morning?"

"Oh, for the love of——!" Stewart scrunched himself half upright against the headboard, pawing at his cobwebby eyes.

"Listen," said Martin exultantly. "Milt Brown, Judge Tibbetts and I have been closeted together all morning. It's just bully what you've done. Just je-wholloper. Your Doctor Cotton has exploded Murrell's defense to flinders. He's turned state's evidence with a vengeance. He's backing up everything in your story, and he's adding some high old touches of his own."

"Then you don't need me any longer," wheezed Stewart, beginning to slump again.

"So what happened—Milton Brown wants to effect a compromise. See, with everything the doctor's spilling, Brown knows Murrell could be charged with murder, treason, God knows what. He wants to throw his client on the mercy of the court." Martin hesitated. "Before I agreed to it, I wanted to ask how you felt about it."

"Me?" said Stewart, astonished to full awakening. "Since when have *I* had anything to say about this business?"

Martin looked a little abashed. "Well, it's like this. If the state accepts, Murrell will get off with a prison term. He won't hang."

"And I'm supposed to want him hung? Is that it?"

"Er—not exactly. But being convicted on this charge wouldn't exempt him from being hauled up again later for something else. And as long as you've got that damning little book of yours . . ."

"Lordy, Lordy," Stewart sighed. "They want me to promise not to make any more fuss? Do you think I'd go through all this hell again? I'll chew up the blamed book and swallow it in front of the judge, if that'll settle anything."

Martin smiled. "All right, then. I'll get back over there and see things squared away. The judge will dismiss the jury and postpone further action until you're refreshed enough to attend."

"I'd just as soon not."

"Well, there are papers to sign. Waivers and whatnot. See, you've got grounds for all kinds of libel and slander suits."

"I wouldn't bring suit, now, against Lucifer himself," Stewart said bitterly.

"And nobody'll be bringing any against you, now that they can't possibly help Murrell's case. That's one of the conditions I'll make Milton Brown fulfill."

"Thankee," murmured Stewart.

"Oh, one other thing," said Martin, as he stood up from the bed. "Lawyer Brown—more to save his own face than any other reason—did suggest bringing perjury charges against your Miss Slocum." Stewart came alert with a start. "No, don't fret. The judge let her off with a sort of stiff lecture."

"Where is she now?"

"Damned if I know. Last I saw of her, she was boarding the southbound stage." Martin evidently misunderstood Stewart's agitation and added soothingly, "It's all right. I didn't give her your money." Stewart threw him a scathing look and collapsed back onto his pillow.

"Look here," said the major. "In a little while, you'll be free to go after her, or back to Tuscahoma, or anywhere you damn please. It's all over. You've done a fine deed, and done it in spite of a hell of a lot of odds against you. You're a hero, man. And folks are starting to talk about a Committee of Safety to finish the job you started. To stamp out everything that's left of the Mystic Confederacy. The country's got good reason to be thankful to you, Stewart. You've been a brave man, and I'm proud to be the first to say so."

The hero did not acknowledge. He was asleep again.

•

A week later, Stewart was still trying to wash his hands of the whole affair and get out of town. But the legal details attendant on John Murrell's immurement were numerous and tedious. And Major Martin insisted on painstakingly making sure that Stewart himself was cleansed of all charges, taints, suspicions and shadows before he would let him leave.

At one time during this period, Martin showed Stewart a handbill, with a smile and the remark, "See? You gave Justice a shove and now she's moving like greased lightning." The paper bore the seal of Cumberland County and a wide black border. The two torn corners indicated that it had originally been tacked on a wall somewhere. In somber black print it gave notice that:

> RUEL JOSEPHUS BLAKE, who has been found guilty at the present term, of the theft of a horse, was this day set to the bar and the sentence of the Court pronounced upon him as follows, to wit, THAT ON WEDNESDAY, the sixth day of August next, he be taken to the place of execution and there to be hung up by the neck, between the hours of ten o'clock in the forenoon and four o'clock in the afternoon, until he is dead, dead, dead. WHICH SAID SENTENCE the Sheriff of Cumberland County was ordered to carry into execution.

Another day Stewart's landlady, Mrs. Finlay, told him (simpering) that "that lovely young lady, Miss Henning," had stopped by, looking for him. He quickly packed up, paid his back rent and moved out. During the remainder of his enforced stay in Jackson, he slept in the livery stable where Israel was quartered.

Ten days after Milton Brown had proposed his compromise deal, Judge Tibbetts handed down his pronouncement. On the morrow, John Murrell would be escorted, in irons, in a closed carriage, by a heavily armed sheriff's posse, to Nashville Penitentiary—and he would not leave there again for ten years. Stewart looked sympathetically at the first expression of downright dismay he had ever seen cross Murrell's face. The man turned almost as pale as the little tick of scar in his eyebrow. When the court had cleared and the prisoner had been led back to his cell, Stewart inquired of Sheriff Cullen if he might have a few last minutes with the man before he was shipped away. And, because Stewart was being given just about every courtesy he asked for these days, his request was granted.

"I'm sorry," he said, when they were face to face at the cell door. "But it was you or me."

The dark man smiled tightly at him. Murrell no longer showed the elegant hauteur he had displayed in court, when the trial was going so smoothly his way. Now his fine clothes were a little unkempt, his jaw unshaven, and his usually immaculate hair uncombed. There were heavy circles under his eyes and an insistent twitch in one cheek.

"Tell me all about it," he said, in a defeated voice. "About how you got Cotton here." Stewart told him. "So old Tip is dead," muttered Murrell, shaking his head. "And gunned down by Sally, of all people. I swear, this whole business is as neat as a Greek tragedy. Full circle. How about Yancey—is he dead, too?"

Stewart shrugged. "If he's not, he wishes he was."

Murrell continued to shake his head, as if the wonderment was too much for him. Stewart mentioned reluctantly that Ruel Blake was scheduled to swing. "Oh, they'll all swing eventually," sighed the fallen chieftain. "All but me. Isn't that the damndest thing?"

"Was I you," said Stewart encouragingly, "I'd be grateful for the flukey way the law let you off."

"Let . . . me . . . off!" grated Murrell. "That bastard Brown and his politicking! He couldn't smirch his record by letting a client hang—not even when the client begged to hang!"

"Hell," said Stewart. "You're not going to be any dauncy old graybeard when you come out. You can start over again, honest, with a clean slate."

"Come out?" Murrell chuckled hollowly, like coffins rubbing together. "Come out of Nashville Penitentiary? After ten years?" He quoted something that Stewart could not place. "I did not die, and did not remain alive; now think for thyself what I became, deprived of both death and life."

"I reckon there ain't many of your men who wouldn't trade places with you," Stewart said. "There are Committees of Safety clubbing together in just about every settlement in this western country."

"And calling for blood, I'll be bound. Yes, the Clan will all be hunted down, poor lads."

Stewart nodded soberly. "Some of these upright citizens *can* be pretty bloodthirsty. Right here in Jackson they're already looking under every rock for somebody to hang. They're eager as animals."

"Animals, Adam, yes." Murrell had forgotten Stewart's real name; now he seemed to forget the man himself. "We're all animals." His eyes were glazed and sighted far away. "You laid me low because I was an animal, a fierce one, and you had to stay my preying. But the folks you saved are animals, as well. You'll wonder why you ever cared what happened to them. What you'll see now will be the jackals and hyenas gathering for a carrion feast. This whole land will run as red as I could ever have made it do. The whole land thereof . . . brimstone and salt, and a burning . . ."

He paused, returned his gaze to Stewart, and said in a terrible whisper, "But this time Black John Murrell won't have done it. 'Twill be you who did."

•

"So it's good-by?" said Major Martin.

"There's nothing to keep me here," said Stewart. "Every time I turn a corner in Jackson I run into a pain I'd rather forget."

"Where do you intend to head for?"

"I don't know. Don't much care. There must be some place far enough away that nobody ever heard of John Murrell or Virgil Stewart. I'll make Memphis first, sell the goods I've still got stored there. Then . . . just drift for a while . . ."

"Give us a thought now and then," said Martin kindly. "Jackson won't ever forget you."

"I doubt I'll forget Jackson," said Stewart, without inflection. Twenty minutes later he rode out of there, and never came back.

•

John Murrell, in his valediction, had spoken nothing but the truth. The fuse Virgil Stewart had lighted was a short one. The Nashville *Banner* laid out Murrell's planned Black Insurrection in lurid detail: ". . . to proceed through the principal towns to Natchez, and then on to New Orleans—murdering all the white men and ugly women—sparing the handsome ones and making wives of them—and plundering and burning as they went." Such newspaper accounts inspired the hue and cry in every smallest locality in the Mississippi valley—against bandits, road agents, land pirates, horse and slave stealers, catchpenny swindlers, gamblers, and every other variety of the outlaw ilk, big and small, real or imagined.

Citizens' Committees, Vigilance Committees and Committees of Safety were organized left and right. They seldom waited for the long drawn procedure of a court trial before meting out their brand of justice to the wretches who fell into their toils. It was the respectable-by-daylight worthies who rode out masked at night to wreak their sadism on some poor prostitute or some penniless and stranded riverboat gambler. Even when cooler heads counseled moderation—there were comparatively few who did—the cry "Root out the Mystic Confederacy!" was sufficient to shut them up. It would have been a chancy thing to suggest to one of these righteous and rabid committees that their style of disposing of unwanted citizens was not very different from that of the infamous Murrell. So it was a bad year for the denizens of Natchez-under-the-Hill and the Memphis Pinchgut and the New Orleans Swamp, and lesser but similar communities all up and down the river.

In a copy of the Lexington, Kentucky *Intelligencer* that he came across somewhere, Stewart read, "The Mississippians are ruining their own State. By their own high-handed and violent measures, they are giving a magnitude and terror to the contemplated insurrection which it otherwise never could have attained."

Almost everywhere that Stewart paused in his wanderings, someone was sure to buttonhole him and recount with relish the latest hanging or tarring and feathering or riding on a rail which that community had to brag about. He made sure to shield his identity, apprehensively expecting that he'd be asked to officiate at such ceremonies if the word got out that here, sure enough, was "the man that got Murrell." But the simple fact that he was a stranger in each of the settlements he passed through made him fair game as an audience for one dreary horror story after another.

"Damndest hanging I ever seen," was one man's comment. Stewart had casually encountered him, a post rider, in a way-side inn, and was being regaled with one more malefaction to add to the already heavy load on his conscience. "I say these string ups should oughta be left to the perfessionals. Amachoors allus botch things. See, they'd caught thisyer feller lallygagging around on somebody else's hoss. So they hung him in a handy barnyard. Not that that's so remarkable nowadays. Seems like ever'body's just going around looking for excuses to stretch somebody else's neck."

Stewart morosely agreed.

"But what happened—this young feller had his hands tied ahind of his back, but someway he worked one of 'em loose. When they shoved him out the loft door, he grabbed with that there hand and caught the rope just above his ear. So o' course he broke his fall and didn't break his neck. He just swung there, holding onto that rope with all his might and main."

Stewart would have been content to have the story end right there. But what the post rider said next made him sit up with a start of recognition.

"Sad thing was, the feller didn't have no *thumb* on that hand, and 'twas purty hard for him to hold on. He just swung there, back and forth, the tears running down his chin, whilst that hand slid slow along the rope. Ever'body was plain struck petrified, watching. They *could* of cut him down and begun all over ag'in. But nobody moved, and the feller slid down the rope to where his neck fetched up ag'inst the knot. It tooken him a long time to strangle thar. And if you've ever seen the jesusly things that happen to a choking man . . . Well, I'd be just as happy not to of seen it."

Stewart eventually had to hear, from one slavering informant after another, how each of his former cronies had come to justice. He heard how old Andy Boyd had gone to the hanging tree with a grin and the comment, "Figgered it was about time," when he was caught doing nothing worse than trying to peddle some pocket watches he couldn't prove title to. He heard about the others: Sanders, hanged. John Earle, hanged. Bill Earle, a suicide in his improvised cell while awaiting hanging. Lee Smith, hanged. Angus Donovan, hanged.

It wasn't until a long time later that Stewart learned, in a letter from Martin, about the fate of Dr. Cotton. While turning himself practically inside out to help put Murrell away, the doctor had apparently confessed too much for a jury to forgive. He was sentenced to hang for his own share of the Mystic Confederacy's crimes. He was probably the only one of the Clan, except Blake, to be legally tried and executed.

But even the legal atrocities committed during that summer and fall of 1834 were enough to sicken the most objective observer. And Virgil Stewart was being anything but dispassionate. Each new instance of villainy, vengefulness, and vileness he encountered made him cringe as if it had been an actual scourge lashing him. The whole nation, he decided, had busted open into putridity like a rotten fruit. He felt he was much to blame for it, and the having to know every last sordid detail was his punishment.

•

From the start of his wanderings, Stewart had more or less let Israel have his head. But somehow, whenever the horse would stray off their rambling southward course, Stewart would unconsciously knee him southward again. Why, he could not have explained. He did not know that he was blindly seeking a balm for his lacerated soul—until he found it.

There was certainly no reason to expect a genuine welcome from anyone in Yalo Busha County. But he went there, probably entertaining the rationale that he was merely stopping by to make some disposition of his farm property. He arrived at first dark, discreetly circled at a distance around the town of Tuscahoma, and saw the light in his little cabin when he was still far off. He picketed his horse, took down his new rifle from its scabbard and crept Indianlike up to the doorway, fully prepared to shoot first and investigate later. What he saw stopped him. Stopped him, not only from firing then, but from ever pulling a trigger in anger for the rest of his life.

She had rebuilt the scattered stones of the little hut's fireplace, and had something cooking in a skillet, and was sweeping the hearth with a turkey wing. When she stood up and turned toward him, her cheeks were flushed from the heat of the flames.

Stewart stared at her—slowly realizing that she was the one

live image among all the ghosts which crowded and clouded his view, the shades of other things too recently seen and experienced. Maybe, he thought, if he was lucky enough to have this vision before him for long enough, those spectres would someday dissolve. Right now, with her nose smudged with soot, her hair disarrayed, her dress dusted with ashes, her eyes brimming with tears of welcome and appeal, she was the prettiest thing he had ever seen.

She swiped at the smudge on her nose and smiled hesitantly. "I've been waiting . . . praying. You said this place was . . . I've kept hoping I could . . ." She paused to collect herself. "I want it to be what you said. Home."

Afterword

Murrell was not exaggerating when he quoted Dante's despairing lines from Hell. His prison term turned out to be a crueler sentence than that pronounced on any of his clansmen. He served the entire ten years, but came out of Nashville Penitentiary incurably insane, and rotted with consumption. Impoverished, wretched and alone, he died not long after his release.

But he had not been forgotten. Even in death, and a full decade after his heyday, the bandit chief was still a figure of awe and fascination. It is told that an enterprising showman plundered his grave by night and made off with part of the man's corpse. He made his living in the years thereafter by exhibiting, to a morbidly curious public, the embalmed head of John Murrell.

G.J.

The Ballad of John Murrell

I rode beside a singin' river,
Windin' through a pleasant land.
Then somethin' chilled me, made me shiver:
I'd stumbled on a dyin' man.

    Go, he said, you cannot save me.
    I am p'inted straight for Hell.
    Git, afore he sends you with me!
    I was shot by John Murrell.

To sin and strife I was a stranger,
So I stayed, I liked that land.
I stayed to build, and laughed at danger.
What here could harm a peaceful man?

    Wish I'd listened to that feller;
    Wish I'd cut and run like Hell.
    Call me coward, call me yeller—
    Even brave men fear Murrell.

I thought I'd found a place to settle,
Friendly neighbors livin' by,
A plot of land—I asked so little!
Here, I said, I'll live and die.

    Never did I heed the warnin'
    That the neighbors tried to tell;
    Turned a deef ear, wouldn't hearken
    To their tales of John Murrell.

I went to fetch my pretty lover,
Her bespoken for my bride.
She swore by all the stars above her
She'd come and live there by my side.

    But then it was I met the stranger,
    One whose name I knowed too well.
    Now, thinks I, I'll play avenger.
    Watch me collar John Murrell!

He said, come with me, son, and revel
With my wild and lawless band.
We wield the power of the Devil,
We plunder riches from the land!

    So I j'ined this limb of Satan,
    Bade my sweetheart fond farewell,
    Left my friends and farm a-waitin'—
    Swore allegiance to Murrell.

But I had left my soul behind me!
Why'd I listen to him tempt
And coax till one sad day would find me,
Like him, a-sowin' seeds of hemp?

    Hemp for rope to bind a nation,
    Rope to toll its fun'ral knell.
    There ain't room in all Creation
    For decent folk and John Murrell.